LIFE IS MY ADVENTURE

To Mary Ryan
With my thanks
for "I did not think
to make music ever
again"
Barbara Mullen

LIFE
IS MY ADVENTURE

by

BARBARA
MULLEN

FABER & FABER LIMITED
24 Russell Square
London

First published in mcmxxxvii
by Faber & Faber Limited
24 Russell Square, London W.C.1.
Reprinted mcmlxiv, mcmlxv and mcmlxviii
Printed in Great Britain by
Latimer Trend & Co., Ltd., Whitstable

To

J.W.R.

Contents

★

Chapter One

The Fair at Topsfield

*

I cannot remember a time when I did not want to run away from home. When I was very young I used to wonder if I could not find a band of gipsies who would take me along with them. Later, as I grew older, I got as far as packing a small bag and saving pennies. But gradually what courage I had was being beaten out of me. I learned that the easiest way was the best way to get along. My only comfort was my books. No one was interested enough to wonder what books I read: consequently, before I was thirteen years old I had delved into every kind of literature, from *True Story* magazines to Jessie James, the *History of the World War*, bits of Shakespeare, and light novels. A good deal of what I read I could not understand, but I came to know of a world different entirely from that in which I lived. I learned of people who spoke nicely to each other, who had shelves of good books, and who believed in helping each other; of others that swore and drank and fought all day, and what decent people thought of them. Slowly I began to understand that I had been wrong to let my mother crush my beliefs and mould my character as she saw fit. "How can I be a person if I think only what I'm told to think and feel only what I'm told to feel?" I asked myself. "I don't want to be trained, I want to be a person." This idea began to take on a definite shape in my mind. I decided to do something about changing my life, but what to do and how to do it I could not figure out. I needed advice, but I had no one to whom I could go; no one I knew would understand how I felt. There was one very remote possibility: my father. Somehow, I was sure that if I wrote and explained things to him he would tell me the right thing to do. But I had been forbidden to have any communication with him, or even to speak of him unless it was to say how much I disliked him. That I never could do. I remembered very very little of my father, but that little was all kindness. I was seven years old when he sailed away to Ireland in 1921, in response to an urgent message from his father. He took with him my brother P.J., three years younger than I. My mother promised to join him the next summer with the baby Winifred, then six months old, and me. But summer after summer passed and we still remained in Boston. Rumours that he was having a difficult time in Aran reached her. But she only became more and more engrossed in the business of making and selling whiskey and eluding the police. She decided, to use her own expression, "To hell with your father and Aran with him," and refused to leave America. She dropped off writing to him, and would not allow me to write either. Puffy, my half brother, having no interest in my father, never mentioned his name. He became my mother's favourite child. The mere mention of my desire to write to my father was enough to precipitate an awful scene and a sound beating. After a few incidents of this sort I became wiser, and I too never spoke of him. Winifred of course did not remember him at all.

For days I pondered over the problem of corresponding with him without my mother's knowledge. Then, after I had almost given up hope, a kind fate took a hand and solved my difficulties, for the time being.

The month of March in 1927 brought with it a streak of luck for me, that lasted a year. An Irish Step Dancing competition was being held in Canton, a small city outside Boston, on the 17th of March. My name was entered and I was fortunate enough to win first prize, a tall silver loving-cup. The following month I won another cup in Cambridge, and in June my luck was still with me and I won another in Boston. My picture had been in the papers after winning each competition, and some kind soul suggested to my mother that I should start a dancing school. My mother leaped at the suggestion and advertised. In no time at all I had more pupils than I could handle. I had reached my thirteenth birthday in June, and though I had the ability to teach, I was not strong enough, at that age, to manage a school of twenty-four pupils a week. I spoke to my mother about it and she permitted me to cut it down to half that number. Though she did her best to help me, converting the parlour into a studio, and doing all she could to give me as much privacy as possible, every now and then a drunk would wander in when I was in the midst of giving a lesson, and with a loud "What th' hell is this?" or perhaps something worse, sit himself down, and no amount of persuasion would get him to leave. During the remainder of the lesson he usually kept up a running fire of remarks, such as "By J—— that's good!" etc. Mothers who came with the pupils did not want their children listening to that sort of thing, and gradually the pupils fell away until there were only two left. Their people insisted that I should go to their home to teach. Both families lived on Spectacle Island, a small island off City Point, near where I lived. Arrangements were made for me to go over every Thursday morning on the eight o'clock boat, the *Woggie*, that brought the workers to the glue factory on the island. I should be given lunch, and should come back in the afternoon at five o'clock when the workers were returning to the mainland. My mother consented to these arrangements, and Thursday in every week became a holiday for me. Off I went at eight o'clock, rain or shine. I spent the morning wandering round the island, had an always dainty but filling lunch at noon, and then taught the two children from one-thirty to four-thirty in the afternoon. While I was there I was very happy and the hours flew by like so many minutes. But like all good things it came to an end much too soon.

Late in July I received a letter from my former dancing teacher, Professor Harrington, saying that the Knights of Columbus were to hold a three-day fair at Topsfield Mass., during the second week in August. One of the events of the fair was to be an Irish Step Dancing Competition for the New England Championship silver cup; this was to take place on the last day of the fair, Saturday the thirteenth of August. He had taken the liberty of entering my name, as he thought I had a good chance of winning. I was pleased but anxious when I read his letter. To win the contest would of course make life at home much easier for me for a while; whereas if I lost, it would be worse than ever. The more I thought of it the more positive I became that my lucky streak was finished and that I hadn't a chance of winning. So I went on arguing with myself, afraid even to hope, until the Thursday before the contest. On that day I went as usual to Spectacle Island. The lessons were very short that afternoon, because most of the time we talked of the forthcoming event and my chances in it. They had read about it in the newspapers, and, unlike my own family, seemed to have a great deal of confidence in me. So much so, that when I started off to get the boat home I was sure of my ability, for the first time. It was just as I was about to get on board that my troubles began. I found I had forgotten my dancing shoes. The workers from the factory were already on board and anxious to be off. At any other time I should have left the shoes till I came again, rather than keep the men waiting. But I had to have them for Saturday. I explained the situation to the men and begged them to wait until I went back to the house for the shoes. They reluctantly agreed to wait fifteen minutes, but no longer. By running as fast as I could, I could just get to the house and back again in that time. Away I went as fast as my short legs would carry my stumpy body. I reached the house in good time, retrieved the dancing shoes and started back. The boat's moorings had been loosed and the engine was running when I returned. The boat itself was drifting in and out at the small quay. I did my best to judge when it would be nearest to the quay so that I could jump on to it, but my judgment was wrong and I slipped and fell and was caught between the boat and the quay. There was an awful pain as though my body was being torn in two, and then I lost consciousness.

Somebody was slapping my hands and shouting at me. I tried to open my eyes, but there was a fog over everything and I closed them again. A voice said: "She's coming round. Get more water quick." I opened my eyes again. This time I could see better, the fog was gone. I looked around. I was on the deck of the *Woggie*, and we were moving. A man gave me a glass of water. "Drink it," he said, "you'll feel better." I wondered why he was being so kind to me, I couldn't remember asking him for water. A great number of men were in a circle round me. "What's the matter?" I asked. The man who had given me the water answered: "You fell when you were getting into the boat and got knocked out," he said.

Then gradually I recalled what had happened. I remembered how I had gone back to the house, the sound of the engine running when I had returned, the awful pain in my back when I had fallen. "Funny," I thought, "the pain is gone now."

"Are you all right?" I was asked.

"Yes," I replied. "I am feeling much better now, thank you."

"You got a nasty bang. We held the boat back for half an hour after you fell; then we figured we had better head for the mainland and take you to the hospital."

I came to myself with a shock. Half an hour's delay! That meant that I should be nearly an hour late getting home. The men coming in on their way home from work for their evening drink—the evening rush as we called it—would be on, and I should not be there to watch at the door or to help serve the customers. My mother would be furious.

We were nearly at the mainland now, and the men were saying that I had better be taken to the hospital at once to make sure that I wasn't badly injured. I refused to go with them, saying that my mother would be worried and that I must get home at once. They insisted but I still refused, and the men, who were anxious to get home themselves after their day's work on the island, finally gave me my own way, and I was allowed to go home alone without any further delay.

The pain in my back had stopped for a little while, but now it started again and grew steadily worse. When I reached the door of my house it was all I could do to keep back the tears.

I had been right when I thought my mother would be angry with me for being late. She was waiting in the dining-room, the usual stick ready in her hand. "What do you mean not coming home till this late!" she shot at me. The pain was growing worse. The room started going round. I couldn't speak. "Answer me," she cried. She raised the stick to strike me and then I found my voice. "Don't," I begged. "Please don't hit me. I fell on the boat and was hurt."

The stick dropped from her hand, but she made no move to come towards me. Instead she looked at me for a long moment. I could see the doubt in her eyes. Then: "I don't believe you. What part of your body was hurt?"

I couldn't hold back the tears any longer. "My back," I sobbed. "It hurts."

"Leave it to you to put the house to and fro, and only two days before the contest. Come here till I see your back." I went to her, and after she had examined me she said: "Well all I can do is strap it up tightly and let you stay in bed for the next few days until the soreness goes out of it."

"But what about Saturday?" I asked.

"You just forget about Saturday. You probably wouldn't win anyway, and I have no money to throw away on car-fare, sending you to Topsfield on a wild goose chase. Besides, we may get something from the boat people if you stay in bed for a while. They'll want to settle the case."

I couldn't believe that she meant what she was saying. She had promised to let me go. Her refusal to live up to her word somehow only served to strengthen my new-found confidence in myself. "You said you'd let me go. Please don't go back on your word now. I'm sure I can win."

"I've told you once. Forget about the contest. Get upstairs to bed and never mind what I said about letting you go."

"But mom, I just know I'll win if you——"

She reached for the stick. It was not her way to stand for argument from any of her children, especially from me.

Mrs. Barret's voice came from the kitchen: "Musha don't hit her mam, please don't. Sure hasn't she been beaten enough for one day without you puttin' more on her?"

I blessed Mrs. Barret from the bottom of my heart as I saw my mother hesitate. Many a time before this I had been saved from a beating in the same way. She, Mrs. Barret, whom we called "Lady Biddy", had been taken in by my mother to live with us when her own children had refused to care for her any longer. She was nearly seventy years old, very tall for a woman, and very straight. For the last six months her sight had been failing her and now she was nearly blind. She seldom left her seat by the kitchen fire unless there was someone to lead her around, and indeed she made a most impressive sight sitting there, a lovely plaid shawl thrown about her shoulders, her rich black hair piled high on the top of her head, the beautiful, nearly sightless eyes always staring straight ahead.

My mother, who was inclined to be superstitious, had always been a little in awe of Lady Biddy. Her reputation had followed her from Ireland. It was said that she would put a terrible curse on anyone who had ever done anything to hurt or displease her. But mother had known Lady Biddy in Ireland and so had taken her in more out of pity than because of any real fear of her. We all had a sort of affection for the old lady, and she in turn liked us. She liked what she called her "Little droppeen", which was really almost a tumblerful of whiskey. At odd times during the day, when no one was looking, I used to manage to give her a drink or two. As a result she had an extra soft spot in her heart for me, and often, when things were bad at the house and my mother was in worse temper than usual, the old lady brought her persuasive powers into play on my behalf, and succeeded in softening things out and getting my mother back into good form again. When coaxing didn't work she used the never-failing threat of the curse. I often thought that my mother had good reason to fear Mrs. Barret. She used a tone of voice so awful when putting the curse on anyone, that it would put fear into the heart of the strongest. One day I asked Lady Biddy why she threatened so often to curse my mother. "Sure darlint," she told me, "isn't it how your ma is that scared of the curse that she will do nearly anything I ask her? All the same I'd never really curse her and she so kind to me with all her temper, but there's no harm in letting her think I would if she put me to it. And sure doesn't it serve yourself well when I do stop her beating you?"

This wise old woman, whom some of our customers called "that blind old fool", had become my only source of protection, and my only confidante. So it was to her that I now ran, feeling instinctively that she alone was the only one who could talk my mother into giving her permission to let me go to Topsfield.

Lady Biddy was standing by the stove, her arms outstretched, waiting for me. "Make her let me go," I whispered.

"Hush," she said in a low tone, and then, aloud: "Why don't ye be goin' to bed as your mother asks ye? Sure ye'll be puttin' the poor woman astray in her mind with your trickstin'! Off with ye to bed and do as you're bid!"

"She'll do as I tell her and without interference from you or anyone else," said my mother. "Go upstairs; I'll bring your supper up to you as soon as I get it ready, and no talk out of you either!"

"Yes mam," I said.

"And never mind the 'yes mam'. You can't get round me with that stuff," she called after me.

I could hear Lady Biddy's voice as I went up the stairs that led to my bedroom. "Sure mam I meant no harm. I was only trying to help." And then my mother's: "Well I don't need anyone's help in raising my children, especially Barbara. She's no trouble." I stopped to listen. I had long ago decided that I was "Mom's pet peeve", and now she was saying that I was no trouble to her. I had to hear more.

Lady Biddy was speaking again: "But you're that hard on her sometimes mam, with the beatings and scoldings ye do be havin' on her, that it makes me heart turn over lookin' at ye. Sure I don't understand it at all and she such a nice, quiet, little thing."

"She's too much like the Mullens with her books, and reading, and queer notions. But I'll knock it out of her."

"Sure 'tis yourself she's takin' after in the dancing, and you once the finest dancer in the County Galway."

"I was that, and the best-looking woman too," said my mother.

" 'Tis a pity entirely that ye won't let her go dancing on Saturday, with yourself being her mother, she would surely win mam. But as ye said, ye need no advice about what to do, still 'tis a pity ye won't let her go and she takin' after ye the way she does."

"Who said I wouldn't let her go?"

"Didn't ye say those boat people might come mam?"

"I did, but I didn't say I wouldn't let her go. Your hearing is going back on you Lady Biddy."

"Ah then, 'tis yourself will be the proud woman on Saturday mam."

I didn't wait to hear more. I thought of Lady Biddy, whom most people considered a fool. There was nothing foolish about what I had just heard. It took clever thinking to get round my mother without her being aware of it, and Lady Biddy was the only one who had ever accomplished it, to my knowledge.

I remained in bed until Saturday morning. My mother brought up all my meals and bathed and strapped my back tightly with adhesive tape. She made several attempts at conversation, and so did I, but they were painful ones. We had never talked together as most mothers and daughters do, and neither of us knew how to go about it. It was a bit late for us to become friendly. I was too much afraid of her, and I think that that Saturday morning she realized it. She brought up my breakfast, and after asking how I was pulled up a chair close to the bed and sat down. I began to shake. I didn't know what she was going to say or do. She had never sat down beside me like that before. She cleared her throat. "Do you still want to go to the contest?" she asked.

"Yes, I do."

"Well, I sent Puffy out to telephone the station and find out about the trains and how much the fare is."

She was speaking in what I felt she meant to be a kind way, and I couldn't believe my ears. I wanted to throw my arms round her, but I didn't dare. I could only say: "Thank you, I am very glad." There was a long silence. She moved about in her chair and let her hand fall casually on to the bed. She wanted to reach over and pat my forehead I am sure, but, strangely enough, she who was able to cope with almost any situation didn't know what to do now, and finally with a sigh she took her hand away and folded both in her lap. She cleared her throat again. "Do you feel strong enough to go?" she asked.

"Yes, I do."

"You're sure now?"

"Yes, I'm sure."

Another long silence. I wished Puffy would come back so that she could talk to him instead of me. At the same time I dreaded his return, because I knew that never again would my mother and I come so near to tearing down the wall of reserve between us. There would never be another opportunity like this for us to establish a friendship or come to an understanding. If only either one of us knew what to say—but we didn't. I racked my brains trying to think of some way to break the silence. Finally, "I'm sorry I couldn't help you for the last couple of days," I said. She made no reply to that; she only looked at me for a moment, and then, "You don't like me do you? You don't need to say whether you do or not," she went on, "I can see it in your eyes. You're afraid of me, that's why you do as I tell you, not because you like me. That's true, isn't it?"

I didn't have to answer; she kept on as if she were talking to herself. "You're too much like your father, reading whenever you get the chance. As if it will ever do you any good. That's the trouble—too much like your father. Well, you better change, because if it's the last thing I ever do, I'll knock it out of you if I have to kill you!" Her voice had risen. It was loud and shrill, the way it always got when she was angry. I sat up in bed. I thought she was going to hit me and I wanted to get out of the room if I could. "You don't need to run at all. I'm not going to touch you," she said. "But from now on you'll give up your book-reading, and be said and led by me. Come downstairs when you're ready." She left the room.

I was greatly relieved when she had gone. I loved my mother, but feared her more. She was in constant pain as a result of injuries which she had received in an accident years before. She had gone to the docks to see an aunt of mine off to Ireland, and the gangway had fallen down and crushed her chest. Added to this was the continual fear of the law and raids. The two together were more than sufficient reason for her violent outbursts of temper, and though I realized this, it did not serve to lessen my fear of her. But thinking about it only made me nervous and apprehensive, so, making an effort to act and feel as if nothing extraordinary had happened, I got up, dressed, and went downstairs.

My mother was busy cooking when I reached the kitchen.

"Did Puffy come back yet?" I asked.

"Yes, he's back. There is a train at one-thirty this afternoon that goes directly to the fair grounds. The fare is four dollars return trip, and unless we get a few customers before that time you'll just be out of luck, because I haven't the money to give you."

"Then maybe I can't go after all?"

"We'll have to wait and see. It depends on how good business is this morning. You know I never have any money on Saturday mornings." Which was quite true. The bootlegger who delivered our stuff to us always got paid on Friday nights. There was no putting him off, because if he didn't get his money he did not give us any more whiskey. He sold us five-gallon cans of whiskey at a very reasonable price. When we sold it, we made what we had paid out on it and as much more besides. He carried on an enormous business, selling his whiskey to almost every speakeasy in Boston. He would deliver as many gallons as we wanted during the week, but he had to have his money "on the line", as he called it, without fail on every Friday night.

We had what was known as good trade. That is, we had more customers than any other speakeasy in the district. There was plenty of money coming in. But as fast as we made it, it was spent again, in paying fines whenever we were raided and the stuff was found, which was frequently. So that every time the bootlegger "Chips", as we called him, was paid, it took all the ready cash that was in the house, and we had to depend on Saturday's business to get Sunday's dinner, or anything else for which money was needed.

By noon that Saturday I was all ready to start off, but there had been only one or two customers and they had not bought enough to make up the price of the ticket. And so the minutes dragged on until twelve-forty-five, when it was time I should be leaving for the station if I was to be in time for the train.

Mr. Lynch, one of our more respectable customers, had come in. He kept watching me for a while, and then he said:

"You look all dressed up with no place to go, Barbara."

"She has some place to go all right," said my mother, who was serving him. "She's supposed to dance in the contest to-day at Topsfield."

"You mean the New England Championship?" he asked.

"That's right."

"She hasn't much time," he remarked, looking at his watch.

"I'm afraid she won't be going after all," my mother returned. "The price of the ticket is too steep."

He thought that over for a minute and then: "Look here," he offered, "why not let me give her her fare down? I'd like to do it," he added hastily as he saw my mother's expression change, "and if she wins I'll feel as if half the credit belongs to me."

My mother looked first at him and then at me. "All right," she said. "I've never let any of the children take money like this before, but she's so anxious to go. . . ."

Without further comment he took a roll of money from his pocket, and handing me a five dollar bill said: "Here you are and the best of luck to you."

I thanked him and looked at my mother. It would have meant so much to have her wish me luck too. "I hope you win," she said. "Now beat it." And I did. "The blessin' of God on ye darlint," Lady Biddy called after me as I raced up the stairs.

The train was an express to Topsfield, and I reached there shortly after two-thirty. Never before in my life had I seen so many people. Endless throngs, milling and pushing each other about. I felt terribly small and insignificant in that huge crowd. "Is this the Fair?" I asked a man who passed near me.

"Whatcha say?"

"Is this the Fair?" I repeated.

"This is it all right," he said, "only you're on the outside. You gotta get your ticket or pay at that gate over there, to get in."

I pushed my way through the crowd until I reached the gate he had pointed out to me. There was a man standing by it, collecting either dollar bills or tickets from everyone who passed through. I joined the line of people waiting to get in and I soon found myself up at the gate.

"Ticket please," said the man.

"I haven't any."

"Then dollar please."

"Is it a dollar for children too?" I asked.

"Huh?" he raised his head with a jerk. "How old are you?"

"Thirteen."

"Sure?"

"Yes sir, I'm sure."

"Okay, fifty cents for you."

I paid him half of the dollar I had left after buying my railroad ticket, and went in.

Inside there were even more people than I had seen outside. Everybody seemed to be with a friend or a group of friends. I had read somewhere that staring was impolite, but I stared anyway. There were so many things to see.

I saw a sign that had painted on it in big letters: "Merry-go-round", and a hand underneath with a finger pointing: "This way." I followed the direction in which the finger was pointing and sure enough I found it. A real merry-go-round, just like the girls in school said they were, only much nicer. I had never seen one before, because I had never been to any of the summer resorts where they were. I stood for at least a half an hour watching it, amazed that the people didn't fall off the horses going round and round at such speed. They did not seem at all frightened however; everyone was smiling and looked happy.

I felt a tap on my shoulder. I looked up: a policeman. There was nothing strange about policemen or cops tapping me on the shoulder, but this was a different kind of tap, and he was smiling. I hadn't thought they could smile. "Are you lost youngster?" he asked kindly.

"No."

"Well are you looking for someone? You're not down here alone are you?"

"Yes, I'm going to dance this afternoon."

"The platform for the dance contests is over on the other side of the grounds. They start at four o'clock you know."

"I didn't know," I said. "Thanks for telling me," and I ran off in the direction he had indicated. I should have liked to have stayed and talked with him, just for the novelty of carrying on a friendly conversation with anyone connected with the law, but I had a dim feeling that in some way he might know who I was and start asking questions. And I didn't dare take any risks.

After asking the way from two men who wore badges on which was written "Committee", I eventually reached that part of the grounds in which the contest was to be held.

A huge platform had been erected in the centre of a large field. It stood about ten feet from the ground and was roughly about twenty-five feet square. A flight of steps led from the ground up to it. Three very official-looking men were standing near the front edge of the platform, examining four silver loving cups, which they placed on the very edge, so that they could be seen without difficulty by the crowd. Farther back, an orchestra was playing Irish airs, and on one side a man was setting up camp stools in a row. In the centre was a large horn—an amplifier, as I heard it called later. Some of the crowd, attracted by the music, began to drift over towards the platform. Others joined them, and soon it seemed to me that nearly all the people who had come to the Fair were gathered round.

I had been wondering if any other of Professor Harrington's pupils would be there besides myself. Standing by the steps I saw three that I knew: a young man, Joe Mulchahy, a girl, Gladys Grover—both of whom had entered in the Senior Contest for those over sixteen years of age—and another girl, Babe Walsh, who was entered in the Junior Contest, as I was. They were all three dressed so neatly and looked so clean that I felt very dirty and shabby beside them.

Miss Grover was wearing a simple, neat, white dress, white stockings, and her black dancing shoes. She had a green band round her hair, and another round her waist. Her face was very clean, and so was Babe Walsh's. But they didn't have the scrubbed look that I knew mine had. They looked instead very comfortable, as though having clean faces and clean fingernails was an everyday occurrence with them. I wondered what they would think if they knew that until this morning my neck hadn't been washed for three days and that my fingernails hadn't been cleaned since the last time I had danced in public, or that I hadn't had a bath for a week.

Painfully conscious of my scrubbed appearance and of the fact that my dress was longer on one side than it was on the other, and that my shoes needed shining badly, I began to wish that I had remained at home and spared myself this ordeal. Certainly I did not belong with these people who looked so comfortably sure that all their clothes were going to stay on, and that they looked just right. I felt that at any moment the pin in my petticoat would give way or that the loose button in my bloomers would fall out. I became terribly nervous and began to fidget. I wished the contest would start so that I could get back home. It didn't matter there how I was dressed. I would have given anything for a needle and thread and a place to go in order to sew myself up and look as neat as the others did. I made up my mind that day that I would have a bath every three days, that I'd wash my neck and clean my fingernails every day, and that I'd sew on the loose buttons every night. Then I'd look comfortable too.

A man was saying that the contest was about to begin, and would the contestants please come up on the platform.

Joe Mulchahy led the way, Miss Grover followed him, then came Babe Walsh and her mother, who kept smoothing Babe's green dress and whispering: "Now don't be nervous dear," all the way up the steps, and I, with thoughts of my loose buttons making me step very gingerly and of course stumble, brought up the rear.

The names of the three judges and the rules of the contest were announced. We were called by name, first the seniors, five in all, then the juniors, two others besides Babe and myself. We were all given numbers, and each one told that we were to be judged for time, carriage, and execution of steps. Babe had a piece of paper with "Number 1", written on it, pinned on her back, and I was "Number 2". I did not know who the other two were, and I did not care. What concerned me most, was Babe Walsh. We were old rivals in dancing. We had danced as partners in several places, but always Babe had been the one to get the most applause. She was shorter than I, chubby, with dimpled cheeks and knees and a round, baby face.

I was fat, not chubby, at least a head taller than Babe, and awkward, except when I was dancing. I always fell over my feet walking on or off the stage and made myself ridiculous. But not Babe. She'd skip lightly on to the stage and throw kisses to the audience with no danger of falling all over herself.

People used to come back stage and say: "Isn't the little one sweet? Did you ever see such dimples?" Once in a while someone would say: "The big one certainly can dance can't she?" And invariably someone else would answer: "Oh yes, but isn't the little one cute?" It had been like that ever since we had been at dancing school together. We both danced and Babe was petted and praised. "If she wins the cup to-day, I'll never live it down," I said to myself, and prayed fervently that the judges wouldn't look at her dimpled cheeks or notice her cute ways, and that my bloomers would stay put until the contest was over.

The seniors had danced, each one a reel, jig, and hornpipe. Joe Mulchahy had danced first and Miss Grover third. Then "Number 1", in the Junior was called, and Babe stepped forward. The orchestra played different tunes for every contestant, and Babe danced perfectly to each time. I had never seen her dance so well before, and she flashed her dimples too. I was heartbroken. As if worrying about my loose buttons hadn't been enough.

But I had no time to think. My number was called, the music started, and that was all I needed.

I had always loved dancing. My mother had taught me the few steps she knew when I was only three years old. It had never been difficult for me to learn new steps, and when I heard music I forgot everything else, and was happy, dancing as long as anyone would play for me. And so it was on this day. All my nervousness faded away, and I danced like merry hell.

When I had finished, the other two contestants were called, one after the other. Then the judges put their heads together, talked and compared the notes they had made, nodded, and then handed the slip of paper with the names of the winners written on it to the announcer.

He walked to the edge of the platform where the cups were and picked up one of the two big ones, then he returned to the centre of the platform to make his announcements.

"The Senior Contest, Irish Step Dancing," he

shouted. "First prize winner and Senior New England Champion!"—he looked at the paper in his hand—"Joseph Mulchahy!"

The crowd cheered and shouted as Joe stepped up to receive the trophy. He shook hands with the announcer and the judges after he had received the cup and went back to his place, a short distance away from where the juniors were sitting.

The announcer was shouting again: "Second prize winner, in the Senior Contest, Gladys Grover!" He handed her the cup. She shook hands all round, bowed to the cheering crowd as Joe had done and returned to her place beside him.

There was now a big cup left like the one Joe had been given, and a smaller one like that now owned by Gladys.

The announcer walked over, picked up the big one, and cried: "The Junior Contest, Irish Step Dancing. First prize winner and Junior New England Champion—Barbara Mullen."

He meant me. I knew I should step forward to get the cup but I couldn't move.

"Number Two," he was shouting. "Barbara Mullen." The crowd was cheering. I looked at the judges. They were smiling at me. The announcer came over and took my hand. "Don't be shy," he whispered. "Come on."

We had started to walk to the centre of the platform, when suddenly I felt the loose button in my bloomers snap. I clutched frantically at my waist, hoping no one would notice. I held on to dress, petticoat and bloomers with one hand, while I took the cup with the other.

"How am I going to shake hands with everyone?" I thought.

The announcer was holding out his hand.

"Please sir," I said, "could I tell you something?" He bent down and I whispered in his ear. "I'm awfully sorry, but the button is gone and if I shake hands my bloomers will fall down."

It took him a couple of seconds to get it, and then he threw back his head and roared with laughter. I could have cried. I didn't see anything funny in it.

"It's all right," he said, wiping the tears from his eyes, "it's all right. Just make a bow. I'll explain to the judges." He patted my head, still laughing, and I bowed still holding on for dear life and returned to my place.

He walked over and spoke to the judges and all three began to laugh. Then he went and got the last cup and announced that Babe Walsh had won second prize.

After she had received the cup and shaken hands all round, the winners of both divisions were asked to bow together. Joe and Gladys went first, then Babe and I: Babe throwing kisses, I holding my bloomers.

The other contestants were then called on and they took their bows in response to the cheering.

The orchestra began to play again as we started to leave the platform.

The last I saw of the announcer and judges was when I looked back, just before I started down the steps. They were looking after me, smiling. "They wouldn't smile if they were losing their pants," I thought.

Joe and Gladys were waiting at the bottom of the steps. I drew Gladys aside and explained what had happened.

"Well you'd better find a place to go and pin them up," she laughed.

"What will I do for a pin?" I asked. "Have you got one?"

"Yes, I have one in this belt that I can give you. But let's find a spot first. It wouldn't do for you to pin yourself together in a public place would it?"

I agreed with her, and we hunted about until we found a clump of bushes behind which I could hide. After fixing the pin so that I felt much safer, we went back to where we had left Joe standing.

"Say, what happened to you two running off like that without a word?" he asked.

"Private business," Gladys explained briefly.

"Well it must have been pretty urgent to make you rush off like that. I thought you were never coming back."

"It was," said Gladys. "But we still have plenty of time on our hands. There is no train till nine o'clock to-night."

The three of us went off together. We looked for Babe Walsh and her mother, but they had disappeared in the crowd and we couldn't see them anywhere.

We came to the place where all the amusements were. There were tents with gipsies outside them, asking the people in to have their fortunes told.

Into one of these Gladys and Joe went, telling me to wait till they came out. Of course I couldn't stand still for more than five minutes with so much going on on all sides of me. I wandered round feasting my eyes on everything till I came to the tent that had the most people round it. There were a great many dolls, blankets, boxes of candy, and various other articles arrayed on shelves inside the tent. This I could see from where I was standing in the midst of the crowd. But that wasn't enough. I had to see more. I pushed my way through till I reached a spot directly in front of the tent.

A man was shouting: "Come on folks, try your luck. Only ten cents a chance on this five pound box of candy. Think of it. A five pound box of the best candy for one small dime." So I parted with ten cents of my fifty, and lost it of course. I forgot that I had to wait until nine o'clock to get a train and that I needed the fifty cents to get something to eat. I parted with one dime after the other without winning anything, and finally realizing that I had nothing left but my ticket home, and the cup I had won, I left my place in front of the tent reluctantly, and went looking for Gladys and Joe.

I found several gipsy tents, but not the one I was looking for, and after an hour or so with still no sign of the pair, I gave up the search.

It was nearing seven o'clock and I was beginning to get hungry. I passed more hot dog stands that day than I've seen since. By eight o'clock, with still an hour to wait before the train left, I felt weak. I hadn't eaten since early morning and I'd had an exciting day. I felt that if I went any longer without food I should fall over. I went up to one of the refreshment stands. A very stout man was ordering a hot dog and a glass of lemonade. I could feel my mouth watering with every bite he took. He finished the first, and ordered a second. I felt I could have eaten a dozen while he was eating only two. Suddenly he turned round. "Say you," he said angrily, "you've been watching me for the last ten minutes. Now what's the big idea?"

"Would you please buy me a hot dog?" I could have bitten my tongue when I'd spoken. I had not meant to say that at all.

"What did you say?" he asked slowly.

Now the damage was done it couldn't be any worse, I felt, so: "Would you please buy me a hot dog?" I repeated. "I spent my money on chances and I haven't any left, and I'm very hungry."

He looked me over, probably wondering if I was being fresh or if I was really hungry. "Where'd you get that cup?" he asked.

"I won it, dancing."

"Humph." Then again: "Humph. Come on, I'll buy you a hot dog."

He gave the order to the attendant. "When did you eat last?"

"Breakfast," I said.

"Wanna glass of milk with that?"

I nodded, my mouth full. He ordered it. "Let's see the cup."

I showed it to him. He examined it. "Pretty nice," he said, "pretty nice." He handed it back to me.

I had finished the milk by now, so I thanked him and turned to go. He put a hand on my shoulder. "Look here kid," he said, "I'm going to give you some advice. Next time you're hungry or in trouble, ask a policeman to help you. And you'd better wrap the cup in something. It will be dark soon and someone's liable to grab it and run. You've got your ticket home haven't you?"

"Yes," I said. "I've got that all right."

"Where do you live?" he asked. I told him.

"And your mother let you come all the way down here by yourself?"

"Yes, I came alone."

"Isn't there anyone here you know?"

"Yes, but I can't find them."

He looked at his watch. "Go ahead and look for them," he said. "If you don't find them inside half an hour come back here and I'll put you on the train. I'll wait here till nine o'clock. It's eight-fifteen now, so you'd better start looking."

"Thanks," I said.

Strangely enough, now that I didn't care particularly whether or not I saw anyone I knew, since I was no longer hungry, I had been walking only a few minutes when I met Mrs. Walsh and Babe, Joe and Gladys—all drinking milk.

"Where did you go?" they asked.

I told them all that had happened to me, leaving out my adventure with the stout man at the hot dog stand.

"We saved some milk and a sandwich for you. You must be starved."

They seemed to take it for granted that I had had nothing to eat, and I saw no reason to tell them, so I gravely accepted the sandwich and thanked them.

It was not till we had boarded the train that I thought of home or my sore back. I had felt a twinge or two during the afternoon, but I was too much interested in everything that was going on about me to pay any attention to it.

It never occurred to me that my mother might be

worried about my long absence, for as a matter of fact I did not feel as though I had been gone more than a few hours. But in the meantime, as I learned later, the scene at home had been something like this:

At seven o'clock my mother had spoken to Mike Broderick, one of the boarders, saying: "Barbara has been gone since one o'clock, it's time she was getting back."

Mike had reassured her, saying that Topsfield was a long way off and that I could not be back any sooner than eight o'clock. At eight o'clock she had consulted Christy, another boarder, who had told her that the train must have been delayed. At nine o'clock she was nearly frantic. Christy and Mike sat in the kitchen drinking. They had been boarding with us for three years at that time and were like members of the family. They treated Lady Biddy to one drink after the other, and then, when my mother started to cry, Lady Biddy, Christy and Mike all cried with her. My mother, who, despite the fact that she handled over forty or fifty gallons of whiskey during each week, had never tasted a drop in her life, got disgusted listening to them and made tea for herself.

She kept telling Mike and Christy what she would do to me when I came home. "Kill her as dead as a doornail," she'd say. Then again: "That one mightn't come home at all if she didn't win the cup. She's that proud." Then she'd begin to pace up and down the floor, crying out that she was sure that I had been killed and why had she ever let me go at all?

Lady Biddy, more than half drunk by this time, began to keen. Christy cried heartbrokenly that his Kathleen Mavourneen (as he called me) was gone, never to return. Mike told all who would listen that he had always thought the world of me, while my mother sadly supped her tea.

I opened the front door with my key, and on hearing all three going strong as if all their relations had died at once, I thought something terrible had happened to one of the family. I rushed down the stairs and into the kitchen.

Mike blinked, Christy sniffed, my mother jumped. And Lady Biddy, hearing me come in, cried: "God be praised. 'Tis herself."

They all looked at me as if they had never seen me before that moment. They had worked themselves into such a state that they couldn't believe I was really there.

"What's the matter?" I asked. "What's happened?"

"Sure didn't we think they would be bringing in your body at any minute," said Lady Biddy.

"What kept you so long?" my mother asked. "I thought something had happened to you, that your back had given you more trouble——"

"There was no train till nine o'clock," I explained.

"Is it first or second?" she asked, eyeing the cup.

"First prize," I said, handing it to her.

"By God," she said as she looked at it, "it was worth letting you go." She passed the cup round to Mike and Christy for inspection. Christy began to cry again when he saw it. "Ah Kathleen Mavourneen," he sobbed, the tears streaming down his cheeks, "I knew you'd win. I knew you could do it."

It was put into Lady Biddy's hands so that she could

feel its size. " 'Tis grand entirely," said she. Then my mother placed it on the middle of the table and sent for the whiskey.

It was a custom, started when I had won my first cup, to fill each new cup I won with whiskey, and for everyone in the house to drink from it.

My mother looked doubtfully at this last cup. It was very large and would hold at least two quarts of whiskey, with plenty of room to spare. Christy noticed her hesitation, and fearing that she might change her mind if she thought any longer about it, said: "Arra get on with it till we drink to my Kathleen Mavourneen. It isn't so often we get the chance and it's well worth it."

"You're right," said my mother, and proceeded to fill the cup to the very top. It was then passed round, first to Christy and Mike and Lady Biddy, then to a few other customers who had come in in the last few minutes. They all drank to my good health, and wished me luck.

Everyone petted and made much of me that night, but though my mother was pleased at the praise bestowed on me by the various customers, still I did not find it a pleasant experience to be slapped on the shoulders by one drunk after the other, and I tried to think of an excuse so that I could go to bed.

"Let ye give over and let the child rest," Lady Biddy cried suddenly. "She did enough to-day without having to put up with the likes of ye at the end of it. Don't ye think so mam?" This last to my mother. Drunk as she now was, the old lady still knew her stuff.

"Yes," said my mother, "I do. You must be tired,"

she went on, looking at me. "You'd better go to bed and have a good rest."

I turned back to say good night, as I was going out of the door. Mike was staring drunkenly into his glass; Lady Biddy was smacking her lips after the last drink; Christy was looking at the cup, crying. Last of all I looked at my mother. There were tears in her eyes. "Good night," she said softly. I felt sort of all choked up. "Good night," I answered. I was happy that night as I fell asleep.

Chapter Two

Riot at McCluskey's

*

The next day, Sunday, was uneventful. Just the usual run of business, the usual remarks from the more respectable customers, the same old cursing and noise from the rougher element.

On Monday my picture was in the papers, and the boat people came. What they said I do not know. My mother did all the talking and I was asked no questions. I believe my mother was given a small sum of money, a few days later. I felt an occasional twinge in my back, but I was not brought to a doctor, which was perhaps just as well, since nothing serious developed from it.

My mother was really gentle with me for the next few days and spoke sharply to me only during the rush hours, when everyone was under a great strain, every nerve on edge, not knowing what minute we were going to be raided.

On Wednesday afternoon there was a strange ring at the doorbell: one long ring. The customers all gave two short rings, members of the household rang three times. Any other ring meant a stranger, and a stranger meant a raid.

My mother grabbed the pot in which we kept the

whiskey and ran with it to the sink. "Go you, and see who it is," she directed. "If it's cops, or anyone who looks like a cop, yell down here, and I'll dump the stuff. Be careful."

"Okay," I said.

Brought up to dread cops and detectives as I had been, I could always tell them no matter how they were dressed. Sometimes they came dressed in overalls and dirty caps, other times they were well dressed, but they always had "law" written all over their faces. They rarely tried to effect an entrance that way because we always knew them. Usually they broke in the door and rushed us. We might have the stuff dumped in time or we might be caught. It was just a gamble.

But our strange caller that Wednesday afternoon was not a representative of the law. It was a woman who had the most impelling pair of blue-black, flashing eyes, that I have ever seen. I went back to the head of the stairs. "Ma," I called, "it's a woman."

"Does she look suspicious?"

"Yes. But not that way."

"Well, if you think she's O.K. let her in and see what she wants," I was told. I did so. I opened the door and the woman hopped, not stepped, but literally hopped in. "Who do you want to see?" I asked.

"I—am Katherine Leary," she said, in a tone of voice that made me feel that I was looking at one of the most important people in the country. "Who is in charge here please?"

To say that I was awed by her appearance and tone is putting it mildly. I was so overwhelmed by the force of her personality, even in the one brief moment that had lapsed since I first saw her, that I felt she had done me a great honour to speak to me at all.

"You'd better see my mother," I said when I had found my voice.

"Take me to her please."

"Who is it?" my mother called to me.

"It's Katherine Leary," I answered. "She wants to see you."

"Never heard of her, but bring her in the dining-room. I'll be right in."

I brought forward the most comfortable chair in the dining-room for our strange visitor, and stood in a corner where I could see her without being seen myself.

My mother entered the room. "Yes?" she said. "You wanted to see me?"

The woman rose. "I—am Katherine Leary," she began. "I am the world's champion accordion player—Irish music, of course. I have come to see the girl who won the championship cup for Irish dancing, last Saturday. You are that girl's mother?"

I could see that my mother was as impressed as I had been. "Please sit down," she said. "Yes, I am her mother. What is it you want to see her about?"

"I will tell you the whole story," said Katherine Leary. "I am on the stage and doing very well, as perhaps you can guess."

My mother nodded. There was no reason why she should have guessed anything, but when Katherine Leary spoke, she made you feel that it would be outrageous to think she was anything other than what she told you.

"I saw your daughter's picture in the paper last Monday," went on the lady, "and I must say, I was more than impressed by it—more than impressed."

I could see my mother raise her head proudly. I felt my own head growing larger.

"My dear woman," Katherine Leary leaned forward and tapped my mother's knee. "My dear woman, your daughter has ability. Great ability. And I am the woman to give her her chance. Inside one year, I can make her as famous as I am myself," she said slowly, impressively.

"I know she has ability," said my mother, "but you have never even seen her before to-day. What makes you so sure about her?"

"My dear Mrs. Mullen," said Katherine with a slight smile, "I can read faces. The fact that she won on Saturday is really almost enough to satisfy me. Of course I'll have to see the girl dance before I decide to offer you a definite proposition. Now, if you'll just bring her here and have her dance for me before we talk any more"—my mother nodded and I came out of my corner.

"Come here please," said Katherine. I went to her. She looked me over carefully from head to toe. "You have a nice face," she said, "let me see what your dancing is like. I'll play for you myself."

She had brought a square, black box in with her. She now bent and opened it, and drew from it an accordion. She began to play, and if my mother had had any doubts about Katherine, they vanished when she heard the first few notes. The lady could play and play marvellously. I have since heard better players, but none have I heard or will I ever hear who from her fingers could get the same heart, the same feeling, the same desire to dance into your feet, as Katherine Leary.

She played first a reel, then a jig, and last a hornpipe. I danced all three. Even my mother was surprised when she saw me, but she didn't say anything. I knew myself that I had never danced so well before, but I couldn't explain that it was this woman's way of playing music that had almost put the steps into my feet.

I was sorry when she put down her instrument. I wanted to ask her to keep on playing, but I didn't dare. I wondered if she had ever made anyone else feel as I did—as if she could ask questions or give directions, as she saw fit. I did not fear her, but I respected her from the first moment I saw her.

She was speaking to my mother. "I am satisfied," she was saying, "more than satisfied."

"Well, what is the proposition you spoke of?" my mother asked.

"As I told you before," said Katherine Leary, "I am on the stage. I have just signed a contract to appear in New York. Now, here is my proposition. I can use somebody else in my act, a dancer. Your daughter would do very well. You understand that it is an Irish dancer I need?"

"Why do you need anyone at all if you're so famous?"

"It is difficult to explain to you Mrs. Mullen, since you have no knowledge of show business, but every season I try to have something new in my act. This season I want an Irish dancer. But of course if you have any objections, I'm sure there are plenty of others to be found, who will be only too willing, and pleased at getting such a glorious opportunity." She rose as if to leave.

"Now don't be hasty," said my mother. "If there is an opportunity for Barbara to make anything of her dancing, I want her to have it. But isn't she too young to go on the stage? She's only thirteen. Still—she's tall for her age."

"A little make-up on her face when she is dancing and no one will ever know that she is not sixteen. You think over what I've said. We need not settle anything right now, I'll call in later in the week, if I may? And we can talk it over again. Is that all right with you?"

My mother nodded her head in agreement with this plan, and Katherine Leary walked slowly, impressively, from the room.

When she reached the front door she turned and held out her hand to my mother. "Good afternoon," she said; "I will let you know by letter what day next week I can call." She smiled at me as she left.

I have often wondered since what made me go to the front window to watch her. I did so, and in that way I caught my first glimpse of the real Katherine Leary—the one I was to know and live with for the next crazy ten months of my life.

I saw her reach the sidewalk, still with her head held high and walking very slowly. I afterwards learned that she unconsciously adopted this pose in any situation or discussion touching on music. But now as I continued to look, I saw her calm manner fall away, her hands begin to tremble. She dropped the accordion box, put her shaking hands up to smooth her hair, then made the sign of the cross and stepped to the edge of the sidewalk. She picked up the accordion box, looked fearfully to the right and left of her, and then, with the air of one who is risking certain death by doing so, she sped across the street at full speed.

I left my place by the window, and went downstairs. There was plenty to be done and I could not wait any longer, anxious as I was to see what other queer tricks she did.

My mother talked over the events of the afternoon with Christy, Mike and Lady Biddy that night. They agreed finally that they would investigate and find out more about Katherine Leary before settling anything.

The next time she came to the house, my mother told her that though she would not prevent me from going away if she thought I should gain anything by it, still she wanted to know more about her first.

We were invited to visit the Leary home in Arlington; where we met Mr. Leary, the husband. He was a small, meek-looking man, whose conversation was limited to two words: "Yes Katherine." We met, too, the daughter Mary and two sons. Their conversation was limited to "Yes Mother."

The house was a small, white cottage, so clean, that it made me uncomfortable to sit down inside it. We were shown through the rooms, each one cleaner than the last. The furniture was very ordinary, what there was of it.

We were then asked to have tea. This was served noiselessly and efficiently by the girl, Mary. It was during tea that my mother suddenly asked: "Just how well off are you Mrs. Leary?"

Mrs. Leary nearly choked. She was silent for a moment; then she said abruptly: "I'm not well off Mrs. Mullen. My husband is not working. When he does work, he drinks. I am keeping my little home together by playing here and there—earning a few dollars wherever I can. But I can't do it any longer. New York is my big chance and I'm taking it. I'm bringing Mary with me. I feel that if I had a dancer, between the two of us we could get an act together and make a success of it. In the meantime, I'll have to put the two boys in a home."

"That's more like it," said my mother. "You bluffed me the first time I saw you, but no one can fool me for long. Have you really got a job in New York? There's no bluff about that is there?"

"No, I have the job all right. What I want to do is really make a success with my music."

"And the dancing," added my mother.

"Then you'll let her come with me?"

"I will. I'm putting her in your charge. The rest is up to you."

Two days before I was to leave for New York, my mother asked me if I wanted to go. Fortunately for me, since I really had no choice in the matter—my mother having already decided for me—I wanted to go, and more than I had ever wanted to do anything before in my life.

Mrs. Leary had gone to New York a week before this, taking her daughter Mary with her. We had received one letter from her, saying that everything had turned out much better than she had expected. She was now leader of the orchestra at "McCluskey's Irish-American Hotel, Cabaret, and Restaurant", at Rockaway Beach, New York. She was receiving a huge salary, her playing was more popular than she had even dared to hope it would be "And", she continued, "Mr. McCluskey is very much impressed by what I have told him regarding Barbara's reputation as a dancer, and has decided to engage her for the remainder of the season."

So it was with high hopes and light heart that I started alone on my journey to New York. What Mrs. Leary had said about dancing there had not really penetrated into my brain. The only thought in my mind as I journeyed to New York, was that at last I should be away from home. I should be able to write to my father without my mother's knowledge. I felt sure he would answer my letter if he received it. I wasn't very sure of his address. "Kilronan, Aran Isles, County Galway, Ireland," I remembered my mother used to put on her letters when she wrote to him after he had first gone away. But that was seven years ago, and maybe he had moved from Ireland. I could only hope that somehow my letter would find him. I wondered what his answer would be like. Would he be able to help me? Perhaps. If he could, he might even fix it so that I need never go back home again. Maybe he knew of a place to which I could go instead—where I shouldn't have to serve whiskey—where there would be no drunkenness or swearing—no constant fear of the law and of raids. There might even be books there. But even in my wildest dreams I dared go no further than that. After all, he might not believe me, and his answer if he wrote at all might just tell me to stop being a foolish child, that my mother was perfectly right and justified in all she said and did, and that I should do exactly as I was told by her. If it so happened that he did say this last, then I should feel he must be right, and I wouldn't fight against things any longer. However, I could not hurry time. I should have to wait until I knew my address in New York before I could write to anyone.

On my arrival in the big city, I was met by my half-cousin, John Lally, or "Crazy John" as he was called, to whom my mother had written earlier in the week. She had asked him to take care of me until I was safely in Mrs. Leary's charge. He had often visited us in Boston, and I liked him. He always made everyone laugh, and even my mother was in good humour while he was there. He took me to his sister's home in the Bronx, and the next day we left for Rockaway.

Rockaway Beach is a typical summer resort, open from the last week in May to the first in September. It is frequented mostly by Irish people, and the majority of the cabarets, restaurants and dance halls are run by Irish people.

We had no difficulty in finding "McCluskey's Irish-American Hotel, Cabaret, and Restaurant", and arrived there in the midst of the luncheon hour rush.

The place was bustling with activity: waiters and waitresses rushing here and there, serving their guests. We enquired for Katherine Leary, but no one seemed to know her. Finally John said: "Well, as long as we are here, we may as well have lunch. Maybe we can get some information from whoever serves us."

Fortunately we found an unoccupied table and discussed the possibility of our being in the wrong place, or of some mistake in address, while we were being attended to.

Deeply interested in what John was saying about continuing our search, I had not noticed the waitress who was serving us. I looked up at her as John began to ask his questions.

She was quite tall and fair; not beautiful, but her face was sweet and gentle and kind. I judged her to be about forty years old.

She waited until John had finished what almost amounted to a cross-examination. One question after the other, without pause. Then she said, in a voice low, but clear: "This is the only McCluskey's in Rockaway, that I know of. But if you tell me who you are looking for, perhaps I can help you."

"We are looking for Katherine Leary, the musician," said John.

"Oh!" cried the waitress, "thank goodness you happened to ask me. I am Katherine's sister, Bridget." She turned to me. "You must be Barbara."

"Yes," I acknowledged. I introduced John. "We've had an awful time," said he. "Nobody seems to know anything about your sister or where she can be found. Is she in hiding or something?"

"Well, it's like this," explained Bridget, "Katherine is the cook here——"

"Cook!" exploded John.

"In the daytime," she continued hastily; "in the evenings she plays in the orchestra. Her daughter, Mary, and I, both work here too, as waitresses."

John said nothing to this. Three people in one family,

working, sounded like money, and money to him spelled success.

Bridget went on: "We've been expecting you, Barbara. Katherine is in the kitchen; so if you'll just follow me please, I'll take you to her."

"Oh no you won't"—this from John. "She doesn't leave me till I hand her over to Mrs. Leary myself."

"But you can't go into the kitchen young man," protested Bridget.

"Then bring Katherine Leary here," John returned.

"But she's busy. She can't leave the kitchen."

"Then it's too bad for Mrs. Leary."

Bridget's mouth opened and closed. John was only doing as my mother had requested, of course. Neither of us had ever seen Mrs. Leary's sister, nor for that matter had we ever heard of her having one.

John refused to let me out of his sight, and Mrs. Leary couldn't leave the kitchen, so that seemed to be that.

Suddenly Bridget's face lit up. "Oh!" she cried, "you know Mary, don't you Barbara?"

"Yes, I do."

"Well I'll bring her here, and then perhaps this young man will decide that you will be safe in my company." She flashed a resentful look at John and went off in search of Mary.

"She looks all right to me John," I said, referring to Bridget.

"She probably is too," said he, 'but just the same I'm not taking any chances.

"My mother must have written a very strong letter."

"Your mother's letter made no difference Babs. I'd

have taken special care of you anyway. And", he continued, "remember this—I mightn't have a chance to tell you again. If you ever get in a scrape of any kind and need help, you can count on your crazy cousin." He stopped suddenly as Bridget returned, accompanied by Mary Leary.

I remember now that I wondered what on earth had got into John to make him talk to me like that. Could he have foreseen the events of the future I wonder? Because there came a time when I found in John an invaluable friend and ally, and when I needed one most, true to his promise of years before.

John, seeing that Mary and I had met, let me go with her.

We went into the kitchen, and there I finally saw Katherine Leary, "World's Champion Accordion Player", surrounded by pots and pans and delicious smells.

She was doing something with a frying pan as we entered the kitchen. She looked up from her work as she heard us. "Why Barbara!" she cried, as she saw me. The fact that finding her in the kitchen as cook when I had expected to see her a star performer had nearly floored me, and that she knew it, did not knock a feather out of Katherine. She advanced to meet me, with queenly grace and dignity, one hand outstretched, the other holding the frying pan. "My dear," she went on, "I'm delighted to see you. Delighted. Have you had your dinner?" I told her that it had been ordered and that I was to go back to the table to eat, after I had seen her. She nodded her head in approval. "That is good," she said. "I'm very busy now as you see. I finish in here at six o'clock. I want you to go to Aunt B., that is Bridget, at that time this evening. She will take you to my room, and we'll put cosmetics on your face, so you'll look sixteen. Don't answer any questions till you see me again. Now, you may go back to your cousin. Tell him that I said you are free to do as you please till six o'clock." She dismissed me with a slight wave of her hand.

On my way back to the table I could not help wondering what would happen when Katherine and John met. I had seen two sides of Katherine Leary's character. The Katherine of amazing dignity and poise in the midst of her pots and pans or a discussion of music, sweeping all before her, and the other Katherine that I had glimpsed from the window on her first appearance, a timid, nervous, middle-aged woman.

But I also knew John. I have never known John to be sincere with anyone but myself. For me, he would fight tooth and nail; perhaps because I believed in him, and no one else did. He delighted in putting people at a disadvantage. This he was well able to do, as he possessed more than his share of ready Irish wit, and a sharp brain. He was in his glory if he could make people laugh, or laugh himself, no matter how he did it. What would happen when he and Mrs. Leary got together?

"Is everything all right?" he asked as he saw me. "Yes," I replied. "Everything is O.K., so far anyway. She says that I'm free to do as I like until six o'clock; then I must come back here."

"The hell she does!" exploded John. "Who th' hell does she think she is giving you orders like that? I don't like her."

"Remember John," I reminded him, "I'm in her

charge now. It's silly your saying you don't like her when you've never even seen her."

I realized that I had made a mistake in repeating Katherine's wishes nearly word for word. They sounded too much like orders to please John. "She's really quite nice, and can play——" I started, but John interrupted. "I wouldn't mind if she just told you to be back at six," said he, "but she sounds as if she has a swelled head. And that won't do."

We had nearly finished our meal, and John suggested that as we had still a few hours to spare we might go for a walk or on some more of the sky-rides. I was not loath to accept, for any of John's suggestions usually meant fun. I called Aunt B. over, and after telling her that I should surely return in time I left the restaurant with John.

He did not refer to Katherine again till we had started back after making the rounds of ice-cream stands, fortune-tellers' tents, etc. It was as we were nearing McCluskey's that he said thoughtfully: "Yes, she's got a swelled head, and I'm going to do something about it." He didn't say what and I was by no means easy in my mind when I left him at the bar and went off to find Aunt B. To make matters worse, he had decided to hire a room at McCluskey's that night, so that he would have an opportunity to get thoroughly acquainted with the Leary family. There would be nothing gained if I told Katherine or Aunt B. that John was up to something. Katherine had never seen him, and Aunt B. only for a few moments. They would probably call me an idiot, and rather than risk that I decided to let matters shape themselves, and hoped that John would get himself drunk at the bar and forget his funny idea, whatever it was.

I found Aunt B. without any difficulty, and she immediately said: "Just follow me Barbara. Katherine and Mary are upstairs in their room waiting for you." And I did. I followed her first through the restaurant dining-room, then through the kitchen, from there across the employees' dining-room, and finally up a flight of stairs.

She stopped me at the top. "At the other end of this landing", she said, "are the front stairs. They lead into the main dining-room. During the day you must use these back ones. In the evening, when you have to mingle with the guests, you use the front ones. You'll be sleeping in Katherine's room, number twelve, on this floor. Are you listening?"

I jerked back to attention. I had heard every word she said, but I had not been following it very keenly in my mind. I was paying more attention to the shouting and noise that were coming from the same number twelve. "What do you suppose all the shouting is for?" I asked wonderingly.

"Oh," said Aunt B. casually, "that's just Katherine having nerves. Don't take any notice of it."

We were nearing number twelve and I could hear the shouting more clearly. I recognized Katherine's voice. "Jesus Ma-a-a-ry and Joseph!" she was saying, "I cannot stand this any longer." Here was a new side of Katherine's character, and I wondered how I was going to get along with it.

Aunt B. raised her hand and knocked on the door. There was a loud "Sssh" from within, the noise and shouting ceased as if by magic, and Katherine opened the door. I expected to see some outward signs of the rumpus that had been going on, but none were visible. Katherine, all poised and queenly, asked me to "Come in, my dear."

The room was bare, except for a bed, dresser, and divan. Mary was standing by the foot of the bed, a patient, long-suffering expression on her face. Her blue eyes lit up when she saw me: I had evidently come at the right moment.

"Your suitcase is under the bed," she said. "You're going to sleep in here with us." She had no chance to say any more, nor had I, for Katherine took hold of the conversation and no one else had a chance to get a word in edgewise. "Of course it will be a bit crowded, Barbara," she was saying, "but you'll be quite comfortable on the divan I'm sure. Mary and I sleep in the bed." She went on without pause: "Now sit down and put on your dancing shoes. Do you know how to make up your face?" I nodded. I had used make-up before when I had danced at different affairs. "Well, there is powder and rouge and everything else you'll need, on the dresser. So get busy. While you're doing that, I can give you your instructions about how to act when you go downstairs."

I rose and went to the dresser to begin my operations. "Mind you put plenty on," she said sharply. "You're supposed to be sixteen years old, and not only must you look like it, you must act like it!"

That was the beginning of the instructions, the telling of which took nearly an hour. It was mostly repetition, and at the end of the hour she had succeeded in drilling into me that I was no longer thirteen but sixteen years old. I was not to play games or run about during the day, as the other children in the hotel did. I must never be seen without make-up on, as somebody might suspect my real age and report me to the authorities. In the evenings, when I should be in the cabaret, I must mingle with the guests, dance with anyone who asked me, and act as the other grown-up girls did. To anyone who asked me how old I was—no matter who —I was to reply "Sixteen."

I stood under the light for examination, and being approved of, sat down on the bed, trying to feel and look a young woman instead of a schoolgirl, and wondering vaguely what had happened to me.

Katherine had been undressing while she was talking, and was now down to the corset and shirt stage. She turned to Mary, who had been sitting quietly on the divan. "What time is it?" she asked.

Mary looked at the clock on the dresser. "Seven-thirty," she said.

I felt as if a bomb had exploded in the room. Katherine, on hearing the time, stood stock still for a moment; then she began to parade the length of the room, shouting at the top of her voice: "Jesus Ma-a-a-ry and Joseph! Here I am, on the biggest night of my life! I must be downstairs at eight o'clock and I'm not even dressed yet. Perhaps my entire future depends on my appearance to-night, and I won't be there. I cannot stand this any longer."

She went on like this for about ten minutes.

It suddenly dawned on me what a ridiculous figure she looked, striding up and down the room, dressed only in corset and shirt, with her loud lamentations. I began to laugh. Mary must have thought the same thing, because she went off into gales of laughter too. The more we laughed, the more ridiculous and pompous Katherine became. "What is the joke, may I ask?" said she. "You look so funny," said Mary weakly.

The astonished expression on Katherine's face when she heard this was comical to behold. She walked over to the dresser and looked in the mirror. "Well," she said solemnly when she saw herself, "I am a lovely sight," and began the loudest, heartiest, most contagious laugh I have ever heard. We laughed till we cried. And then thoughts of the time and our appearance downstairs returned.

All was confusion. Katherine could not find her dress, and cried dramatically that she was going mad. She wanted the curling-tongs, and when she got them, burned her hair; her shoes would not fit her feet, because of a fractious corn. This time she was being driven to an early grave.

I have never been able to understand how we managed to leave that room at eight o'clock, dressed and ready for the evening's work, that night—or indeed any night after that, because each night brought the same scene, the same laughs, and the same shouting. But we did, and we entered the cabaret with great dignity, our heads held high, according to Katherine's orders.

The music had not yet started and there were but few tables occupied. John was seated at one of these, a glass and a half-emptied pitcher of beer on the table in front of him.

I pointed him out to Katherine, and was rewarded

with a slight smile and a coy tilt of the head; she told me to go and sit with him—she and Mary would join us in a few minutes.

John greeted me with a roguish smile and a wink, and I knew that my worst fears had been realized: he was ready for mischief. "Sit down little cousin," he said jovially, "sit down with John." He was worse than I thought. He beckoned a waiter. "Bring my little cousin a glass of lemonade," he ordered. Out of the corner of my eye I saw Katherine approaching.

"Ah!" she said in her best Lady Katherine voice, as she joined us: "So this is your cousin?" indicating John.

"I am," said John trying to sound important, "I am Barbara's cousin, John Lally."

Katherine went into her act. "I", said she, "am Katherine Leary, the World's Champion Accordion Player."

But her act was wasted on my worthy cousin. "Oh no you don't!" he cried. "You can't fool me. I know you're the cook."

"Young man," said Katherine frigidly, "I am the cook in the day-time. In the evenings I am, as I told you, the World's Champion Accordion Player."

"Naughty, naughty, Katy," cried John, wagging a finger playfully, "you're leading a double life. You just said so, tch, tch!"

Katherine's eyebrows rose at least an inch. "Are you mad, young man?" she asked in a tone of voice that had it been used on me would have made me shrink. But not John. He refused to take anything she said seriously. If she became angry, he said she was flirting with him. A woman of her age, tch, tch! If she spoke icily, he insisted that she was being coy, and when finally she put her hand on his arm and asked him to please act more sensibly, he cried: "Oh, now she wants to play!" That was all she could stand. She could say nothing, but gave vent to a very choked "Oh!", clenched and unclenched her hands spasmodically several times, and walked off with Mary.

Poor Katherine, she never had a chance.

"That wasn't fair, John," I protested after she had left.

"Fair?" he repeated slowly. "Oh it was fair enough, Babs. If I hadn't played her, she would have played me."

"What do you mean by that?" I asked.

"Well", he explained, "if I had let her carry off her champion pose, and been as impressed as she wanted me to be, I'd have had to buy her a drink in the first place, and you would have been more completely under her thumb than you are now, in the second place—understand?"

"No," I shook my head.

He went on. "Because she wasn't successful in our first meeting, she knows she can never pull her champion business with me. That, I think, is where she hits her stride—when anyone believes her—and she holds everyone in the palm of her hand. But she knows now that I've got her labelled, and she'll take good care of you, because she knows you can always come to me if she doesn't. Now do you understand?"

"If you think Mrs. Leary was posing when she was here a moment ago, you're wrong," I told him. "Mrs. Leary doesn't pose—at least, not knowingly. That is the way she really is, when she thinks or talks of music."

"Well, maybe so," he admitted. "But I'm looking out for you anyway."

We had no chance to continue our discussion just then, for Mary came over to tell me that I was to be ready to dance at any moment.

The place had been filling gradually, and when the orchestra began to play at nine o'clock it was fairly crowded. American and Irish music were played in turn. Katherine led the orchestra in the Irish music, and well able she was, too. She received great applause after each number.

John had been listening to her for a few minutes: "By God she's a damn good player, Babs," he said.

"Would you like to dance in a set with me?" I asked.

He shook his head slowly: "No," he said, "no. I'm not in the mood. I'll only dance waltzes all night."

I paid no attention to that. I knew from experience that John always got into moods on one pitcher of beer. It took another pitcher to get him out of them, and start him off. I only had to wait for the next pitcher.

I looked over at Katherine. She was jerking her head in the direction of the floor. A waiter was making an announcement, to the effect that there would be entertainment by Barbara Mullen. Katherine began to play, and I danced. The crowd apparently liked it because I was asked to dance again. I then returned to my seat at the table, and noted with satisfaction that John had called for the second pitcher of beer. Aunt B. was sitting with him. "Meet my friend," he said as I came up, "she's going to dance with me."

"Do you mean me?" Bridget asked.

"Yes, you're the one."

"Oh no!" she cried. "Oh no! Why, I never dance. Thank you all the same."

"What?" said he, "you refuse? But I insist."

Poor Aunt B. looked bewildered. I'm sure no one had ever spoken like that to her before. "Is he angry?" she asked me in a whisper.

"No," I said. "That's just his idea of fun."

Her lips formed a little "O".

The orchestra was playing a jig, and John, who was growing livelier with every mouthful of beer, began to lilt. He kept up a continuous "fol dol di dol", keeping time with his feet. Aunt B.'s head began to move rhythmically from side to side. Unconsciously, I began to drum out the beat with my fingers on the table. People at tables near by began to tap their feet; others to clap their hands in time to the music. John's lilting grew louder and louder.

Everyone in the place, with but few exceptions, had been drinking, and all were in a jolly mood. In a few minutes there wasn't a person in the cabaret who wasn't either trying to lilt with John or else doing their best to stamp out the time of the tune by banging their feet on the floor, or hitting glasses against the table. The orchestra was drowned out completely. All that could be heard was a steady thrump, thrump, thrump, with here and there a drunken "Whoopee!" or "Three cheers for McCluskey's!"

All would have gone well, if one man had resisted the temptation to beat time on another man's back in his enthusiasm—or perhaps if he had been more gentle in his pounding.

There was a loud crash as an overthrown table hit the floor, and the two men were struggling fiercely. Some women screamed, others fainted; some stood up on the tables in order to get a better view of the fight, over the heads of the crowd. Waiters and bouncers came rushing up to separate the two men. Friends of both parties resented the interference, saying that the men should be allowed to fight it out. Arguments and scraps started on all sides of the room. It was developing into a riot.

A waiter ran over to the musicians' platform and spoke to Katherine. She nodded her head quickly, gave a signal to the orchestra, and the musicians, who had stopped playing when the table went over, started again, trying to distract the attention of the crowd from the fight. But it only served to make the noise worse, and they stopped.

Aunt B. was so fragile-looking that I was sure she was going to faint at any moment. She kept saying: "Oh dear me, oh dear me. How rough these men are," over and over again.

John was having the time of his life roaring with laughter.

Mary was elbowing her way through the crowd towards us. "Gosh," she said excitedly. "It's awful. Someone said the police are coming. We'll all be arrested."

The drummer was banging on the cymbals for attention. "Ladies and gentlemen," he was shouting, "ladies and gentlemen!" But it took at least five minutes before the hubbub died down enough for him to make himself heard. "Ladies and gentlemen," he started again. It was Aunt B., bless her, who clapped her hand over John's mouth just in time. It would have pleased him very much if he could have yelled something at the drummer and started the whole thing up again.

The drummer shouted to the effect that the police had been notified, and asked the crowd for the sake of the management as well as their own to sit down quietly, or else they would all be pulled in for rioting.

The siren of the police cars was heard in the distance. The effect it had on the crowd was amazing. Everyone scurried here and there; a few ran out; the women who had fainted made suspiciously speedy recoveries.

There had been a few more tables overturned in the mêlée. These were quickly righted, the bits of broken glass swept into a corner and the music started for the third time. Two or three couples began to dance, and when the police rushed in a few moments later, everyone was conducting themselves in a most respectable manner, and no fault could possibly be found.

The sergeant in charge began to question a few people. "Who's been fighting here?" or "Any fighting been going on here?" He received the same reply from everyone: "Fighting, in here? Oh no."

The police made a circuit of the room, questioned a few waiters, and then left after a warning: "On the next complaint, everyone in this joint gets pulled in anyway, whether you've got things fixed before we get here or not. There's been too many complaints about this place."

The crowd was very subdued and quiet for a while after the police had gone. But there was a tenseness in the air. Everyone felt that something else was going to happen. There was an expectant expression on all faces.

It was Katherine who told us what to expect next. She came over to our table, and her first words as she sat down were: "Mr. McCluskey is drunk, and he is locked in a room upstairs. The waiter told me."

"Why have they locked him up?" I asked.

"He goes absolutely crazy when he drinks," said Katherine briefly.

"He gets violent," said Aunt B.

"He sets fire to things," said Mary.

"There'll be a hot time in the ole town to-night," prophesied John.

There was a crash of splintering wood. "He's out!" cried Katherine. Then came a sound of thundering footsteps on the stairs, and shouts of "Hold him! For God's sake hold him!" Then there was a loud banging and screaming from the bar-room, and McCluskey—with two waiters trying vainly to hold him back—burst into the cabaret.

The patrons, gasping, half rose from their seats. "Sit down," he shouted. They sat. "Silence!" he shouted. There was silence. He shook off the two waiters and strode into the centre of the room, held up his hand and cried: "Drinks for the house are on me."

The crowd didn't know whether to cheer or run. Apparently McCluskey's drinking sprees were well known in Rockaway Beach. McCluskey himself settled it by shouting: "Three cheers for Mattie McCluskey. The best man in the Rockaways." The crowd gave the three cheers. "Bring on the drinks," they cried.

There were at least two hundred people in the place with 25 cents the price of the cheapest drink. The cost of McCluskey's spree would be enormous. "He must be crazy to do a thing like this," I said. "He's drinking all his profits."

"You don't know good nature when you see it," John remarked. "Sure the creature can't help it."

"Good nature!" cried Mary. "You won't think he's good-natured before the night is over. Just wait."

Suddenly Katherine flew into action. "Hush," she whispered, "he's coming over here." She laughed a bit. "As I was saying," she said aloud, in the manner of one who is continuing a conversation, "there is no place in Rockaway that I'd rather work in than here. Mr. McCluskey is the finest man I have ever met." An amazed look was spreading over John's face. He opened his mouth to speak, but Katherine made a slight movement with her hand and stopped him. "He's getting nearer," whispered Mary.

"Mr. McClusky is a splendid man," Aunt B. said, playing up for all she was worth.

"Why Mr. McCluskey," cried Katherine, as if in great surprise, as he reached us, "we were just talking about you."

"We certainly were," from John, and my heart jumped into my mouth.

"And what were you saying?" asked Mr. McCluskey, as though he hadn't heard nearly every word.

"I was telling Barbara here what a fine, generous man you are," said Katherine.

"You were, like hell," John muttered.

"No better man in Rockaway," said Aunt B. quickly.

A pleased smile spread over McCluskey's face. He turned to me.

"What do you think of me?" he asked.

"I think——" I began.

"She thinks"—John interrupted—"that you're crazy as hell and that you drink up all your profits."

Katherine nearly fainted. Mary began to giggle. "He'll go mad altogether now," I thought.

I don't know what I expected McCluskey to do—to lay John flat or begin throwing punches. But whatever it was he didn't do it. No, he began to cry. "Ah, no one appreciates me," he sobbed. "No one. Not even my wife. I haven't a friend in the world. Not *one* friend." He put his arms round John. "Will you be my friend?" he asked.

"I'll be your friend," said John, and put McCluskey's head on his shoulder. Katherine's eyes nearly popped out of their sockets as John, over the head of his new friend, thumbed his nose at her.

Mary was giggling again. I didn't blame her. McCluskey was a huge man, and he did look silly with his head on John's shoulder, crying as if his heart would break. Even Aunt B.'s lips were twitching. She reached over and patted McCluskey's shoulder. "Come girls," she said, "we will leave these two friends alone."

John looked at me pleadingly. He was all right while he had an audience, but being saddled with McCluskey and left there, by no means pleased him. He appealed to Katherine, as Mary and I got up. "Don't go Mrs. Leary, stay here and have a drink with us."

"Why John," she said sweetly, "I wouldn't dream of such a thing. I'm sure Mr. McCluskey wants you all to himself. Don't you, Mr. McCluskey?"

"My friend. My *only* friend," was the reply.

"I'm sure you'll have a very pleasant evening together," went on Katherine, and got her own back by thumbing her nose at John as we walked away.

A tall stout woman came hurrying towards us. "Here comes Mrs. McCluskey," said Mary. "I wonder what she wants."

"The poor thing," said Aunt B. "She looks worried."

"Oh, Mrs. Leary," cried Mrs. McCluskey. "You're just the person I want. What am I going to do?"

"My dear," Katherine reassured her, "you need not worry about him now. He's with John. He's crying and I'm sure he'll be nice and quiet for the rest of the night, and not make any trouble."

"It won't last," said Mrs. McCluskey. "Whoever John is, he'll never be able to make McCluskey stay put."

"John is Barbara's cousin," Katherine explained. "He came with her this afternoon."

Mrs. McCluskey looked at me. "I saw you dancing," she said. "You're the best we've ever had here. You and Katherine make a good team. I hope you won't leave because of Mr. McCluskey. We're really all one big happy family when he is in his sober senses. You poor child. All this drinking and excitement must be quite a shock for you. Boston is a very law-abiding city, I hear."

"It is a nice city," I replied. What would she say if she knew I had been fed on drinking and excitement all my life? I wondered.

"Wouldn't you like a cup of tea?" she asked. "We'll go in the kitchen, just ourselves, and have it in peace. We have an exciting night out before us. Are you coming Katherine?"

"No," said Katherine. "I must go and play now, but I'll join you as soon as I've finished, if you're still there."

"How old are you, Barbara?" Mrs. McCluskey asked, when we were seated round the kitchen table.

"Sixteen," I told her.

"Have you ever danced in a cabaret before?"

"No, not in a cabaret."

"Do you smoke?"

"No."

"Drink?"

"No."

"What a shock all this must be to you," she said. "I've never been in Boston, but I've heard a lot about it. You've probably never seen a drunken man before in your life. Have you?"

"Well——" I passed this off with a smile. I wondered what part of Boston she was talking about.

"You must not take any notice of all this," she went on. "You won't after a while, you'll get so accustomed to it. My only advice to you is, just be careful of the men. They are inclined to flirt with every girl they see, and don't you go and get taken in by any of them. You are old enough to know what I mean," she added knowingly. I nodded. I didn't know what she was talking about, but I thought I'd better agree with her for safety's sake. She was asking too many questions and she might ask a lot more if I did not pretend to understand her. Later I could get an explanation from Katherine or Mary.

Before I could get more deeply involved, Aunt B. changed the subject by bringing Mr. McCluskey's name into the conversation. His weekly drinking sprees were discussed at great length. During his last one, I learned, he had gotten the fire bug mania and had set the building afire. It was put out before any great damage was done, however. The time before that, he had chased customers, guests, and employees out into the street and locked all the doors. Most of the roomers had left the next day.

"My dear Mrs. McCluskey," announced Katherine as she entered the kitchen. "Our worries are over. Your husband and John are talking very confidentially, and I'm positive that he will go to sleep soon, and wake up sober."

"Are there many people outside?" she was asked.

"Not more than twenty now. The waiters are getting them all to leave very quietly, one by one. The rest will be gone soon."

"We lose more and more money every time he does this," said Mrs. McCluskey. "It's not midnight yet and still we must close up, when we wouldn't close till three if he wasn't drinking. That means at least two hundred dollars lost, and if he does any damage before the night is over, another couple of hundred. Besides all those drinks on the house. We've lost every cent we ever made through his drinking." She paused. We all sighed deeply in unison, in sympathy with her. There was silence, broken only by the occasional clink of a tea-cup against a saucer. Katherine yawned. I followed suit.

The hours dragged along. Nobody did anything much: the orchestra was silent, the bar-tenders washed their glasses and bottles quietly. McCluskey and John were still seated in the cabaret, talking confidentially. They were the only occupants of the room. When the clock struck three, they were still at it. I was growing sleepy, Aunt B. was nodding. According to the reports of various waiters who came in and out of the kitchen, everything seemed peaceful enough. It seemed as if McCluskey was at last going to finish a drinking bout in a civilized manner, so following Mrs. McCluskey's suggestion Katherine, Mary and I went up to number twelve. Aunt B.'s room was in another wing of the building, and though she said she thought she might get some sleep after all, she decided to come to number twelve with us, "just in case".

There was not much talk as we were undressing. It was decided that I should squeeze in between Katherine and Mary in the bed and give Aunt B. the divan, and one after another we settled down to sleep.

I felt somebody shaking me. It was Katherine. "Quick Barbara. Get up. Get up," she was saying in a loud whisper. I looked at the clock on the dresser. It was just past 4 a.m. Mary and Aunt B. were standing by the door in their dressing gowns.

"What's the matter?" I asked as I got up.

"I heard a scream and someone shouting," said Katherine.

"It's McCluskey, I'll bet," said Aunt B.

I listened intently, but could hear nothing. We waited for a few minutes, but all was silent.

"Maybe you were dreaming," said Aunt B.

"No," said Katherine. "I hadn't gone to sleep at all. I'm sure I heard a scream. I don't think we'd better go to bed again."

Katherine was sitting on the edge of the bed, in her nightgown. She hushed Aunt B.'s suggestion of a dressing gown. We sat there waiting for something to happen, but nothing did, and at length Aunt B. said that we might as well go back to bed. Whatever it was, it was all over.

Then there was a knock at the door. We heard Mrs. McCluskey's voice. "Are you awake Katherine? For God's sake let me in." Katherine jumped to the door and opened it. Mrs. McCluskey nearly fell in. She was white and panting. "It's him," she gasped. "He's got an axe, and he's after me." Aunt B. and Katherine led her to the bed. "He's never turned on me before," she went on. "I saw him in the dining-room. He was waving the axe over his head. He chased me. I ran up the front stairs and came here."

"Where did he go?" Katherine asked.

"I don't know. I didn't wait. I just ran."

"The brute," exclaimed Katherine indignantly. "I'd just like to get my hands on him."

She didn't have to wait long to get her wish. There was a loud clamouring on the back stairs. We could hear McCluskey's voice as he ran along the hall. Katherine in her anger forgot her fear, and dressed only in her long flowing nightgown, rushed madly into the hall, leaving the door open behind her.

She came face to face with McCluskey. But the sight of the axe and his mad eyes were too much for her, and with a shriek she fled down the front stairs, shouting: "Jesus, Ma-a-ary and Joseph save me."

The unexpected apparition of Katherine, and her shriek, did queer things to McCluskey. Utterly unnerved, he dropped the axe and ran furiously for the back stairs.

Aunt B. began to wring her hands. "Oh," she moaned, "they'll meet at the bottom. She'll surely be killed." She turned to John, who had come out of his room at the end of the hall and joined us. "Can't you do something?" she cried. "Don't stand there laughing. She'll be murdered." For John was hootling with laughter. "She frightened poor McCluskey out of his wits," said he. Katherine's screaming suddenly became wilder. "He's got me," we heard. She and McCluskey had met at the bottom.

Mary was becoming hysterical. Mrs. McCluskey was rocking back and forth. I turned to John. "Please go down," I pleaded, "you can do something with him. He likes you."

"No one dares go near him," moaned Aunt B.

"Please go down," I said again.

He took the stairs three at a time, shouting, "Mac. Hey Mac. It's John. Where are you?" He reached the bottom, and collided full tilt with Katherine. "Are you hurt?" we heard him ask. But Katherine couldn't speak. "Hey Babs, come down and get her," he called to me. "I'm going to find McCluskey."

Mary came with me, and between the two of us we managed to half drag, half carry the shaking Katherine upstairs and into the room. We put her sitting on the bed and gave her water. Gradually her trembling ceased and she became quiet.

It was she who spoke first. "That man. Oh! He scared me half to death. Never have I had such an experience. I'm sure he would have killed me if John hadn't come. Where is he?"

"Where is who?" I asked.

"John. Where is he?"

"He's coming upstairs with McCluskey," reported Aunt B., who had left the door open a crack, and was peering through it. "It looks as though McCluskey is all right again."

We could hear the voices of the two men. "I'm really a gentle soul, John," McCluskey was saying. "I only wanted a little fun."

"I know, I understand," said John's voice. "No one appreciates you but me." The voices faded away, and all inside number twelve breathed easier.

"I hope John puts him to bed," said Mrs. McCluskey. "Thank God you weren't hurt Katherine. What happened when you met McCluskey at the bottom?"

"That's the strangest part of it," said Mrs. Leary. "I bumped into him at the bottom. I was sure he was going to strangle me or something, but he did nothing at all. He just stood there, his eyes nearly popping out of his head." We all expressed our amazement at her narrow escape. "Do you think John will come back here?" Mary asked.

"I suppose so," I said. "He'll want to know how Katherine is."

Nearly half an hour had passed before we heard his knock and low voice: "It's me, John." Katherine, now in her dressing gown, opened the door and let him in.

He informed us, to our great relief, that Mr. McCluskey was now in bed and sleeping as peacefully as a child. "He wouldn't hurt a fly," he concluded.

"You wouldn't think so if you saw him with that axe," said Katherine.

Off went John in roars again, when he heard this. "What's so funny?" she demanded.

"You," said John. "D'you know that you scared poor Mac out of his senses when you met him outside the door here and shrieked? That's why he dropped the axe and ran. You nearly finished him altogether when you came together at the bottom. He couldn't move."

It did sound funny as John told it, and Katherine, always the first to appreciate a joke on herself, began to laugh heartily. Mary, Aunt B. Mrs. McCluskey and I joined in the laughter—and loud and long it was.

There was no sleep for any of our group that night. It was nearing six o'clock, and daylight, when John left us to dress. We agreed to meet in half an hour in the kitchen for breakfast. John had told Katherine that he thought she was O.K. after all. Katherine said that she didn't think he was so bad either, and the end of the meal saw the two firm friends—to my great delight, as I liked them both.

Chapter Three

Cakes and Water in New York

★

Katherine's duties as cook began at 7 a.m., Aunt B.'s and Mary's at seven-thirty, and John and I, finding the time hanging heavily on our hands, went for a walk along the shore.

How long we were to be at McCluskey's was the question uppermost in my mind. During our walk, I asked John what he thought, though I did not tell him why I was so anxious to know. He told me that it could not be more than two weeks, since Labour Day, the first Monday in September, brought the close of the season.

Later that afternoon, sitting alone with Katherine in number twelve, I asked her where we were going from McCluskey's. She answered that Aunt B. was leaving the following Sunday for the city, to put the apartment in order in which we were to live while we were in New York.

"Do you think we will be in the apartment very long?" I asked after a pause.

"You seem more than interested," said she. "Have you any particular reason?"

"I have," I admitted. "I want to write to my father."

"Your father?" she interrupted in surprise, "why, I thought your father was dead."

"No," I told her. "He's in Ireland. My mother doesn't want me to write to him."

"Then why do you want to do so?"

I could not tell her the real reason—that I wanted his help—so I gave her another. "I want to find out what he's like," I said.

"How long has he been in Ireland?" she asked.

"Seven years."

"Haven't you ever written to him before?"

"No, I haven't."

"I don't know why I should take it for granted that he was dead, but I did," she said. "Perhaps because your mother did all the arranging about you coming away with me. She seemed to run everything herself, and never spoke at all about consulting your father. Why doesn't she want you to write to him?"

"I don't know," I told her. "She just doesn't."

"I don't think any child should be kept from communicating with its father, and certainly I can understand that you want to know what he is like, but what will your mother say?"

"She will be very angry if she finds out," I said, and I shivered. My mother's anger would know no bounds, and well I knew it.

"Well," said Katherine at length, "I don't stop Mary from writing to her father, and whatever reason your mother may have for not writing to your father herself, she should not forbid you to do so. I don't know what your mother will say to me if she ever finds out, but you go ahead and write your letter when we get to the apartment in the city. We'll be there for a good spell, while we are getting the act into shape, and arranging for a contract, long enough for you to get your answer anyway."

"And you won't tell my mother?" I asked eagerly.

"No," she replied. "I'll keep it quiet. Though I'm not sure whether I'm doing the right thing or not, going against your mother's wishes," she went on doubtfully, "but time will tell about that part of it, and for the present I will not tell her anything about it."

I was very grateful to her and said so. Then the thought struck me that while I had the chance I had better talk to her about school.

Under the laws of the State of Massachusetts, I should continue to go to school until I reached the age of sixteen. School life had never been pleasant for me. More than one of the nuns who taught at the school I attended were prone to give lectures about the evils of whiskey and the awful fate that would befall those who handled it in any way. During these lectures I could feel the glances of both teacher and pupils upon me, and I squirmed in my seat.

In the past year I had been very busy dancing, generally having engagements for three out of five nights in the week. On these nights, in the rush of running home from school, dressing, eating dinner, getting to wherever I had to dance, and then coming home late at night, I was unable to study. It was not unusual for me to fall asleep over my desk the next day at school, and I found it much easier simply to stand up and say that I did not know the answer to any question that was put to me, than to stumble through it. No enquiries were ever made of my mother about the reason for my drowsiness and lack of interest in my lessons; no one seemed aware of the fact that in the last year I had gone from amongst the heads of the class, where I had been for the entire eight years of grammar school, down to the bottom. Both teacher and pupils evidently expected me to fail, and I was never asked at home if I studied my lessons. I had begun to feel "if they laugh when I fail, and look so surprised when I pass that they scare me, and if no one here seems to think I'll ever know anything, what's the use?" I became so self-conscious, that in my first and only year at high school I avoided all contact with both teachers and girls as much as was possible. Whether I knew my lessons or not I deliberately failed in them, rather than stand up before the class to give a correct answer.

One afternoon the teacher, one of the few who seemed to understand that school had become a place of torture for me, kept me in when the class had been dismissed. She asked me what was wrong, and why I wouldn't make an attempt to keep up in my studies; begged me to try not to mind the sneers and jibes of the girls, and to get back amongst the leaders of the class where I had always been. She said that she would help me, but it was no use—I was too bound up inside. I shrugged my shoulders and told her that I would try, but both of us knew that I did not mean it, and she gave me up. Perhaps she realized how cruel schoolgirls can be. She may have known of the time when during a morning recess period in the school playground, one of the girls had pointed a finger at me and cried in front of the class that my mother had been arrested. I could not answer her because I did not then know how to fight a battle with my tongue, so I demanded that she should either take back what she had said about my mother or fight it out. She elected to fight it out, and proceeded to slap my face, which was a mistake on her part, because years of battling with Puffy had taught me to use my fists as well as almost any boy. I dived into her and beat her so beautifully that she had to be sent home for the rest of the day. She never told either her parents or the nuns who had torn her dress to ribbons and given her a bloody nose, because I threatened her the way Puffy often threatened me, that if she told who had beaten her, I would give her twice as much.

This was only one of the many such incidents that made up my school life, and whether or not the teacher knew it, she never again offered to help me. If she had, the girls would surely have noticed it and jumped at the opportunity of hanging another name on me, probably "teacher's pet". I couldn't ask my mother to let me leave school, or to send me to another; she wouldn't have understood how I felt if I had told her, and I couldn't explain in words how the girls had hurt me.

Now I was over two hundred miles away from all of them, and Mrs. Leary seemed sent from heaven. She had taken me away from Boston, and she had cleared the way for me to communicate with my father. I suspected that I was not to return to school, but it seemed too good to be true and I was not yet sure of my ground, so one day I told her that I should be returning to school in a few weeks. She put me on solid ground when she said: "Oh you have had enough education. You must now think of your career as a dancer."

"Do you think the nuns might want to know why I don't go back?" I asked.

"Your mother will tell them that you've gone to New York or to Ireland or some place. The authorities in New York will not bother you so long as you look and act sixteen years old."

My way seemed clear at last. I was away from whiskey: true, I was still surrounded by it, but no longer part of it as I had been. These thoughts brought to my mind the free and easy way in which the drinks were sold over the bar and served to the customers at McCluskey's. They apparently had no fear of raids as we had in Boston. Maybe Mrs. Leary could explain this. "How come McCluskey's aren't afraid of getting raided?" I asked her. "They don't need to be," she replied. "The police seldom if ever make raids. Prohibition is a national law, but it hasn't been adopted by the State of New York as it has been by Massachusetts."

"It sounds a bit mixed up to me," I said. "I don't understand."

"Well that's what Mr. McCluskey told me one day when he was sober. I don't know whether I've got it all mixed up or not. But I do know that all the speakeasies and dance halls in New York are wide open."

"What does that mean?" I wanted to know.

"It means", she explained, "that they all sell drinks with no fear of being raided unless by the Federal Officers, and that rarely—if ever—happens. Your mother would make a fortune here."

I shook my head. "She might make a fortune here, but she'd never like it whether she did or not. She likes

Boston and the battling she has with the cops, and proving that she can beat them. It wouldn't have the same kick in New York. It would be too easy."

Katherine was about to speak when Mary poked her head into the room.

"Have you seen John?" she asked. "Aunt B.'s looking for him. It's getting near his train time. He told us to be sure and not let him be late. He wants to get back to the city early this evening."

"We've been up here most of the afternoon," said Katherine. "Barbara, you go and look for him, he should be around somewhere. Bring him into the kitchen, he'll want a cup of tea before he goes."

I found John at the bar, trying without any apparent success to open up a conversation with his friend of the night before, Mr. McCluskey.

On the way from the bar to the kitchen John was silent. He looked puzzled as though he was not sure whether he should be angry or laugh. "What is wrong?" asked Aunt B. when she saw him. "McCluskey," he said. "I went up and spoke to him at the bar, and he looked right through me, as if he'd never seen me before in his life."

"He doesn't remember you, John," Katherine told him. "Mr. McCluskey's mind becomes a blank whenever he drinks. He remembers nothing."

"Not even the axe," said Aunt B.

"Sure I thought there was something gone haywire," said John. "There's a lot of people like that. Can't remember anything after the first two or three have been dusted off—oh well," and he sighed. Whether or not he himself experienced that he did not say.

Katherine and I walked to the station with him. The train was already in. "Walk on down the platform," directed John. "I'm going in and get a seat, there'll be none left in a minute. I'll get a seat next to a window, and we can talk."

"Don't forget to call on us when we get to New York, John," said Katherine, when having found a desirable seat he poked his head out of the window.

"You can bet on that," said he. "I have the address put away in my wallet. So long," he shouted as the train began to pull out. "Take care of Babs."

"I will," cried Katherine. "Good-bye John."

"Good-bye John," I called.

We waited till the train had left the station and then walked back to McCluskey's.

For the next week there was much talk between the Leary family and myself concerning the apartment that Aunt B. was going to put in order for us. Curtains, dishes, our prospective neighbours, all were discussed with enthusiasm.

"Isn't it going to cost a lot to buy everything that we need?" I asked on the day Aunt B. was to leave.

"Oh the apartment is completely furnished already," I was told. "We just rent it, as it is, for ten dollars a week. Aunt B. is going to arrange it in her own way to make it as attractive and homelike as possible, and get acquainted with the neighbours, so that when we arrive there everything will be very pleasant."

The nearest I had ever been to an apartment, were the "flats", in the tenement district of South Boston. We had never lived in one, but my mother had sometimes hired one, for the sole purpose of hiding or storing whiskey or bottles.

But the way that Katherine said "arranging curtains, adding a few personal touches", made me picture in my mind a smallish home, perhaps three rooms, bright and airy, and, recollecting Katherine's former home in Arlington, spotlessly clean. There would, no doubt, be a potted plant or two, and some flowers—they would be one of the personal touches.

I looked forward eagerly to my life in New York. I had always lived in a big house. Living in an apartment, especially the kind I was thinking of, would be something new. And it certainly was.

The Wednesday after Labour Day, Katherine, Mary and I arrived at Pennsylvania Station in New York City. When I had come from Boston, John had met me at Grand Central Station, and had whisked me out of some side entrance and into a cab so quickly that I hadn't a chance to look round. In Pennsylvania Station, however, it was different. Katherine and Mary knew as little about New York as I did, having rushed off to Rockaway without giving the big city a second glance. Thus it was our first real look at New York and we were astounded. There seemed to be no end to the crowds of people who were rushing like mad for trains, or through doors or round in circles. Everywhere we looked, people were running or walking at great speed. The noise that exists wherever there are crowds and activity got on Katherine's nerves as we went upstairs to the street. Here the noise grew into a positive roar. All around us were taxis, hundreds of them, and it sounded as if every taxi driver was tooting his automobile horn. Street cars were clanging up and down the street; ambulances, fire engines, and police cars were chasing each other all over the place. We were bumped into and jostled dozens of times; the day was very hot and sultry, and we were hungry and weighted down with luggage.

Aunt B. had written to Katherine telling her that the apartment was on Second Avenue near Thirty-Second Street, and giving directions as to what street car would take us there. We were to take a cross-town car and get off at Second Avenue. It sounded very simple, but Aunt B. had neglected to say whether Second Avenue was on the East or West Side of New York, and two hours after our arrival in New York found Katherine, Mary and me hopelessly lost somewhere on Tenth Avenue. We were all on the verge of tears. Katherine refused to take a taxi, saying that she had read of many cases in which women, having hired taxis in New York, had been whisked off somewhere and never seen again.

At length it was decided that we should walk back to Pennsylvania Station, if we could find it, then walk in the other direction for a few blocks, and if we did not then find Second Avenue, risk a taxi. "And", said Katherine, "if we're not kidnapped we'll surely be charged five or six dollars over the real fare." She was sure that we were going to have our pockets picked or purses snatched at any moment, and kept continually looking into her purse to make sure that she still had her money. Several times during the afternoon she was on the point of asking a policeman where Second Avenue was, and which car to take, but each time she changed her mind at the last minute, saying: "No, I won't, we'll take this car, I'm sure it's the right one——"

By the time we reached Pennsylvania Station again we were all so tired that we couldn't walk any farther unless we abandoned our luggage, and so in desperation Katherine signalled a taxi. We reached the apartment in less than twenty minutes, and the meter read something like fifty or sixty cents. The driver deposited our luggage in a dark, smelly hall. Katherine rang one of a dozen or more push bells, and we struggled up a flight of stairs, to be met by Aunt B. as she was coming out into the dirty corridor. When we all entered the apartment I got the drop of my life. It was one large room, divided in the middle by a pair of long, dark-green curtains. On one side of the curtains were a bed, a bureau, and a closet; on the other, a couch-bed, a large table, a gas stove, and a box, with a shelf across the middle on which were a few dishes. The room had one window, which looked out on a fire escape, a tiny patch of yard, and five stories' worth of brick wall, dotted here and there with windows. The apartment was stiflingly hot. The window was open, but no breeze could possibly find its way over or between the buildings and into the room. Now and then a slight puff of air would manage to get in, and with it came odours of garlic and onions, or fish, and sometimes garbage. Aunt B. looked worn and dusty. "I'm afraid the dinner is spoiled," she told us. "I expected you much earlier." We explained what had happened. "I've been riding in New York taxis off and on for years", Aunt B. said to Katherine, "and I'm still in one piece. You'll get over your fear of them after you've been here a while; they go with the city."

I longed for a cool bath. I asked Aunt B. if there was a bath. No, there wasn't; just a tiny sink, in a tiny closet next to the gas stove.

So much for the bright airy rooms, potted plants and flowers of my imagination.

Katherine spent the evening with her feet in a basin of cold water. Aunt B., Mary and I unpacked, and it was decided that Mary and I should sleep on the couch-bed, Katherine and Aunt B. on the bed. There was some talk about producers and agents who would have to be seen at the earliest possible moment, and we turned in to spend a hot and uncomfortable, sleepless night.

I spent the following afternoon in writing my first letter to my father. I wrote several, only to tear them up after reading them over. I did not know how to address him. Finally I consulted Katherine, who in turn consulted Aunt B. It was so long since he had left America that I could not remember what I used to call him. At length we dismissed "Dear Daddy", and "Dear Papa", and decided that "Dear Father", was the proper thing. I cannot now recall the contents of that first letter, but I do know that it was a most unhappy one. It was posted that evening, and with it went my prayers for a speedy reply.

Katherine had a long list of producers' names and theatrical offices. It was our plan to go from the top to the bottom of that list, seeing every producer and every agent. "I'm sure", said Katherine, "that we will not have to try more than two offices. People will be only too glad of a chance to engage us after they see what we can do." We had no set routine. Katherine would play a few numbers, I would dance, or perhaps one or the other of us would sing. Neither of us could sing. Katherine's voice was hoarse, mine broke on every second note. But if we were asked in any of the offices whether we could sing or not, the reply was to be: "Oh yes indeed," and such was Katherine's optimism that she really believed we could manage to put it over.

Before starting on our way to Stardom, Aunt B. told us that our venture should have the blessing of heaven, else we should have no luck. Accordingly the four of us began a Novena at the Little Flower Church on East 29th Street. Aunt B. went to the afternoon service; Katherine, Mary and I went in the evenings. It was through one of these afternoon services that Aunt B. first met Mr. Martin. Mr. Martin was a little old man, with long white hair, big blue eyes, and a very innocent, honest face. He was almost as religious as Aunt B. The latter was fond of buying flowers to lay on the altar of the Little Flower. Mr. Martin was fond of doing the same thing. They both bought flowers from the same flower woman, every day at the same time. Each was impressed by the undoubtedly sincere piety of the other, and in a while Aunt B. was bringing the little old man to the apartment to hear Katherine play and to see me dance. We performed for Mr. Martin regularly every evening, after the Novena services. In this way we met Mr. and Mrs. Gleason, who had the apartment above ours, and old Maggie Murphy, who lived behind one of the doors across the hall from us.

We first became aware of the Gleasons' existence when during a pause in the entertainment for Mr. Martin, we heard what sounded like an Irish Reel being played on a violin. Katherine went out on the fire escape in order to hear better, and directed by the sound of the music looked up and saw Mr. and Mrs. Gleason sitting on the fire escape, outside their apartment window. The violinist was Mr. Gleason. "Hello up there," called Katherine, "come on down the two of you and we'll play a few tunes together." They came down, and nearly every night after that either we went upstairs, or they came down.

Maggie Murphy was all of eighty years of age. She was tall and powerfully built, though a trifle bent, and lame. She introduced herself by the simple expedient of banging on the door and asking if there was any reason why she shouldn't join the party. There wasn't, and she walked in and made herself right at home.

Katherine and I had formed the habit of practising every morning, from nine to ten o'clock. We felt no compunction about disturbing any of the other tenants in the building, as there was always enough noise or shouting coming from one apartment or another to give us sufficient reason for contributing our share to the bedlam, if reason were needed.

Beyond Maggie Murphy and the Gleasons, we knew no one else in the building, not even their names or what they looked like. Therefore it was with some surprise that one morning during our practice hour we heard a steady gentle tapping on the door. Katherine opened the door and saw a strange man of medium height. "Yes?" she said inquiringly.

"I'm Michael," said the man in a hushed voice. "I live in the apartment under yours."

"Well?" said Katherine.

"I don't like to disturb you," went on the man, "but my uncle died last night and there are quite a few people in the house this morning, all our relations. We can hear the music very plainly, and it sounds so strange, hearing jigs while we are watching a dead body, that I came up to ask if you would mind not playing any more till after the body has been taken to the undertaking parlour this afternoon?"

"Oh I'm so sorry," said Katherine, "I had no idea ——"

"I didn't like to ask you, but you see how it is?"

"Yes, of course. You should have told us before."

Katherine was genuinely upset over this incident. "Imagine, Bridget! Why, such a thing could never happen in Arlington! If a person died there, all the neighbours would know about it in less than an hour," she said, shocked.

"My dear Katherine," said Aunt B., who had lived in New York for years and wouldn't dream of living in any other city, "this is not Arlington, it's New York. People here are not interested in their neighbours' lives or how they live them. They mind their own business, which is the proper thing to do."

Katherine was not appeased however, and from that morning she hated New York, and was loud in criticism and dispraise of it whenever she got anyone to listen to her.

We lived high for the nine days of the Novena. Katherine did all the baking and cooking; she was a fanatic on cleanliness and health. We never bought bread or canned vegetables, for Katherine had a horror of anything in a can. She was constantly deploring the fact that modern women, New York women in particular, knew nothing about cooking. "The national emblem of this country should be a can-opener," she would proclaim loudly. But then, Katherine could afford to talk, or boast. Her baking was delicious, and she could make carrots and spinach melt in one's mouth the way she cooked them.

Then came the close of the Novena and the discovery that nine days of idleness had put a good-sized dent in the family purse. Katherine was not alarmed. "We have been extravagant," she admitted, "but there is no need to worry. Barbara and I will start to-morrow and visit the agencies. I'm sure we'll have a job before the day is over."

The next morning saw Katherine and me at Times Square. We went from one booking office to another; we tried Keith's and Loew's and at least a dozen others, and in each office we were told to "Come back to-morrow".

"Well," said Katherine hopefully as we trudged homeward after an unsuccessful day, "they must do all their big business to-morrow, so we'll try again." At the end of the week we were both limping. We knew the Times Square district as well as we knew our apartment, we faithfully visited every office on our list every day, and were regularly told to come back to-morrow, but still Katherine's hopes were high.

"Why don't you try one of the smaller booking agents instead of trying to get a contract with Keith's or Loew's circuit right away?" suggested Aunt B. at the close of the second week of fruitless searching.

"People sometimes try for years before they get a contract or even a try-out with either place."

Aunt B.'s store of gentleness and patience was inexhaustible. To Katherine's frequent outbursts of "Jesus, Mary and Joseph I'm being driven to my grave!" Aunt B. would reply with a quiet smile, or a casual remark, that worked wonders with Katherine's temperament. She was never too busy to listen to our recital of the day's adventures, and was ever ready with sound advice. No one was more overjoyed than she on the night we told her that we had, after acting on her suggestion, made arrangements for a try-out in a small theatre on the West Side. It was the beginning of our fifth week in New York. The try-out was to be on the following Friday. We had four days in which to practise as much as possible so that there should be no chance of failure.

On Friday afternoon, Katherine, Mary and I started out for a short walk. Aunt B. who usually spent her afternoons in church, decided to stay in, saying that she wanted to give our costumes a final look over. As we reached the street, Katherine suddenly remembered that she had not told Bridget to regulate the gas oven. She feared that Bridget might not think of it and that our dinner would be burnt, and nothing would do but that we should all three go back again. Katherine reached the apartment first, and Mary and I, still in the hall, heard her cry "Bridget! My God! What's the matter?" Mary and I rushed into the room. We saw Bridget with an expression of awful agony on her face; she had one hand pressed against her breast, the other was grasping the edge of the kitchen table. "It's nothing, Katherine," she said weakly, "just a slight pain." She walked over and sat on the couch-bed. "It's gone now." But the expression in her eyes belied her words.

"Tell me what is wrong," demanded Katherine. "No slight pain would make you look as you did when we came in here." Aunt B. refused to tell us, but Katherine declared that she would not leave the house that night, try-out or no try-out, till she knew what ailed Bridget. All Aunt B.'s protestations were of no avail. Katherine wouldn't give an inch till she knew what was wrong, and eventually she won.

Some few months before, related Aunt B., when the Leary family was living in Arlington, she had paid them a short visit. During her stay she had helped Katherine to move some furniture, while arranging a room, and had accidently hit her left breast against a sharp corner of a dresser. It had been very painful at the time, but she had said nothing about it, as she did not want to cause Katherine anxiety, and besides she was sure it would be all right in a few days. It was some time after this that the pain had become intense and that she had noticed a lump growing on her breast. Knowing how apt Katherine was to worry, Aunt B. had continued to suffer in silence. Since going to Rockaway the pain had grown worse. She had not gone to a doctor because she felt that we should need the few dollars she would have had to pay him. Katherine insisted that Aunt B. should show her her breast, saying that perhaps she could do something to ease the pain. It was a hard, purple lump, about the size of a half-dollar, on the upper part of the left breast. It was an ugly looking thing, and Katherine's face paled when she saw it. She did none of the things you would expect from a person of her temperament: to faint, or go into hysterics. In a very calm voice she said: "You should have spoken about this before. We'll go to a doctor to-morrow and find out what it is. It is probably nothing but pus that has formed into a ball and hardened. Mary once had something like that in her ear," she finished casually.

"Do you think it will have to be lanced?" asked Aunt B.

"It might," Katherine told her. "I'd bathe it but bathing may be the wrong thing to do for it. We'll see what the doctor says."

"We cannot afford to spend money on doctor's bills," protested Aunt B. But Katherine silenced her by saying that there was no doubt about us getting work after the try-out that night. She directed Aunt B. to lie down and rest, and said we would go on with our walk.

Outside the apartment door Katherine nearly collapsed. She staggered and caught hold of Mary for support. "My God!" she said hoarsely. "My God!" Mary and I said nothing. We just stood there, one on each side of her, holding her as best we could. Somehow we both knew that we should not go into the apartment for water; that Aunt B. must not know. We helped Katherine downstairs and into the street. The air served to revive her, and though her face was still pale she seemed steady enough. "Is it Aunt B?" I asked in a whisper. She nodded.

"Do you know what it is?"

"Yes, I know," she said. Her voice broke, but she was very quiet. "I've seen it before," she went on, "it's cancer."

"Gosh!" I said.

"Why didn't you tell her?" Mary asked.

"How could I?" said Katherine. "Besides, Bridget would not want me to know. She'd be happier if she thought I didn't." She turned to us. "The doctor will tell her to-morrow. Maybe she will tell us what he says, and maybe she will not. If she does not tell us, we must never let her guess that we know what it is. It would kill her if she thought we were worrying about her at all. We must pretend there is nothing wrong, and keep her cheered up as much as possible, while we have her."

Katherine was badly shaken; between herself and Aunt B. there existed a deep, sincere affection. To Katherine her sister's death was already a certainty, but she bore up under the knowledge with an amazing, calm courage, that stayed with her all the long months of Aunt B.'s illness.

The try-out that evening was successful. We were one of several acts, there for the same reason. The booking agent was out in front. He was well pleased with us and gave Katherine his card, saying: "Come in and see me to-morrow afternoon."

In the morning Aunt B. went to the doctor. True to Katherine's prophecy, she dismissed the account of her visit with a casual "very ordinary case. I shall have to go to the hospital for a few days till they attend to it. Nothing to worry about."

The afternoon brought an interview with the booking agent, and several engagements—all "one night stands"—in small theatres in New York City and Long Island.

The evening brought Mr. Gleason, and Mr. Gleason's uncle, "Uncle Tom" McGiveney. Mr. McGiveney was short, stout and bald-headed. Five minutes after we met him he was calling us all by our first names, and we were calling him Uncle Tom. He was about fifty-five years of age. There wasn't a reel, jig, or hornpipe that he couldn't whistle to perfection, and he didn't know one from the other. He was as much wrapped up in music as Katherine herself, and just as keen on dancing. He enjoyed himself tremendously, and it was long after midnight when he left us, after asking if he could come again the next evening. Our apartment became the nightly meeting-place of Mr. McGiveney and his friends. All his friends were Irish musicians, and good ones. It was not unusual to see Maggie Murphy, Mr. Martin, Aunt B., Uncle Tom, and Mary, sitting close together, side by side on the couch-bed, while Katherine, Mr. Gleason, Jimmy Hines and Arthur Fulcher (two young violinists) and several other musicians, sat on chairs or boxes in the middle of the kitchen floor, playing jigs and reels at top speed from eight o'clock till after midnight, stopping only at intervals to discuss the points of different tunes, or for tea and cakes at ten o'clock. Uncle Tom insisted on playing host after the first evening, and we soon grew accustomed to hearing his knock, his query of "Are you home?" and then his entrance into the room, a large bundle under each arm containing tea, cakes and sugar. It often happened that Katherine and I had left for the theatre before Uncle Tom or his friends arrived. We usually got home about eleven o'clock to find the table laid for tea, and an interested audience waiting to hear how we had fared.

"It would mean a lot to me", said Uncle Tom one night, "if my two sons could dance or play music."

"Have they had lessons in dancing or music?" Katherine asked.

"They both studied the violin for two years, and at the end of that time they couldn't do more than murder 'Yankee Doodle', so I stopped the lessons. As for dancing, well, I'm afraid they wouldn't be any better at that than they were at the fiddle."

"Why not let Barbara have a try at teaching them?" Katherine suggested. "She can give them a few lessons and one never knows, they may turn out very well."

"It's an idea," said Uncle Tom thoughtfully, "and as you say, one never knows. How much do you charge for a lesson, Barbara?"

"One dollar," I told him.

"That's reasonable enough," he said. "Can you come to-morrow afternoon about four? They'll be home from school then."

"Yes," said Katherine, "she can."

The hours from four to six the next afternoon were the most exasperating I have ever known. "Raise your right foot," I'd say, and the two boys would shuffle awkwardly, and then raise the left one. "Keep your hands close to your sides," I'd direct, and they would begin to scratch their heads or suck their thumbs. They nearly drove me mad.

Uncle Tom arrived home from work a few minutes after six o'clock. "How did the lessons go?" he asked.

"Not so well," I admitted.

"Humph!" he said. "It isn't your fault, I'm sure of

that. Come on into the dining-room and have some dinner. Jimmy Hines and Arthur are here too."

After dinner we went into the front room. I sat by a window, trying to decide how to take my leave: whether I should say: "Well I must go now," or begin as Katherine always did and say: "I've enjoyed myself so much" —but my teaching that day I certainly hadn't enjoyed. I settled it by saying: "Mrs. Leary will be worried if I stay any longer. May I have my hat and coat please?"

I had noticed Jimmy Hines and Arthur looking earnestly at me during dinner and while we had been sitting in the front room. They made me very nervous. I was sure there was something wrong with me and I was anxious to get away as quickly as possible. I said good-bye to Uncle Tom and his wife, whom her friends, young and old, called "Aunt Sarah", and was about to leave when Arthur started over towards where I was standing. At the same moment Jimmy made a dash in my direction from the opposite end of the room. It was he who reached me first. "Will you let me take you home?" he asked. I looked at Arthur. He evidently had the same idea. "Good God!" I thought frantically, and turned and ran. I kept running until I reached 52nd Street and Third Avenue, a block south of where Uncle Tom lived. Then feeling safe I began to walk. I felt a tap on my shoulder. It was Jimmy Hines. "Wait," he said. I waited, because I didn't know what else to do. He hailed a passing taxi, gave the driver the apartment address, and turned to me. "Get in," he said. I was in a panic. Mrs. McCluskey's advice came back to me; I thought of kidnappers and sudden death, but I got into the taxi. I stayed huddled in a corner of the cab till we reached what I called home. I don't know what was said, or indeed if anything was said during that ride. My one thought was to get to Katherine.

"Why are you so frightened?" Jimmy asked as we were entering the hall. I didn't answer. I raced up the stairs, only to have him race up after me. He caught hold of my wrist. "I won't let you go", he said, "till you tell me that you're not afraid of me. You know you needn't be. I wanted to take you home because I like you, and—Gee! your eyes are nice. Big and blue."

"My goodness gracious!" I gasped. "You better leave go my wrist before Katherine catches you! I'll tell her."

"You look like a kid of thirteen when you talk like that," he said. "When am I going to see you again? Please say I may."

"My goodness gracious!" I said again. "You leave me go now."

"Barbara," Katherine's voice came from within the apartment. "Come in here at once. What are you doing out there? Who are talking to?"

Jimmy had released my wrist at the sound of Katherine's voice, and finding myself free, I turned and fled.

"I'll never let you out alone again," said Katherine, when I reported the incident to her. "You look sixteen all right," she went on. "What did he say?"

"He said", I told her, "that I have big, blue eyes, and not to be afraid of him and that I'm cute."

"Well, you just forget about that. You didn't tell him your right age did you?"

"No," I said. "I didn't. Oh!" I went on, "and I think Arthur wanted to take me home too."

"Mmn——" said Katherine dryly.

"I wouldn't worry about it Katherine," put in Aunt B. "Jimmy seems a very nice boy, and I see nothing wrong in his taking her home."

"You forget", returned Katherine, "that Barbara is only a child, thirteen or fourteen years old."

"But supposing he wants to take me home again?" I asked.

"You'll never go out alone again," she said. "And if he wants to do any taking home, he'll take the two of us, or three of us, or no one."

And while I lived with the Learys I never did go out alone again; either Katherine or Mary was always with me.

Aunt B. refused to enter the hospital until Katherine and I were well on the road to success, insisting that we should be lost if she were not there to press our costumes and give us advice. She held out for two weeks, and then one day she informed us that she was to enter Bellevue Hospital that afternoon, for a "slight operation".

Katherine, as Aunt B.'s nearest relative, was allowed to visit her for a few minutes the next day. Mary and I waited for her in the hospital waiting room. When she reappeared her face was pale and set. She did not speak until we had reached home. Then in a very shaky voice she told us that Aunt B.'s left breast had been cut off in the hope of circumventing the spreading of the disease. She had seen the doctors after leaving Aunt B., and though the operation had been successful in itself, they shook their heads and said that they could hold out very little, if any, hope of Aunt B.'s recovery. If she had attended to it six weeks, or even a month before, yes she would have had every chance, but she had let it go too long. They had done all in their power, but they could not say definitely whether or not the disease had been checked.

Katherine told us that Aunt B. was in great pain, but there were no apparent signs of her suffering when we saw her. She looked up at us and smiled, and when we asked her how she was feeling, replied "very well indeed". We knew that she worried about our welfare, and so, to allay her fears, we told her that we had engagements for every night in the week. This was not true. Our booking agent had more would-be stars on his hands than he could possibly find work for. He recommended us to another agent, and between the two of them we managed to work often enough to keep us fed and housed, without debt, for a couple of weeks. But we woke up one morning, to find that though we were up to date in rent, we had no money in hand, and no food except what Katherine called "the emergency rations": a small supply of flour, tea, and sugar. Hopefully we applied for a job, but the agent regretfully said: "You've got a good act Mrs. Leary—splendid material. I've played you in some of my best houses, but I can't keep on booking you because the act is too short, and it needs polishing. You can't get into big time either, until you fix it up."

"Would another dancer do?" Katherine asked. "Miss Mullen here has been training my daughter."

"Is she good enough to go on?" asked the agent.

Katherine told him truthfully that Mary was not quite ready.

"I tell you what I'll do," he said. "You go up to New Haven. I've got a friend up there who books small time only. I'll give you a letter to him. After you've played the sticks, got your new dancer broken in, and your routine all set, come in and see me and I'll fix you up with bookings."

"Well," began Katherine, and hesitated. Then, gathering her courage, she told him that because of Bridget we could not leave New York at present, and that even if we could, we hadn't the necessary money.

"That sure is tough," remarked the agent when he had heard the story. "But"—and he shrugged his shoulders—"I don't see what else I can do for you." Hard luck stories were to him everyday occurrences.

"I'd suggest your playing amateur," he continued; "you'd probably win enough cash prizes to keep you going—but as you've been professionals all along the line so far, you'd only damage yourselves. Why not try broadcasting? You might make some money that way." He dismissed us with: "Brush up your act and come back, say, in a couple of weeks."

Thus we began making the rounds of the broadcasting stations. Here we met with immediate success, where engagements were concerned. After our first two broadcasts we were asked to appear on the station programme at the World's Radio Fair, to be held in Madison Square Garden. We were not going to be paid for it, but even so, Katherine was very pleased. It would be valuable publicity, she said.

The day we were to appear in Madison Square Garden, we were in a fever of excitement. Again and again Katherine played her choicest tunes, and I danced my best steps. The hours simply flew by. I was to wear my regular costume, a short, sleeveless dress of green and white sateen, trimmed with gold-coloured braid and glittering, spangled shamrocks. Katherine would wear what she called her antique.

While we were dressing that night at the apartment, Katherine was extremely nervous and excited. She grew more so with each passing moment, and when we reached Madison Square Garden she was in a state bordering on hysteria. We were directed to W.G.B.S., now W.I.N.S., and we pushed our way through the throngs of people crowding the Garden till we reached it. We were a quarter of an hour ahead of time, and during the next fifteen minutes I saw tears of nervousness start to Katherine's eyes more than once.

The broadcasting took place in a large, glass-enclosed sound-proof room. So far as I remember, only the artists were allowed within this room. On the other side of the glass were hundreds of people, craning their necks, trying to see over each other's heads and into the room. All this did not help to calm Katherine.

At last the announcer came over to us. "We have not brought the floor board for you to dance on, Miss Mullen," he whispered. "Can you dance on top of a desk?" I nodded. He went back to the microphone, announced our names, and then beckoned furiously to Katherine.

Till that moment I had feared that she would be unable to go on. But the moment she heard her name mentioned, she became a different woman. Suddenly, she was no longer shaking and nervous; she was Katherine Leary, World's Champion Accordion Player.

The dress which she called her antique was a real

Irish costume, over a hundred years old. The wide skirt of the dress reached to the ground, it had a high neck and leg-o'-mutton sleeves, and it suited Katherine to perfection. She had had her hair specially dressed that afternoon. It was jet black and framed her face in soft waves, and was coiled into a bun at the nape of her neck.

She was positively beautiful as she rose from her chair, swept across the room till she reached the chair in which she was to sit while playing, and bowed, as only Katherine could bow, to the gaping crowd. And with a slight smile of self-confidence she sat down, complete mistress of herself and of the situation.

I was lifted up on top of a desk that had been placed before the microphone. The surprise of the crowd was pictured on their faces. I suppose dancing on a desk top was something new. In any case, our performance went off without a hitch from start to finish. We could see the crowd applauding, though we could not hear them. They heard the broadcast by means of a loud speaker.

Katherine could hardly contain herself, and almost ran from the Garden after our time was up. "Do you think it was all right?" she asked breathlessly. "We'll find out how it came over from Mary," I said. Mary had been listening in on Maggie Murphy's radio, and their report was favourable indeed.

Although Katherine was sure that our appearance at the World's Radio Fair would result in our getting a great many offers, nothing came of it. We were not advertising any commercial product, so we were not paid for broadcasting. Nor were we hired steadily by the station, though we broadcasted once a week on an average.

Our rent bill was increasing, but for food we managed well enough. When our tea supply gave out, we existed on dry pancakes made of flour and water, and pint bottles of milk which were left by the milkman every morning outside the neighbours' doors, and which became ours by the grace of God and Katherine's quiet footsteps. We wangled invitations for supper from the Gleasons or Uncle Tom, or else filled up on the tea and cakes that the latter brought when he and his musician friends came to spend an evening. The size of Uncle Tom's bundles and the anxiety with which we eyed them as he came in, became a standing joke between Katherine, Mary and myself, as did the dry pancakes. These we always ate very furtively, ready to hide them at a moment's notice, should there be a knock at the door. This manner of dining did not help our digestion, but it did keep us alive and gave us many hearty laughs.

Katherine was really getting worried about the situation. What if the landlord took it into his head to tell us to pay the back rent or get out? It would not be so bad for the three of us, for we should get along some way or another, but there was Aunt B. to think of. She would have to have a place to live in and good food when she came out of the hospital. We decided that the best thing to do was to tell Aunt B. that we were not getting as many jobs as before from the agent. Perhaps she might think of some way for us to make enough money to keep going until Mary was trained well enough to come into the act. We did not tell her that we were absolutely broke: it was she who told us. "I guessed it," she said. "All your stories of prosperity, and getting along marvellously, sounded too good to be true."

We did not stay the full visiting hour that day. The

dry pancakes and Uncle Tom's bundles were twice as funny when Aunt B. knew about them too, and the nurse came over and told us that we had better leave, as we were making the patient laugh too much and it was bad for her: the wound might open.

That evening Mr. Martin was our only visitor, for Maggie Murphy went to visit a sick friend, and Mr. and Mrs. Gleason were going to the theatre, as they had won two tickets in a cross-word puzzle competition. He seemed to have something on his mind, and was very nervous and ill at ease. He fidgeted in his seat and twiddled his thumbs. We couldn't imagine what was wrong with him, and his constant moving about began to exasperate Katherine. "Is anything the matter with you, Mr. Martin?" she asked in a very loud voice.

Poor Mr. Martin jumped, and his face grew very red. "N-no," he quavered. "But", he ventured timidly, "I want to tell you—I—I hope you won't be offended Mrs. Leary?"

"My dear Mr. Martin, please speak out and say what is on your mind," said Katherine smiling. "I don't see how you could offend anyone."

Mr. Martin was certainly having a bad time of it. After several unsuccessful starts, he blurted out, his words tumbling over each other. "I was in to see Miss MacNiff just after you left her to-day, and she told me that you could not get any more work in the theatre till your act is polished up, so I telephoned a friend, who knows a producer, and he spoke to him, and the producer is going to come down here and see you. If he thinks your act has anything in it, he'll fix it up himself and arrange bookings for you. My friend has great influence—that's how—I hope you're not angry with me for taking such a liberty?" he finished breathlessly.

We were speechless with amazement. Mr. Martin, of all the people in the world to arrange an interview with a producer! Little Mr. Martin, who somehow suggested bed-time stories and peppermint candy.

"Angry with you?" said Katherine at last. The little man's action had touched her heart, and she was very close to tears. "I don't know what to say, or how to thank you."

"My goodness!" he exclaimed. "It's quite all right. Really——" and Katherine let it go at that. "When is the man coming?" she asked.

"Some afternoon this week," replied Mr. Martin, obviously relieved that Katherine did not persist in thanking him.

"You don't know exactly what day?"

"N-no; you see, he's a very busy man, but whatever afternoon he gets a chance, he'll come. Before Saturday."

It was then Tuesday. Katherine spent Wednesday morning in giving Mary and me advice on how to act when the producer came. She borrowed fifteen cents from Maggie Murphy, which was spent on half a dozen small tea-cakes.

From two o'clock that afternoon until past six o'clock that evening the three of us sat round the kitchen table, dressed in our best clothes. Cups, saucers, etc., were placed on the table, the tea-cakes in the middle; we were not to touch the tea-cakes. Katherine's plan was this: when we heard the knock, she would open the door, and after the introductions were over, say: "We were just having a cup of tea. Won't you have some?" The producer would then be given the cakes. All this would dispose him very favourably towards us. We rehearsed several times. Katherine, in response to an imaginary knock, would open the door and say her little piece. Mary would contribute her part to the performance by saying: "Do sit down Mr. ——" whatever his name was. And my bit was: "Won't you try one of these?" "these" being the tea-cakes.

But the producer did not show up that day, or the next, or the next, and on Friday evening Katherine said: "Well, we can dismiss that from our minds altogether. Poor Mr. Martin; he meant well."

Saturday morning brought an orgy of house-cleaning. Every bureau drawer was turned out, thoroughly cleaned, the contents rearranged, and put back in place. Kettles, pots, and pans were scoured till they shone, the floor was scrubbed, and the window washed. All three of us were dressed in old house dresses, now very dirty, and old dust caps, also dirty. About noon we sat down to a lunch of one pancake each, and black tea. We were all in a jolly mood, Katherine especially. She said that she must have swallowed a feather, because she couldn't stop laughing. Every time she went off, Mary and I were off too. It was talk of the preparations we had made and the little act we had rehearsed so often that started us off first, but when Mary brought out the now green-moulded tea-cakes, and with a stately bow presented them to Katherine, saying: "Won't you try some of these?" we positively roared. No one heard the knock on the door, or heard it open. We were first aware of a visitor when a deep voice said: "I beg your pardon. Is

Katherine Leary at home?" With one accord we grabbed the dry pancakes and threw them under the table. Instinctively we knew that the producer had arrived. In spite of our appearance, which was anything but preposessing, we made an attempt to rise to the situation. Only Katherine succeeded. She forgot, or else disregarded, her dirty face and garb, and said grandly: "How do you do? We were just having a cup of tea. Won't you have some?" This was too much. Simultaneously, Mary and I looked at the stale cakes, we looked at each other, and unable to restrain ourselves, burst into laughter. Katherine, suddenly realizing what we must look like to the producer, and catching sight of the pancakes, which were plainly visible on the floor, could not control herself either. The producer was frankly amazed at our behaviour and looked it. Still, we couldn't stop laughing.

The result of Mr. Martin's efforts was a two-minute talk with the producer which ended in his saying: "I'll call around again sometime—maybe." Needless to say, we never saw or heard of him again.

I awoke one morning to find Katherine holding an envelope before my eyes. "It's a letter for you, Barbara," she said, "from Ireland."

"From Ireland?" I repeated, "honest?"

"Honest," she smiled.

I knew it must be from my father, but I couldn't open it. All power seemed to have left my hands, and I kept staring at the envelope as though I had never seen one before.

"Shall I open it for you?" Katherine asked.

The sound of her voice brought me back to life. "No," I said. "No thanks. I'll do it."

It was a long letter. What the exact words were, I cannot remember, but it started "Babs dear," and it contained a wealth of love and tenderness and understanding. He was going to write to a friend of his whom he thought might be able to help me. He told me to have courage and to fear nothing. He had given an order for two Irish costumes to be made. One was for me, the other was for Mary Leary. As long as she was to be my partner, it wouldn't do for him to send one to me and leave her out of it, he said. He hoped they'd fit, as he had only guessed at the sizes. P.J., my brother, was grown into a fine, strong boy. When I wrote again would I send a picture? as they both wanted to see what I looked like. It was signed: "Father."

For a few minutes after reading the letter I was silent, looking at it; then I read it again. "Gosh," I said at last, "he's a very nice man to have for a father."

"Is it a good letter then?" asked Katherine.

I told her about the costumes. "Ah!" she cried joyfully, "it's a good omen. Our luck is going to change when those costumes get here. I feel it in my bones."

Her big idea this time was to take the agent's advice and go up to New Haven. There, Mary would join the act, we would fix a routine, and when the Irish costumes came, write to our former booking agent in New York telling him that our act was polished and ready. "Then", cried Katherine, "on to New York and we'll knock 'em cold."

It was a great idea. There were only two things wrong with it. In the first place, we hadn't a thin dime between us, let alone the railroad fare to New Haven; and in the second place, even if we did have enough money to get us there, suppose we didn't get a job right away, what should we live on? Above all, there was Aunt B. to consider. She would soon be leaving the hospital, and would need good food and attention. If we could only get some kind of a home fixed up for her in New Haven, everything would be all right. Both she and Katherine had lived there in their twenties. They had plenty of good friends there who would make it their business to see that Aunt B. was well taken care of, if Katherine, Mary and I didn't make enough to do it ourselves. "But we won't have to ask anybody for help," said Katherine confidently. "Even if we have to play one night stands for a year, we'll make enough to get along till Aunt B. gets better." The three of us always spoke of Aunt B. as if she were going to get well again, even though in our hearts we knew differently.

"It's all very well to talk," put in Mary at this point, "but Aunt B. won't be well enough to travel for weeks yet, and what are we going to do in the meantime?"

There we struck a blank. What were we going to do in the meantime?

We were interrupted in the midst of our discussion by Maggie Murphy. She came in carrying a paper bag, which she left on the table, saying: "A friend of mine brought me a basket of food. I thought you might be able to eat some of it. The spaghetti is for Mary. I'll be in to-night," and walked out.

The bag contained two cans of soup and one of spaghetti. The can of spaghetti was covered with dust and looked very old. "Ugh!" said Katherine when she saw it. "We'll throw this one away. It looks as if it might be bad."

But Mary would not hear of it. Her one weakness was spaghetti, and she insisted on having it for lunch. Despite the grimaces which Katherine made while drinking the soup, I could see that she was really enjoying it as much as I was. She just would not admit that any canned food could possibly be tasty. It was the first taste of anything besides the dry pancakes and Uncle Tom's tid-bits that we'd had for days, and we called down all the blessings of heaven on the head of Maggie Murphy.

Later that day, we went to visit Aunt B. "I have good news," she told us. "I am going to be sent to Burke's Foundation—a convalescent home up in White Plains. I shall be there for two weeks, or more, and it won't cost us anything." Here was one of our difficulties solved.

Katherine explained our plans to Bridget. "Why, in that two weeks", she said, "we can have a nice little home all ready for you to come to, in New Haven. We'll get plenty of work there: the booking agent here said that he would give us a letter to one up there, and armed with that we won't have to wait more than a couple of days till we get put to work. It will be so nice to be amongst all our old friends again too. We could start to-morrow. Now all we need is the money."

"Oh, is that all that's keeping you back?" asked Aunt B. dryly.

"I thought she might be able to suggest something or advise us in some way," Katherine said as we walked back from the hospital. "Bridget can usually find a way out of any difficulty."

"What are we going to do, though?" asked Mary.

"Something will turn up," said Katherine cheerfully, "I'm sure of it. Anyway we still have a roof over our heads, even if we may be ordered out from under it at any moment, and we'll worry about that when it happens."

That evening we had a surprise visitor. Uncle Tom had arrived with his musician friends, Maggie Murphy had seated herself between the Gleasons and Mr. Martin on the couch-bed, and the "orchestra" had taken their usual places, tuned up, and started off the evening concert with a jig. Suddenly the door was thrown open, and we heard John's voice say: "I'm in the right place, begob!" Five minutes after he had arrived, he was dancing with Maggie Murphy, overriding all her protests of having a game leg with: "Sure if you can walk you can dance. We'll have a go at it." Mary was paired off with Mr. Martin, and the Gleasons were partners, as were Uncle Tom and I. The table was pushed into the "bedroom", the musicians crowded together near the door, and the eight of us with plenty of shouting, laughter and noise, danced an Irish set. "Oh!" cried Maggie Murphy breathlessly when we'd finished, "I haven't danced that much in nearly forty years!"

It was nearly two o'clock when the party broke up and good nights were said.

During the latter part of the evening, I had noticed Mary looking very pale. We were about to get into bed, when suddenly she screamed and doubled up in pain. "Oh, my side," she began to moan. She couldn't move at all, and Katherine and I had to lift her into bed. "Come with me for the doctor, Barbara, quickly," said Katherine. She was pulling a coat over her nightdress.

Hurriedly I did the same, and together we raced down the stairs and into the street.

Even at three in the morning it is not difficult to get a taxi in New York. We hailed one. "The nearest doctor at once," Katherine told the driver. That driver was one in a million. At break-neck speed he sent the cab shooting ahead, tearing up one street and down another, while Katherine, who was usually terrified in cabs, thought that he was not going fast enough. In a very short time he stopped. "Up those steps," he pointed out. "I'll wait."

"We have no money," Katherine told him on the return journey.

"It's okay lady," he said. "I hope everything turns out all right."

He let us out at the apartment door, tipped his hat respectfully, and bade us good night. One would have thought from his manner that it was quite the thing to drive half-clad, frantic females in search of a doctor in the wee hours of the morning, without being paid for his services.

It seemed hours before the doctor arrived to put a stop to the agony Mary was suffering. "What's she been eating?" he asked after he had examined her.

"Spaghetti," Katherine told him. "A very old can."

"You should have known better than to give her a very old can of anything," he said tersely.

For three days Mary was very ill. The doctor came every day, and arranged for one of the district nurses from Bellevue Hospital to call in every day, too.

Katherine was furious. "The only time I have ever given in to Mary about canned foods, and look what happens," she raved. She didn't tell Maggie Murphy what had made Mary so ill, saying: "It isn't Maggie's fault. It was the can, and there's no sense in having Maggie blaming herself for it."

At the end of a week Mary was allowed to sit up.

"I've arranged to have her sent up to Burke's Foundation," said the doctor, who happened to be on the Bellevue Hospital staff. "She needs a couple of weeks of rest and fresh air in order to get her strength back."

"I'm pleased about that," said Katherine after the doctor had left. Aunt B. had been sent to Burke's Foundation during the week. "Mary being there too will make it easier for Bridget. She won't feel so alone."

Mary's departure left Katherine and me sole occupants of the apartment. Katherine grew more impatient with every hour that passed in New York. She was sure that New Haven was the land of opportunity. The question was, how to get there? Again Mr. Martin came to the rescue. One evening he blushingly handed Katherine an envelope containing seventy-five dollars, stumbling through a little speech: "I—I hope you won't be angry with me for taking such a liberty. Miss MacNiff told me about New Haven, and I'm so grateful for all the pleasant evenings that you've given me. It's a little present to you both," after which he sat down like a man exhausted.

The next afternoon Katherine and I, with the aid of Maggie Murphy, smuggled all our luggage (with the exception of one very large trunk, which we feared we could not move unnoticed), out of the apartment and into a waiting taxi. Maggie promised to watch our letter box, and to send on any mail that came for us to New

Haven. We did not know what to do about the trunk. We knew that the landlord, who lived in one of the apartments on the ground floor, would never let us take it out of the building. We owed a seventy-dollar rent bill, and if he knew that we were moving he'd hold the trunk and all the rest of the luggage as well until the bill was paid. Getting the suitcases out had been fairly simple. They were not very large ones and were easily handled. The trunk, however, was a different story. It couldn't be brought downstairs without making a racket that would surely bring the landlord out to see what was happening. Katherine and I couldn't lift it, and Maggie Murphy vetoed Katherine's suggestion of hiring two men and telling them to take it down as silently as possible. "They might think you'd got a dead body or something in it," said Maggie pleasantly, "and run for the police. No, you can't work it that way. If you could get someone you know and can trust, and tell them why you've got to sneak it out, then it could be managed. What about Uncle Tom? Would he be able to get it out?"

"Uncle Tom?" said Katherine, "why, he couldn't possibly lift the trunk, let alone get it down a flight of stairs."

"I know that," returned Maggie. "But if he had a couple of his musician friends and Mr. Gleason with him, it could be done, and you can trust all of them."

"I couldn't get in touch with them before train time."

"Give me the key to your apartment," said Maggie impatiently. "Get your train this afternoon, and when you find a place to live in New Haven, send me your address, and I'll see that the trunk is sent on to you.

Uncle Tom and I will manage it some way. When the trunk is safely out of the building and on its way, I'll give the landlord the key, and tell him that you sent it to me, but I won't tell him where you've gone. If we can get the trunk out without making a racket, he won't know whether you're here or not till he comes up to collect his rent or to give you a dispossess."

So we gave the apartment key to Maggie, and with her wishes of "God-speed and good luck go with you", Katherine and I were off to Grand Central Station, New Haven, and new adventures.

Chapter Four

Hard Lodging and Return

★

Katherine knew her way about in New Haven, and within an hour after our arrival in that city she had rented a large room in the Central Hotel.

The Central Hotel was an overgrown rooming house, and was managed by a little woman of about sixty years of age. Her name was Mrs. Whitney. She had been on the stage—a ballet dancer—in her youth. All her roomers were "people of the theatre". We learned this and more on our first evening there. We learned, too, that she had been married four times, that her first three husbands were dead, and the fourth now dying in some hospital. "Poor man, I visit him every Sunday," said Mrs. Whitney. Katherine clucked sympathetically. That was all she could do. I have never heard anyone talk so fast or for so long at a time as Mrs. Whitney. We heard about every other roomer in the hotel. "The man in number eighteen is an acrobat. The man in number sixteen is a juggler. There are two opera singers across the hall and a clarinet player. They practise every day, but you won't mind that, you'll be practising too I suppose. That's an accordion box isn't it? My second husband played the accordion, poor man."

We listened to her for a solid hour, and then Katherine yawned and said pointedly: "We've had a tiring day, Mrs. Whitney. Won't you come in some time again? We'd love to have you."

Mrs. Whitney was so sorry, she should have realized that we were tired. Oh indeed she would come in again, to-morrow afternoon. It was so nice to have someone to talk to, and after another half-hour of good nights she left.

We sent our new address by telegram to Maggie Murphy, early the next morning. We received a letter from her, and the trunk, three days later. Maggie's letter gave us the first good laugh we'd had since we left New York. It was all about the trunk and the manner in which it had been sneaked out of the apartment.

Apparently, on the evening of the day we left, Uncle Tom and Jimmy Hines had arrived at the apartment at their usual time. Maggie had been watching for them, and just as they reached the apartment door she attracted their attention with a loud "psst!" She motioned silently that they were to enter her apartment, which, wonderingly, they did. She closed the door in a very furtive manner, and whispered to them that we had gone to New Haven. She explained about the trunk, and how it must be taken out without the landlord's knowledge.

They were very much surprised at the suddenness with which we had moved, but Maggie gave them no time to talk about it. "The trunk must be sent on its way to-night," she told them. So they called Mr. Gleason down, and put their heads together to figure out a plan of action.

At length it was decided that they must have a taxi

waiting outside the front door. Uncle Tom would watch the door of the landlord's apartment, ready to give warning if he should be coming out, and Jimmy and Mr. Gleason would carry the trunk downstairs. They were quite sure that they could manage it without making a sound.

Jimmy went out, and came back in a few minutes to report that the taxi was ready and waiting. The entire company, with the exception of Uncle Tom, then proceeded on tip-toe across the hall from Maggie's apartment to the one in which we had lived. Maggie produced the key and a flashlight, and with a whispered "We mustn't put on the lights" and "I've oiled the lock", she led the way into the bedroom where we had left the trunk.

Their plan started to go astray when Mr. Gleason tripped over something that he had not seen in the dim glow of the flashlight, and both he and Jimmy began to laugh. In vain Maggie cautioned them to be silent: the more she whispered and gesticulated, the more difficult they found it to be quiet. Finally, after much tripping and bumping over odd pieces of furniture, they managed to get the trunk to the head of the stairs. Tom, from his post in the hall below, gave the signal that the way was clear, and the two, with Jimmy in front and Mr. Gleason behind, started down the stairs carrying the trunk between them. They were half-way down the stairs when Mr. Gleason, with a shout of "Look-out Jimmy," dropped his end of the trunk and sat down on the stairs, helpless with laughter. Jimmy sprang to one side, flattening himself against the wall, and the trunk banged and clattered down the stairs, "making", as Maggie put it, "enough noise to rouse the dead".

The landlord of course rushed into the hall, and with a loud "What's the big idea?" demanded to know what was going on. Uncle Tom began to argue with him, while Jimmy and Mr. Gleason, with Maggie berating them from behind, got the trunk as far as the front door. There it stuck. It took them a good ten minutes before they managed to get it out and strapped on to the back of the taxi, and all the time the landlord was insistently demanding to know who was moving, and whose trunk it was. Uncle Tom kept telling him that it was none of his damned business, and asking if he wanted to make something out of it.

Where the trunk went to that night Maggie didn't know; Uncle Tom and Jimmy had gone off in the taxi with it. But the next afternoon she had told Jimmy of our wire. He was sending the trunk on at once, and she was giving the landlord another few days to forget about the trunk episode before letting him have our apartment key.

We were put to work at once by the New Haven booking agent, and were given enough dates to keep us busy every night in the week. Katherine spent the days in looking up her old friends. She found a great many of them and was cordially welcomed by them all. They were shocked when they heard about Aunt B. and Mary, and agreed with Katherine that the Central Hotel was no place for two convalescents. Katherine told them of her plan to rent and furnish an apartment. We were making enough money to do this if we bought second-hand furniture. Her friends, however, advised her against renting an apartment, saying that what we needed was a small house all to ourselves so that Aunt B. would not be disturbed. One of them knew of a place she thought might do—a five-room house on Howard Avenue, the rent of which was twenty-five dollars a month. Katherine went with her friend to see the landlord: they were shown through the house, and Katherine, very pleased, decided that it was to be our new home.

Her friends overwhelmed us with gifts and offers of pieces of furniture that they were not using at present. One woman came forward with two chairs, another with tables and dressers, and still another insisted on presenting us with a ton of coal. The bed question was the hardest to settle. Aunt B. definitely must have comfort, so for her we bought a new bed and mattress—on credit. Two more beds, and other odd pieces of furniture that we needed, we bought second-hand.

Mary was dismissed from Burke's Foundation sooner than we expected she would be. She came to the Central Hotel to stay until the house was put in order, and one week after her arrival we unostentatiously took up housekeeping in our new home.

On the very first night of our occupancy, things began to happen. All Katherine's women friends banded together and burst in on us at eight o'clock. They were loaded down with pots, kettles, dishes, blankets, cutlery and food. One brought an oil stove and two gallons of oil, specially for Aunt B.'s bedroom when she returned from the convalescent home. Their husbands and friends arrived two hours later. With them came two violinists. They all vied with each other, seeing who could dance oftenest and longest. They wanted to know why Katherine didn't open a dance hall; the entire Irish population of New Haven would patronize it, they said. If they held dances once a week at their homes, each taking a turn, would Katherine play? Katherine promised that she surely would. It was dawn when they left and Katherine, Mary and I went to bed.

We heard from Jimmy Hines that he had forwarded an Irish letter and package, addressed to me, to the apartment. Both he and Uncle Tom had been to see Aunt B. She was looking well and expected to be able to start for New Haven in a fortnight.

The letter was from my father, and this time I did not hesitate before opening the envelope.

"Another nice letter, Barbara?" Katherine asked.

"Yes," I told her. "He sent the costumes, the same day as this letter."

"That must be the package!" she cried. "Is there any other news?"

"He has written to a friend of his and asked her to come and see me."

"Your father's letters make you very happy, don't they?" she asked suddenly.

"They do," I said. "I wish I could go to Aran."

"I suppose you'd do anything your father told you, now?"

"I would."

I noticed that she was looking at me in an odd manner when I spoke; however, she said nothing more, except: "The costumes will probably be in the afternoon mail," so I thought nothing of it.

The costumes did come that afternoon.

Except in colour—one was dark-green and the other white—the two costumes were alike. The dress of each one was simply, but beautifully made. A large shawl, oblong in shape, went with the dress.

The shawl was to be attached by a very old Celtic brooch to the left shoulder of the dress, brought down and across the back, under the right arm, up and across the chest, and fastened by another Celtic brooch, a few inches below the other on the left shoulder. This brought into play all the exquisite embroidery of the enormous Celtic design on the shawl, and the effect was very beautiful.

There was a bit of a dispute about the costumes. Katherine said that Mary being the darker of us should wear the white one; but my father in his letter had said that he particularly wished me to wear the white one because it was a princess's colour, so I refused to have it otherwise.

"You'd do anything he told you all right," said Katherine, as she reluctantly agreed to let Mary wear the green one.

Mary and I tried them on; they fitted perfectly, and Katherine was so pleased with them that she immediately sat down and wrote a letter to the booking agent in New York, saying that Mary was now part of the act, that we were fully equipped with new costumes, and that the act was polished and ready for Broadway.

A few days later she received a reply from the booking agent, naming Wednesday of the following week for the try-out, which was to take place at a "breaking house" uptown in New York.

As may be well imagined, we were on tenterhooks for the next four or five days. We decided that to start the act off Mary and I would dance a hornpipe, then

Katherine would play a solo, after which I would dance a reel, alone. And to finish the act, Mary and I would dance a jig, Katherine of course playing for the dancing.

We practised this routine for hours on end. When Mary and I were tired, Katherine would spur us on, saying: "We must be perfect. This is our big chance. Everything depends on it." And we'd go over the whole thing again.

We arrived in New York early on the next Wednesday morning, and engaged rooms for the night at a small hotel. We did no practising until just before we left for the theatre, and then we went through the act once. We met the booking agent just inside the stage door. He looked pleased when Katherine told him how we had arranged the act. "Who does the singing?" he asked.

"Singing?" Katherine repeated blankly.

"Sure," he said. "You had dancing and music before. Two dancers sounds O.K., but a song is what's needed. Variety, you know. Who sings?"

"I do," said Katherine. The time had come for us to put over the bluff she had once spoken of.

"O.K." he said. "Go down and give your music to the piano player."

Katherine went down into the pit and conferred with the piano player, while Mary and I proceeded to our dressing-room.

"I told him I had no music," she reported to us, "but I hummed the air of the song for him, and he'll be able to follow me all right."

"But what are you going to sing?" Mary and I asked together in amazement.

" 'Back to Donegal'," said Katherine.

Mary and I said nothing, because we didn't know what to say. Katherine had never sung in public before, any more than Mary had danced. Of the two, Mary was the less nervous.

We quickly decided how to fit in the song. Katherine would go on first and sing. The song finished, she would take a bow and walk off, then she would walk back on to the stage again and play the introduction that would bring Mary and me on. The rest of the act would be the same as we had previously arranged it. It looked to us like a good plan. But the bluff failed.

She walked on to the stage, and made two false starts before she could get going. Her voice broke before she was half-way through the song. She could not control her trembling, and beads of perspiration stood out on her forehead. All that she was fighting for really depended on that song, and it failed miserably. But in some way, what she was enduring must have communicated itself to the huge audience: she was so evidently doing her utmost to put the song over. They did not laugh when her voice broke or when, conscious of her failure, she choked on the final note. In the entire theatre there wasn't a sound. When she reached us in the wings she was half-fainting. "Do you think you're able to go out there again?" one of the stage hands asked.

Katherine's head went up. "I may not be able to sing," she said fiercely, "but I *can* play music." And she marched defiantly on to the stage again.

The rest of the act was a huge success. There was a spontaneous burst of applause when Mary and I appeared, dressed in the Irish costumes. Mary danced her steps unfalteringly; Katherine played perfectly; we were encored twice and took four bows. But the song had done for us. "With singers like you in it, I wouldn't touch your act with a ten-foot pole," said the agent. "Get a good singer before you come to see me again, and even then maybe I couldn't give you another try-out."

So much for the try-out that was to be the forerunner of fame, fortune and success.

Thoroughly disheartened we returned to New Haven. We had no difficulty getting jobs there, but they were all one or two night stands and not big time. Still, it brought us money: not very much, but enough to keep us fed, clothed and housed. We were kept very busy between jobs and dances run by Katherine's friends.

Aunt B.'s arrival in New Haven was the signal that started a steady flow of visitors. Quite suddenly she began to show great interest in my father's letters and insisted that I should show them to her. After reading the letters, which I was now receiving regularly, she and Katherine used to hold lengthy conversations in Aunt B.'s bedroom. I suspected that they were discussing my correspondence with my father, but at the time I thought nothing of it, putting it down to curiosity on their part.

One day Katherine was asked to play at an Irish dance which was to be held in a small-sized hall in West Haven. She agreed to play, and Mary and I went along to dance. As Katherine did not get paid until the dance was over, we were nearly the last persons to leave the hall. It was very late at night, or rather, it was early in the morning, and the street cars had stopped running. We were considering the prospect either of walking home—which we rejected because we were not sure of the way—or of waiting until five o'clock or whatever time the street car service started again. We had decided on this last when Katherine suddenly espied a taxi coming slowly along the street. She hailed it and the driver pulled up to the curb; she gave him our address, and we climbed gratefully and wearily into the cab.

The first intimation we had that anything was wrong, was when, after going over a bump, Katherine looked out of the window. "Jesus, Mary and Joseph save us!" she shrieked. "We're up on the sidewalk." Mary and I jumped to the window, and up on the sidewalk we certainly were. Katherine opened the slide window connecting with the driver's seat. "Are you trying to kill us?" she cried. "Stop this cab immediately." The driver turned completely round in his seat and faced her. "Keep your eyes on the road for God's sake!" she screamed. "Oh I wish we were home."

"Home?" said the driver drunkenly, "I'll have you there in two minutes," and he stepped on the gas. Mary and I watched the speedometer. It went from thirty to forty to fifty, it reached sixty and stayed there. We sped round lamp-posts, up on the sidewalks, and back into the street. By a miracle he missed the walls of a cemetery and went through the open gate. We flew down the cemetery road, avoiding the tombstones by a narrow margin, the driver madly tooting his horn. We didn't know what minute we were going to be dashed to pieces, but even so, when Katherine began to laugh and shouted that we might as well die laughing as crying, Mary and

I began to laugh too. On we sped, through and out of the cemetery. Again the driver forsook the street for the sidewalk, and we rolled merrily on. The cab suddenly jerked to a halt at Church and Chapel Streets. We tumbled out hastily. "I'm out of gas," reported the driver mournfully, as Katherine paid him. "If you'll wait here, I'll fill her up and take you home."

"Indeed you won't," said Katherine quickly. "We'll walk the rest of the way."

When we arrived home at last we reported the incident to Aunt B., who said that we must kneel down at once and say the Rosary in thanksgiving for our safe deliverance. The Rosary however, was not finished that night. It was interrupted by giggles from Mary and me and hardly subdued laughter from Katherine, as thoughts of the ride home recurred to us. Aunt B.—the corners of her mouth twitching suspiciously—declared herself disgusted with our behaviour and packed us off to bed.

Katherine was a firm believer in very early rising, and as much fresh air and exercise as possible. She very rarely slept or allowed Mary or me to sleep later than eight o'clock, no matter how late we had been out the night before. Still half asleep, Mary and I would hear Katherine's voice: "Get up, get up!" she would cry, "it's a lovely morning." Opening the windows wide (this in the middle of winter) she would mumble "should have been up hours ago", and pull the clothes off our bed. Mary and I would hop up as if we had been stung, dive for our basins, indulge in an icy sponge, dress, and go out into the crisp morning air to walk for an hour before breakfast. This, with rare exceptions, began our daily programme.

Katherine did the cooking, supervising and instructing. She arranged a house-cleaning schedule, and rigidly enforced it. When we returned after our walk, Katherine would set about making the fire. Mary's duties were the downstairs rooms, kitchen, dining-room, bathroom and hall. I was assigned to do the three upstairs bedrooms, including Aunt B.'s. The cleaning of the entire house took from forty-five minutes to an hour. Then, while Katherine inspected the work, Mary turned out and rearranged the contents of bureau drawers and closets, and I gave Aunt B. her exercises. She chose me to attend her instead of Katherine or Mary, because she said my hands were smaller than theirs, and my touch lighter. Her exercises consisted in raising and lowering her left arm forty times. She was powerless to move it since her operation, and the doctor had recommended this exercise to help restore circulation. I had then to pat a soothing ointment over the wound and bring her a basin with hot water and towels. By the time she had finished her toilet, breakfast was ready. An hour after breakfast was set aside every morning for washing and ironing; this done, boilers of water were heated for our baths. We were then free to do as we liked, if Katherine approved of what we liked, for the rest of the day. Katherine, as I said before, arranged this schedule, and while I was there it was never interrupted.

Despite the fact that Katherine was doing all in her power to help Aunt B. regain her lost strength, she was getting no better. She was given strengthening foods;

all the directions of the New York doctor were carried out to the minutest detail, but she did not improve. She never complained, and only an occasional painful gasp that she could not suppress betrayed the fact that she was suffering.

Deciding to leave no stone unturned, though the doctors could do nothing more for her, Katherine made an application to the Sisters of Mercy Convent in New Haven. We could not afford a trained nurse, and the Sisters of Mercy were the next best thing. Some of the nuns at this convent were trained in nursing, and they visited and attended the sick free of charge.

Shortly after Katherine's application, two of these nuns came to see Aunt B. After their first visit they came and ministered to her every afternoon, but though Aunt B. seemed more cheerful after they had called, she got no better.

Then Katherine began to think that if we were making more money, perhaps something could be done with it to help Aunt B, so we opened a dance hall. All the cash on hand was put into it. We hired it for two nights in the week, Thursday and Saturday. Katherine and the two violin players were the orchestra, admission was twenty-five cents, cloakroom ten cents. Mary and I had charge of the cloakroom, and took turns in walking round the hall to see that everything was going smoothly. We often wondered what we should do if a riot started. We never found out. The dance hall failed in two weeks. At the fourth dance there were but ten people. All the money we had was gone, and we were on the rocks again.

We were now playing one night stands only, and we usually had two or three free evenings in the week. We were fairly sure of making enough to pay the rent, but not so certain of being able to buy food. To guard against a possible shortage, Katherine began to accept invitations to parties. If we happened to be playing somewhere, we accepted the invitation and went to the party after we'd finished at the theatre. We went to parties every night in the week, and the plan was this. At the supper Katherine, Mary and I would eat as much as possible, but unobtrusively. "We mustn't look vulgar no matter how hungry we are," Katherine would say. A bag was put inside the accordion case. We would arrange to be the last at supper if possible, and Mary or I would bring the accordion case to the table, ostensibly for Katherine to encase the precious accordion while we were eating. Instead of the accordion, all the cakes and cold meats that we could get without being seen were fitted into the case. On leaving the house, Katherine herself carried the case; Mary or I carried the accordion. Several offers to carry the box would be made to Katherine, but she always refused, saying: "No thank you. Really it isn't at all heavy. The bottom of it is a bit weak, and the girls are carrying the accordion, so it won't drop out, you know." We were never caught, and we escaped the threat of food shortage. Another way of avoiding this was to accept three invitations in one day. If asked for tea, Katherine had a convenient appointment and wangled an invitation for lunch instead. Sometimes we managed to have lunch, tea and dinner at three different houses on one day. Thus we feasted royally with very little expense, while we managed to get the best of food for Aunt B., and to keep up appearances in general.

About this time I began to receive letters from Jimmy Hines; these, as well as all the letters I got from my father, underwent Katherine's censorship. When one day I received a note from my father's friend, inviting me to come and visit her for a while, Katherine said nothing, but she seemed preoccupied and thoughtful for the next few days. Then one afternoon she had a long private talk with Aunt B. Entering the room to tell Aunt B. that the two nuns had arrived, I heard the words: "Wait until after Saint Patrick's Day," then they abruptly changed the subject.

Saint Patrick's Day dawned crisp and clear. All was hustle and bustle about the house, in preparation for the ball we were to attend that evening. Several times during the day I noticed Katherine looking at me doubtfully. Then, just before the taxi which was to take us to the ball arrived, she sat down and with an expression of great determination on her face wrote and sealed a letter. This she posted herself, before we entered the taxi.

The ball that night was a huge success. Katherine's playing was enthusiastically received and applauded by the crowd. Mary and I danced twice together, I danced twice alone, and our offerings too were very well received. We arrived home at dawn, and after the usual talk with Aunt B. tumbled tired into bed.

My mother arrived two days after Saint Patrick's Day. I was of course very glad to see her, but at the same time my heart sank. That she did not come especially to see me, I knew. There was another reason, and I felt that my father's letters had something to do with it. I was right. I quaked, knowing what I was in for, and then I saw coming up the stairs behind my mother my half-sister, Nancy. I had not seen Nancy for a long time—not since she had been married. I liked her, a liking that was born when I was a toddler, and "Nanna" used to give me candy and dress me in my Sunday clothes and take me walking. I remember raising a row about having my neck washed unless it was done by Nanna, who could wash behind my ears and never hurt me. Now I saw her as a safeguard against my mother's wrath.

I was questioned harshly and closely by my mother about the contents of the letters. What had I said to him? How dared I write to him? Where were the letters he had written to me? Did I think I'd ever get another chance to write to him? Well, I should, but she would dictate the letter, and I'd write it or I'd know what she'd do to me. My mother was furious. It took the combined intercession of Katherine, Aunt B., and Nancy to save me from a beating. I refused to answer her questions about the nature of my letters. I made only one statement to her—that I had not mentioned her in any of them unless to say that she was in fairly good health. Nothing could convince her that I was telling the truth, and knowing even then the futility of arguing with her, I either evaded her questions, replied in monosyllables, or just said: "I don't know."

"What made you write to him in the first place?" she thundered furiously.

"I don't know," I said stupidly.

"What did you say to him?"

"Just—how was he feeling? and a couple of things."

"What things?" she demanded.

"Oh, I wanted to know how P.J. was."

"What else?"

"Just things."

"What things?"

"Oh just things. I can't remember."

It went on like that without pause for hours, till we stopped for lunch. In the afternoon she resumed the cross-examination. "Who is this friend he speaks of?"

"I've never met her."

"You must have met her or she wouldn't write to you. You probably met her secretly," she accused.

"I didn't," I denied.

"How many times have you written to your father?"

"I can't remember."

"Why did he send you those costumes?"

"To wear dancing."

"Do you like them?"

"I do." Those costumes were my most precious possession and she knew it; she knew too how she could hurt me more than if she had beaten me. "Well, you'll never see them again. They're not yours any longer. I'll use them as kitchen cloths, that's what will become of your fine costumes. And when they're covered with grease and dirt we'll see how proud you'll be of them."

I stubbornly refused to give her the satisfaction of raising my voice, or crying, and though I felt as if my heart would break, I simply shrugged my shoulders. Dig after dig she gave me, about the costumes, about my father, and still I refused to do anything but shrug. And at long last she gave up, saying scathingly: "You'll never be any good. You lying, deceitful fool. You'll never amount to anything, because you're too much like your father."

Abruptly her manner changed and she became almost gentle. "What is wrong with you?" she asked. "Why do you hate me so?"

"I don't hate you," I said. "You know I don't."

"Then why can't we be friends?"

"You never talk to me——" I said hesitatingly. "I can't tell you things." I saw a flicker of suspicion in her eyes. "What have you done?" she demanded.

"Nothing," I said.

"You must have done something or you wouldn't say that you couldn't tell me things. Out with it. What have you done?"

I shut up like a clam. We were right back where we were before.

She was quite sure now that I was guilty of something, and she tired herself out in questioning me for the rest of the day. Even when Katherine said that the only thing I had done was to write to my father, with her permission, and that it was absolutely impossible for me to have done anything wrong because I had never been allowed to go out alone since Jimmy Hines had taken me home from Uncle Tom's in New York, my mother still eyed me with suspicion. But she did not beat me, and it was years before she raised her hand to me again. Whether or not Aunt B. had anything to do with it I do not know, but I think so.

There was much further talk that night, before my mother, Nancy, and I left for Boston. I said very little and asked no questions, but kept listening to the conversation trying to find out why my mother had been told about the letters; and before the night was over I knew.

Aunt B., fearing that I might impulsively rush off to

New York to visit my father's friend, which I should be very apt to do without thinking of the consequences, or of their position as my temporary guardians, had written to my mother, telling her to come at once and either take me back to Boston with her, or else drill into me the fact that I was not to write to my father again. Aunt B. had gone so far as to say that she thought it advisable for me to return to Boston, as my love for my father was so strong that if he wrote and told me to do this or that I should do it without question, despite anything that she or Katherine could say. There was no harm in the letters so far as she knew. But she knew nothing of my father's friend, and for all Aunt B. knew, this friend might even be a kidnapper. No, she and Katherine could not take the responsibility. They would have told me to stop writing to my father, but they were sure I should refuse to obey them. Besides, there were young men writing to me from New York. One in particular, Jimmy Hines, was noticeably attentive. This certainly was not my fault, but their own, for making me look and act as if I were sixteen, when I was only fourteen and couldn't say so. Well—did my mother understand? Yes, my mother had understood. She had lost no time in packing a bag, telephoning to Nancy, and travelling to New Haven.

That night saw the last of my association with the Leary family.

Just before we left the house, Aunt B. called me to her bedside. "Barbara dear," she said, "I want you to take this Rosary. Keep it always with you. I know I shall never see you again, but my dear, if it is possible for me to help you, I shall, and never forget it."

"But Aunt B.," I protested.

"Stop child," she said impatiently. "And don't say: 'You'll soon be well again, Aunt B.' because I know differently. We've done you a good deal of harm", she went on, "growing you up and making a woman of you when you are still a child. Go back to your games if you can Barbara, but I'm afraid you are too much of a woman now ever to be a child again. We have taken your childhood away from you, and because of that you have a hard road ahead, with your young mind full of old ideas. I have only one bit of advice to give you. Control your impulsiveness, and your stubbornness, and try for my sake to be friends with your mother. Will you promise me?"

"I can't promise to do it Aunt B.," I said, "but I promise to try. Is that all right?"

"Yes," she said. "Now kiss me good-bye. God bless you and guard you my dear child."

My mother went in then to Aunt B.'s room. Her interview lasted only a few minutes, and she was crying when she came out.

Katherine did not come to the station with us. She and Mary waved their good-byes from the door of the house.

There was very little said while we were travelling to Boston. My mother made no remarks, save that I should write a letter to my father, dictated by her, as soon as we reached home. Nancy spoke very little during the journey. Once she told me that I looked well, and that it was nice to see me again—the rest of the time she read the paper. She was afraid to say very much, I think, because of my mother being present.

Chapter Five

The Police Play Whiskey Poker

*

South Boston looked dirtier and shabbier than it had before I left, by comparison with New York and New Haven. But there was no doubt that I was welcome back. I was nearly knocked over by an avalanche of arms, legs and kisses, paws and barking. I disentangled myself from the first to see Winnie, my little sister, a miniature edition of myself. The paws and barking came from our Alsatian, Lassie.

Winnie I hugged till she was breathless, then I stood her on a chair to have a really good look at her. She had not grown at all since I left and she was very pale. Only her eyes seemed different; they were darker and bigger, and the lashes were longer than when I had seen her last.

To Lassie, I pretended to pay no attention. I do not know what had made Lassie my dog in the first place. She had come to us as a two-months-old pup. My mother had told us that we were not to tease the dog because she was an Alsatian and therefore dangerous. We played with her while she was still small, after that we left her strictly alone. She obeyed my mother and Winnie, and Mike and Puffy, but it was me she followed everywhere.

Because of her viciousness, my mother was often going to send Lassie to the Dog Pound to be shot. But gradually the dog became invaluable, though it was a good while before we realized her real worth. She could smell a cop or a stranger even if she were at the other end of the house. By her growling, and her headlong dash for the door or window—wherever the cops happened to be—we gained a priceless moment or two that gave us time to have the whiskey destroyed or dumped. But it took three or four raids before we became aware that the dog never barked unless she had reason to, and that she never bared her teeth unless she meant to spring.

After leaving my luggage in the bedroom, I went downstairs into the kitchen. Lady Biddy was in her chair by the stove. "Hello, Lady Biddy," I said.

"Is it yereself that's in it asthore?"[1] she cried joyfully. "Oh thanks be to God and His angels that ye've come back again to us. Come here till I see ye. Are ye well darlint?"

I went to her and put my hands on her shoulders. She stood up. "Ye're thinner," she said, as she ran her hands over my face and body, "but ye're hard, and solid too," she went on. "But what's on yere face darlint? Sure 'tisn't the same face ye went away with, that ye have comin' back."

"I have make-up on," I told her. So accustomed had I become to wearing cosmetics, that from force of habit I had made up my face before leaving New Haven and renewed the make-up while on the train, and it had never once occurred to me that it was no longer necessary. My mother had made no remarks about it either.

[1] Darling.

"Make-up on yere face?" said Lady Biddy, "and is there anything wrong with ye that ye do be havin' to make up yere face asthore?"

"No, there's nothing wrong with me. It's rouge and powder I have on my face," I explained.

Lady Biddy sat down with a bump. "An' is it paintin' and powderin' ye are now?" she asked. "Oh go an' wash it away. Sure 'tis the divil entirely if yere face is so poorly that ye have to paint it to cover it up."

"But all the girls do it Lady Biddy," I protested, "you know, putting colour in their cheeks——"

"Faith," said she, "is it a monkey ye are, that ye must paint because other girls do it? Go and wash it off let ye, and leave yere face as God made it!"

It began to dawn on me then that I was no longer a young lady; I was a girl again. I left off make-up completely, but my face had acquired a sickly white pallor; I tried hard to readjust myself to games, and even tried to face the prospect of going back to school, but it was no use. I had worn high heels and ladies' dresses for ten months; I couldn't go back to flat heels and pinafores. Aunt B. was right when she said that they had taken my childhood away from me. They had. I decided to remain a young lady and go to work. I'd try for the stage again, and on my own this time. I had passed for sixteen in New York, there was no reason why I couldn't do the same in Boston.

I was a week at home before my mother made me write, at her dictation, to my father. She spent the week in threatening dire things if I did not obey her, and in the end I gave in and wrote to my father, saying that I no longer wanted to hear from him, as I had no use for him and preferred my mother. For weeks after sending the letter off my every movement was watched by my mother and Puffy, to make sure that I did not write to my father and tell him that I had been forced to write that awful letter. I was nearly heartbroken, and I determined that if I ever got the chance I would go to my father and stay with him.

My mother was trying by threats to make me obey her, to think as she wanted me to think, and that way only, to live as she decreed, and say only what she wanted me to say. By forcing me to write that letter to my father she had brought out all the stubbornness in my nature, for I fiercely hated to be forced to do anything. I made up my mind that from that time on I would do as I pleased. If I couldn't get it by asking, then I'd fight for it in any way I knew. My mother said that I should return to school and complete my education. She was right, and I knew that she was right, but I promptly began to make the rounds of the theatrical booking offices in Boston. She told me to discard cosmetics, and in spite of Lady Biddy's and her protests, I used more than ever.

We were doing good business at home. I was kept busy washing and filling bottles and serving customers till I got to know all the new ones, then I was put back to my old post "on the door". Lassie was always with me, except when I sent her with Lady Biddy. Lady Biddy sometimes went into the back yard to walk on fine days. To get out to the yard it was necessary for her to go across the kitchen, into a vestibule connecting the kitchen with the pantry, through a wood-shed, and thence to the yard. Between the vestibule and the pantry was a step. Lady Biddy was never sure where the step was, so usually Puffy led her out to the yard and back. If Puffy couldn't attend to it, I did, and if we both happened to be very busy, I'd send Lassie. The dog would walk slowly beside the old woman till they neared the pantry step, then she would run ahead, plant herself squarely before Lady Biddy and bark once, just before Lady Biddy came to the step. Lassie never left Lady Biddy's side till the latter was safely back in her chair in the kitchen.

I determined to plunge into things and keep myself as busy as possible between dancing and helping in the house. Our trade had increased to such an extent that we could hardly handle it. There was plenty of money being made, and practically no raids. In spite of this my mother grew more and more worried and anxious. "It was better when they raided us every other week," she said, "then we knew what we were up against. Things are too quiet to be safe." She approved of my interest in the business, and daily I learned more about it. I knew how to dilute whiskey to the ninety-five proof, at which we sold it, how to colour it to make it look like genuine Rye or Scotch, and how to flavour each bottle so that it would taste like what it was supposed to be. Once and again some member of the family would be stopped on the street and questioned by a detective or a policeman. I learned how to give vague answers, to reply to questions with other questions, and how to talk for an hour without saying anything. One afternoon I was accosted by a cop just as I was about to enter the house.

"Just a minute," he said, "I want to talk to you, Miss Mullen."

"Yes?"

"Yes, how's business?"

"Business?" I repeated blankly.

"Come on, you don't have to be afraid of me," he lowered his voice confidentially, "I tipped your mother off to the last raid. I'm your friend."

"It's nice to have friends."

"I notice you have a lot of people going in and out all day—hundreds of them. How many gallons of booze do you sell a day?"

"All those people are our friends," I told him.

"Do they all buy booze?"

"Booze? In my house?"

"Yeah, booze in your house."

"How could they buy anything when we don't sell anything? They're our friends."

"Your mother has her kids well trained," he said. "You can go into the house. I'm not going to follow you in—not this time," and he walked away.

"They're planning something big," said my mother when I told her. "I'm sure of it. We'll have to be extra careful."

Accordingly, we increased our vigilance. The doors were doubly and trebly barred. Lassie slept inside the back door, which we assumed the night squad would smash in first if we were raided at night.

Every second day after my arrival home, my mother sent me to telephone to New Haven to enquire after Aunt B. Katherine had taken a job as a cook, and was earning good wages; Mary was doing general housework. For the first few weeks Aunt B.'s condition remained unchanged. Then one day I was told that she had been moved to the hospital. I telephoned every day after that. For a week I was told the same thing: "Condition unfavourable." She still took the greatest interest in what Katherine was doing and in our telephone conversations, enquiring anxiously each day about my welfare. Then abruptly her name was placed on the "dangerously ill" list. "I go in as often as possible to see her," said Katherine, "and I'm holding myself in readiness for the news I know will come any day now." Still Aunt B. lingered on, suffering. Then one day I was told: "She's dying, Barbara. It will probably be to-night or to-morrow. I was at the hospital all night. She knows she's going, and all she says is: 'My dear Katherine, you're not to worry. It distresses me to think that you are anxious about me. How is Barbara? Give her my love when she calls again.'" When I called the next afternoon there was no answer, and that evening I called again. Katherine was there; her voice was tired and she sounded very old. "It's over," she said. "She died at three o'clock."

As I left the telephone booth a voice said: "You're Mullen aren't you?"

"What?" I said.

"Are you Mullen?"

"Mullen? Yes, why?"

"The B.P.D.'s headin' up the street."

I ran out of the store and looked down the street. Still a block away I saw the Boston Police Department car, as the man had said, heading up the street. I raced for the house. Mike was on the door. He saw me running up the front steps and had the door open; "B.P.D." I gasped, "coming this way." Mike slammed the door shut behind me: "Here they come," he shouted. "Dump. Dump." I rushed downstairs to the kitchen. In the middle of the kitchen floor was a five-gallon can full of whiskey. The bootlegger had just delivered it and there was not time enough either to hide it or dump it. Mike was still shouting "Dump. Dump."

"We're sunk," said Puffy, as he looked at the can.

"Like hell we are!" cried my mother defiantly. "Stand up Lady Biddy."

"Are they in yet?" asked Lady Biddy as she stood up.

"Don't talk," said my mother sharply. "Do as I tell you." She lifted up the four or five large, heavy petticoats that Lady Biddy always wore under her black billowy skirt, and taking the can of whiskey, placed it between Lady Biddy's legs, then pulled her petticoats and skirt down again. We heard the crash and shouting as the cops smashed through the front door. "Don't move. Don't sit down, no matter what happens," said my mother.

"You can trust me, mam," returned Lady Biddy.

We heard the sound of swift heavy footsteps on the stairs; Lassie was growling viciously. The cops didn't wait to turn the knob of the kitchen door. They smashed it through, and Lassie sprang for the throat of the first cop that entered; her teeth tore through the coat sleeve of his left arm which he threw up as a shield.

"Go down, Lassie," I cried.

The cop reached for his gun. His face was white. "Keep that god dam dog off or I'll shoot her," he cried.

I caught hold of Lassie's collar. It took all my

strength to hold her. The rest of the raiding squad swarmed into the kitchen, and the sergeant gave them orders: "You take such a room. You take the yard. You tap the walls," etc.

Lady Biddy began to sob softly: "Oh the Lord save us this blessed day, what is it that's happening at all mam?"

"It's all right, Lady Biddy," said the sergeant, who knew her of old. "We won't hurt you. We're raiding the house, looking for whiskey. Do you know where it's hidden?"

"Whiskey is it? Oh the Lord bless yere poor head. An' how would I know sir, and I blind this many a year. Isn't it little ye have to do to be puttin' yere questions at an old woman like me, blind an' all as I am," and she began to cry loudly.

One of the cops had been, with the sergeant, tapping the kitchen walls and searching the closets; they even unscrewed the drain pipe in the kitchen sink. They came at last to the stove. The sergeant looked in the oven and the cop went to Lady Biddy. "Move out of the way," he said sharply.

For a moment you could have heard a pin drop in the room.

"Move," said the cop impatiently, and he put his hand on Lady Biddy's shoulder as if to shove her out of his way. To us it was apparent that Lady Biddy had been waiting for him to touch her, for the moment she felt his hand she set up such a howling and roaring that she could be heard plainly out in the street. You would have thought she was being murdered.

"Oh what is it ye're trying to do to me at all sir?" she

cried as she rocked her body back and forth: "What is it ye're trying to do to me? Oh can't anyone save me? Have ye no mother of yere own? Oh have pity on a poor old woman at this hour of me life. May the Lord forgive ye for puttin' yere hand on me, as though I wasn't bad enough before, bein' blind and all. Where are ye mam? Isn't there anyone at all to save me? Oh what am I goin' to do at all?" On and on she went, her voice growing louder and louder, her body rocking faster and faster, but not for a second did she move her feet. She still held her position over the whiskey, hiding it successfully.

"For God's sake let her alone," snapped the sergeant. "If you want to get behind the stove go around the other way. Can't you see that the old woman's blind? You've got her scared silly."

The cop meekly obeyed, and the sergeant began to speak to Lady Biddy. "Sit down, Lady Biddy," he said soothingly, "no one will hurt you."

But Lady Biddy continued to cry and roar and ask him if he hadn't a mother of his own, and finally he gave her up as a bad job, and let her alone. But she kept on doing her stuff until the police, after an hour of unsuccessful searching, left the house.

"They're gone," said my mother as she took the can of whiskey from its hiding-place. "You worked well, Lady Biddy."

"Me throat is that dry from all I cried mam, could ye spare me a little droppeen, just to take the thirst off me?" asked Lady Biddy as she sat down. My mother began to laugh. "By God, you can have all in the house," she said, filling a large glass, "you're well worth it."

Except for an occasional direction given by my mother, no one spoke for the next ten minutes. We were all busy, each doing our share of the work of getting the whiskey out of the five-gallon can. Some of the whiskey was to be hidden, the rest would be kept in the house ready to sell. The five gallons of whiskey were poured into a large pot. From this Puffy filled two one-gallon jugs, I filled quart bottles, and my mother filled pint bottles. One gallon of whiskey was left in the pot. Puffy then went "on the door", relieving Mike, who took the one-gallon jugs and quart bottles and put them in a burlap bag. He then went out into the yard, crossed it, climbed over a high fence into another yard, and entering through an open back window of an empty house, stored the whiskey under some loose boards in the floor of its cellar. In the meantime my mother was occupied in hiding on her person eight pints of whiskey.

Often, when we were being raided, my mother walked about the house with the cops, talking to them while they were searching for the evidence which she had hidden in her corsets. She always got away with it. She was stout, and if she bulged in places, the cops apparently just thought that she was growing stouter. In any case, she was never searched.

The pot containing the whiskey was placed on a table, next to another pot in which was disinfectant. At the slightest warning of raid, the disinfectant would be dumped into the whiskey, effectually destroying it as evidence.

Because we sold whiskey, landlords in South Boston were reluctant to have us as tenants. For them there was always the danger of the house being "padlocked" by the police, which meant that we should have to move and the house could not be occupied again for six months or a year, whenever the period of padlocking expired.

The empty house in which Mike had stored the whiskey was rented by one Mrs. Graham. That is to say, it was rented in Mrs. Graham's name. My mother paid the rent.

Mrs. Graham was one of the two women employed by my mother to work in our house. All the house-cleaning was left to them, and they sometimes assisted in serving customers or filling bottles. They were both absolutely trustworthy, but of the two Mrs. Graham, or Grahamy, as we called her, was the more reliable in a crisis. Grahamy was short, with a round chubby body set on a pair of matchstick-like legs, and bobbed black hair, streaked here and there with grey. She was full of good humour, always bubbling over with laughter, and continually looking for something to wash, or dust or pick up. She never walked if she could run and had a peculiar gait all her own, that my mother often described as being "a cross between a gallop and a slither, with a step of a jig thrown in for good measure".

The other woman, Mrs. Mary Ward, was Grahamy's direct opposite. Tall and thin, she affected long dresses that fell away loosely from her sparse figure, and antiquated hats that she perched at a precarious angle on the side of her head. Her hair was long, brown and stringy, and seemed continually falling down in front of her face. She was afflicted with a mild fotm of tic, her mouth and hands jerking spasmodically. She was a fine houseworker and very loyal; at the mention of "cops", however, she lost all control of herself. The twitching of her mouth and hands would become violent, and she would dive for the nearest bottle of disinfectant. The word "cops" always affected Mary in the same way, whether it came up in conversation, or whether they were actually hammering at the door.

Between herself and Grahamy war was ever being waged. Each wanted to outdo the other in whatever work there was to be done. For instance, Grahamy might have just put the finishing touches to a certain room. Mary would wait until Grahamy had put brooms, dusters, etc., away in the closet, then, with a resigned expression, she would go into the room, survey it critically, fetch a duster and dust it all over again. Grahamy would then run after Mary demanding furiously that she mind her own business. That room had been cleaned thoroughly, and what was the big idea? Mary would begin to jerk and twitch and say: "I'm-the-only-one-around-here-that-can-dust-a-room-properly-and-some-people-I-know-know-it-too." Grahamy would get her own back by washing out whiskey bottles while Mary was otherwise occupied, and then saying to her triumphantly: "Well, I'm the only one around here that can wash bottles properly, and a certain party *I* know can put that in her old tin hat."

Grahamy came in this evening just before the evening rush. "How is your New Haven friend, Barbara?" she asked as she donned her apron.

"Good Lord!" I said, as I suddenly recalled Aunt B.

"What's the matter?" my mother asked.

"Aunt B. died at three o'clock this afternoon——"

"And you said nothing about it?"

"The raid. I couldn't think of anything. I meant to tell you after the cops left."

Grahamy began to hop about. "Were we raided?" she asked excitedly. "Were we raided?"

My mother tried to talk to Grahamy and me at the same time. "Yes. How did Katherine seem to be taking it?"

"She sounded all in," I said.

"Did they get anything?" Grahamy asked.

"See me after the rush is over," my mother said to me, then turning to Grahamy she began to tell her about the raid.

I went upstairs to my bedroom. "Aunt B. is dead," I said aloud to myself. And suddenly New Haven, Katherine and Aunt B. grew very dim in my mind, as though it had all happened years before. "I'm sorry about Aunt B." I thought; "I liked her." But somehow I didn't feel sad enough to cry. I was more surprised than anything else. To me, Aunt B. had seemed so permanent.

"Barbara-your-mother-wants-you-downstairs-to-help." It was Mary Ward, trying as usual to look dignified between jerks.

"I didn't know you had come in, Mary," I said.

"I-just-this-minute-got-here."

"Have you seen Grahamy yet?"

"No—I haven't. And-I-don't-want-to."

We began to descend the stairs. "What have you got against Grahamy?" I asked. "I'm sure she likes you." I liked to question Mary about Grahamy and Grahamy about Mary because they gave identical answers. At the same time we all knew that each liked the other, although neither would admit it. "That woman," said Mary in reply to my question. "She-can't-do-anything. What-your mother-keeps-her-for-I don't-know——"

"Mary dear," Grahamy called sweetly from the foot of the stairs: "Did you know that the cops were——"

That of course was as far as she got. Mary jerked, slid, and squealed her way down to the foot of the stairs and rushed madly into the kitchen, where fortunately my mother, who guessed what had happened, caught hold of her before she had time to reach the pot of disinfectant.

"Who's trying to be so funny?" my mother demanded.

"I only asked her if she knew that the——" began Grahamy.

"That's enough," said my mother. "You did it deliberately. You ought to have more sense."

"I'm sorry," said Grahamy meekly.

My mother knew that Grahamy was far from feeling as meek as she tried to look, but said no more than: "Indeed, you look it, you do." In her own way, Mary would soon be one up on Grahamy.

That night we held a council of war, and decided to move. Mike was definitely against moving, pointing out that we had a good place where we were. "We've got a good front door, a better back door, and a great hiding place for the stuff," he said. "The doors are so strong that we could have the stuff dumped while the cops were breaking in."

"It was just luck that we weren't caught to-day," my mother told him. "They have raided us here so often that they know every inch of the house as well as we know it ourselves. No, we've got to move. We'll try a flat this time instead of a house. Are you game, Christy?"

" 'Tis all the same to me mam," said Christy. "I'll go anywhere. Sure I'd be lost living with any other family."

"I think you're wrong," Mike insisted.

"Who the hell cares what you think!" said my mother. "I say we move."

So we moved, twice in one week. The first move was into a house. It was a grand house. My mother was extremely pleased with it and considered herself very fortunate in finding it vacant. She had no trouble with the landlord about renting it, and it was ridiculously cheap. Even Mike liked it.

We stayed in the new house one night, and were flat-hunting again the next day. About midnight, Lassie had begun to howl. Lady Biddy ran all round her bedroom screaming that the fairies were after her, and nearly broke her neck falling over everything. The house was infested with huge, horrible-looking rats. They ran over the beds, up the walls, on the tables and chairs, between our legs and over our shoes. We all stayed together in one room and no one dared venture out of it. We couldn't do anything but pray for daylight. As fast as we beat off one rat, three or four others would take its place. Winnie had hysterics; Puffy walked about looking rather pale and saying: "What a joint." Mike and Christy sat or walked together, smoking and saying: "No wonder, no wonder," and I listened to my mother cursing the day she'd rented "this goddam house". It was awful.

We saw Grahamy early the next morning, when exhausted and frightened we trooped out into the street.

She was waiting outside the front door, and her face was a picture when she saw us. "You slept in there all night?" she asked in an amazed voice.

"We stayed in there, but we certainly didn't sleep," said my mother.

"You look queer, what's the matter with you? And why didn't you show up yesterday?" We were crossing the street towards a restaurant, where we could breakfast and telephone for the furniture removal men. Grahamy explained that her daughter Catherine had been ill the day before, and couldn't be left alone. She was much better to-day. "I didn't realize that you meant that house," she said, "or I would have told you about it. I wouldn't go in there myself for any amount of money, and I'm a poor woman."

"Why?" my mother asked.

"Well," related Grahamy, "years ago, when my grandmother was a child, she used to play in the cellar of that house, and one day when she was digging under a heap of rubbish she saw a small human foot. Terrified, she ran home and told what she had seen. The police were notified, and when they went to the cellar they found, under the rubbish heap, the body of a child. You've heard of Jesse Pomeroy?"

My mother nodded.

"It was he", continued Grahamy, "who murdered that child, and that house has not been lived in since the body was found. It's supposed to be haunted and full of rats."

The low rent and the eagerness of the landlord to have us as tenants were explained.

Before she had seen the "rat house", my mother had

been searching for a flat. She had decided on one and had started for home to send Grahamy to take it. On the way she had seen the "To let" sign on the house, hunted up the agent who had the keys and made him show her round. She fell for it immediately and told the agent that she would take it, and didn't bother to go back to the flat at all. While we were having breakfast she directed Grahamy to go and see if the flat was still vacant. If it was, she was to park on the landlord's door-step till she had paid the rent and got the keys from him so that we could move in at once. If the flat was occupied, she was to come right back and we would figure out something else.

A very flushed and angry Grahamy returned in two hours. "Did you get it?" my mother asked.

"And how I got it!" said Grahamy.

"What happened? Did you have any trouble?"

"I'll tell the world I had trouble. He didn't want to give me the flat. He heard that I work for you, and he said he'd rather not let it. It took me an hour to convince him that I was O.K. If I were you Mrs. Mullen I wouldn't take that flat. The landlord is sure to order you out as soon as he finds out you are there."

"Who collects the rent?"

"The agent."

"Then as long as we keep the rent paid," said my mother, "we won't see the landlord. In any case, we've got to get in some place. Did you see Mary Ward any-where?"

"I did," said Grahamy; "she was sitting on a camp stool outside the haunted house when I left here to see about the flat. She's still there."

"Why didn't you tell her we were in here?"

"I was in such a hurry Mrs. Mullen. I was afraid the flat might be gone, and I thought I'd better not stop for anything."

I went over and fetched Mary. Sooner or later she'd find out about Grahamy's seeing her and letting her wait, and then she would start something. I hoped I'd be around when the two of them went at it.

Puffy telephoned to the furniture removal men and they arrived on the scene in about a quarter of an hour. There was no one at the flat to give them directions and they were not very particular about where they put things. When we got to the flat we found all the beds in the kitchen, the kitchen tables in the bathroom, a couple of trunks piled on top of two or three barrels of crockery, etc. My mother walked from one room to another raging and storming at the way the things had been thrown; then abruptly her mood changed. She became good-humoured and capable, issuing an order here or a direction there, working like blazes herself and making sure that everyone else followed suit. Even Winnie did her share, running about with nails, hammers, etc. We didn't stop for lunch. Grahamy went to see the gas and electric people, and she brought back some sandwiches and coffee which we finished in a few minutes. By nightfall the flat was presentable, and business was being carried on as usual. Letting the customers know of our change of address was, as Winnie would put it, "merely a minor detail". Mike simply stood on the corner of C Street for five minutes, long enough to start the word around, and in the evening every customer came directly to the flat.

The most important matter, and one which had to be attended to at once, was that of finding a new hiding place for the whiskey. This was left to Mike, who taking a flashlight and Lassie with him, started on his quest at eight o'clock. It was nearly midnight when he returned, looking very dirty and covered from head to feet with cobwebs and dust. He announced that he had found a perfect hiding place but that he could never get into it again.

"That's great news," said my mother. "It's going to be a lot of help, isn't it, if you can't get into it again?"

And then Mike explained. Our flat was on the second floor of the house. To get to the hiding place, one had to go down three back flights of winding stairs into the cellar, then across twenty feet in the open. This led to what appeared to be the securely boarded up windows of another cellar, that was under one of a row of five houses which had been condemned by the board of health as unfit for habitation.

"Looking at them from the outside", said Mike, "you'd think that each house had its own separate cellar. Instead it's just one cellar for all five houses, and it extends nearly the length of half a block. I had to bend double to get around in it, it's so low. It's full of old packing cases and boxes, and all kinds of rubbish and dirt. We can hide the whiskey at the end farthest from this house. I've picked the spot. When we get in a load of stuff, I'll take it down and put it away. But I couldn't go down every time you want a gallon, because I'm too big and it would take me too long——"

"How did you get in there in the first place?" my mother asked.

"I loosened two of the boards over the cellar window. I loosened three first but it was too noticeable, so I had to nail one back on when I came out. Somebody small can squeeze in now. I left two boards just loose enough to move. When I go in I'll have to take off the third one and put it on again when I come out. But whoever is smallest, that's who'll have to go down every day for the whiskey when it's wanted."

My mother looked at me, then at Puffy, and then at me again. "It's up to you," she said. "You're the smallest. O.K.?"

"O.K.," I answered.

"Don't go down without Lassie," Mike advised. "Let the dog go before you down the stairs and into the other cellar. Just in case someone finds out about it and puts the cops wise, Lassie will give you plenty of warning."

"Remember", said my mother, "you'll have to be very careful. If we're caught it means a stiff fine, with maybe a couple of months in jail thrown in. But if they get you, you'll be sent away till you're twenty-one years old, because you're under age now. I wouldn't let you do it if there was any other way, but there isn't."

Chapter Six

Capture and Release

★

We soon grew accustomed to our new home. Business flourished, and my mother, believing as she did that the cops could never find the whiskey, began to feel safe. We never kept more than one gallon of whiskey in the flat. When that gallon was gone and another needed, I went and got it. "Supposing", I said to my mother one day, "that the cops break in here while I'm downstairs getting the stuff. I won't know they're here and I'm liable to walk right in and practically present them with the evidence."

"I'll leave some towels out on the clothes line," said my mother after a moment's reflection, "and if anything happens I'll begin to take them in and drop one or two."

"What if I don't see them?" I asked.

"I'll shout to you to bring up the towels; whether you see them or not you'll know what I mean."

I used to go down to that old cellar at least five times a day, and each time I had to go through a sort of routine of getting dressed for it before I could start. First, I would don one of my mother's size fifty-six housedresses and tie a string round my waist to keep myself from getting lost within it; next I would put on one of Puffy's old caps, and then to complete the outfit, a pair of cotton gloves. Despite all this covering, every visit into the cellar saw me dirtier, and by nightfall I would be positively filthy.

My dancing engagements increased, and it became a rare thing for me to spend an evening at home. I was constantly thinking and devising plans to write a letter of explanation to my father, but there was no opportunity to carry them out. Jimmy Hines wrote to me steadily from New York, and occasionally I heard from Uncle Tom and John Lally. John wanted to know why my family didn't move to New York, where we should be safe from raids. Every letter that I received was read by my mother, and she wanted to know what John meant by this. I told her what Katherine Leary had said about New York's being wide open, so that we could make a fortune there. "Well," said my mother, "things look quiet enough now, but if it ever gets too hot for us here, we'll go to New York. Maybe this friend of yours, Uncle Tom, would find an apartment for us. Anyway, it will be time enough to think about that when it happens. We'll see."

I was asked to dance at an "Irish Fair", which was to be held in Boston Garden. It was a week's engagement, and the terms were most agreeable—only two shows a day, one in the afternoon, and one in the evening. Between them I had plenty of time to return home. I usually brought my costume home with me for Grahamy to press while I was having a very necessary bath after visiting the cellar.

I was passing through the kitchen one afternoon when

Grahamy called me. "Your costume will look extra good to-night Barbara," she said. "I pressed it in a very special way and it came out beautifully. I laid it across your bed so that you'll see it the minute you enter your room." I went in to look at the costume, and it certainly had "come out beautifully". It looked like a new costume instead of one that was two years old. "It looks swell, Grahamy," I said.

My mother came into the room. "Doesn't my costume look good?" I asked. "Yes, yes," she said. "I'll look at it later on. There was an unexpected rush and we're out of stuff. Hurry and get some. We've some customers waiting."

"But I've just come out of the tub," I almost wailed.

"Well, you can go back into it just as easy as you came out. Hurry on. We can't keep the customers waiting."

Much against my will I hastily got into the cellar outfit of house-dress, cap and gloves, took the flashlight, and went to the kitchen table for the large crockery pitcher in which I always carried the whiskey. In case I did see a cop, a crockery pitcher could be smashed against a wall or the ground and the evidence destroyed at once, whereas a heavy glass jug wouldn't always break at the first knock it got. I didn't have to call Lassie, for she was so accustomed to going to the cellar with me by this time, that the moment she saw me take the pitcher off the kitchen table she was ready and eager to be down the back stairs.

All went well until I started to cross the twenty feet of open ground. I wasn't half-way across when I was sure that Lassie had gone mad. She was about ten feet or more in front of me, when quite suddenly she began to growl and bare her teeth viciously; abruptly she turned and ran towards me and jumped on me with such force that I was knocked down. I dropped the pitcher and it smashed into pieces. I got up and looked at the dog. She ran madly towards the two loose boards over the old cellar window, stopped dead for a second and then began to growl furiously. I was sure my hair was standing on end. For the first time since she had come to us, I was terrified of Lassie. I thought of my mother waiting upstairs for the whiskey and decided to have another try at getting it. I could bring up one of the gallon jugs. "Get away from there Lassie!" I cried. "Go and lie down!" Again she ran and jumped on me and knocked me down—and this time I stayed down. The dog sat on my chest and I was afraid to do anything else. A couple of minutes had passed before I realized the meaning of Lassie's strange behaviour. "Get off Lass!" I cried. And as though she sensed that at last I understood what she had been trying so hard to tell me, she jumped up and raced before me for the door that led to the back stairs. From somewhere in the regions above me came my mother's voice: "Barbara, bring up the towels that dropped off the line."

"Okay," I shouted back. I glanced hurriedly around but couldn't see the towels, so I didn't bother to search for them. I just ran up the back stairs as fast as I could.

I made sure that Lassie wouldn't spring for anyone's throat this time by catching hold of her collar as we reached the door of the flat. I opened the door with one hand and did my best to hold Lassie with the other. She began to struggle fiercely to get away. Someone, I think it was the sergeant, pushed the door shut against me from the other side. "If you bring that dog in here I'll shoot her," he called to me.

"For God's sake don't bring her in!" my mother cried. I knew she meant "Don't bring in the whiskey". "She must think I'm awful dumb," I thought as I tied Lassie to one of the stair rails just outside the door. "Well, you can't get in now Lassie, and they can't get out—not this way. You can let me in now," I called aloud, "the dog is tied." The door was opened by one of the cops. He dragged me forcibly into the kitchen when he saw how near Lassie was, for she nearly went crazy altogether then.

"Hey, you. No rough stuff," said the sergeant sharply.

"She didn't tie the dog," the cop protested.

"I did so," I cried. "If you don't believe me, go and look." But he didn't open the door again.

"What did you do with the whiskey?" the sergeant asked.

"I don't know what you're talking about," I said.

"What were you doing downstairs?"

"I went down to pick up some clothes that fell off the clothes line."

"What did you do with them after you picked them up? Hide them?"

"I couldn't find them."

"Where's the whiskey?"

"I don't know what you mean."

A welcome interruption came from my mother. "Did that cop hurt you when he dragged you about?"

"He hurt my arms," I complained. My arms were

not hurt at all, but I thought it better to say that they were, for then the sergeant might not question me so closely.

"A nice way," said my mother angrily, "great strong men having nothing better to do than to go pulling the arms out of that innocent child."

"She should have called off the dog," snapped the sergeant.

"You call off your dogs and we'll call off ours," my mother snapped back at him meaningly.

He turned his attention to Grahamy. "You're still here I see," he said.

"I am," said Grahamy, "and very glad to be. I must say I've never worked for nicer people."

The sergeant began to laugh. "Where's Mrs. Ward?" he asked.

"She won't be in for another hour," said my mother, "she went in town, shopping."

"She's the one that gets the jitters whenever she hears 'cop' isn't she?"

"Mrs. Ward is a good respectable woman I'll have you know," said Grahamy, up in arms immediately. "She doesn't get the jitters, she's just a little nervous, and well she should be. The way you people come crashing in here is enough to give any woman a nervous breakdown."

"And I thought you two didn't like each other."

"Who's been giving you all the information, sergeant?" my mother asked suddenly.

"You've got all kinds of customers, Mrs. Mullen," he said.

"I see," said my mother. "Thanks."

He went to the back window and called down to somebody who was evidently waiting in the yard below, "Get it?"

The answer: "No, nothing around here," came floating up to him.

"Meet us at the car," he directed. He called to the three cops who were searching the rooms, questioned no one any further, and left.

The idea of one of our customers being an informer caused great excitement. I took a quick bath, and when I came back into the kitchen they were all—my mother, Grahamy, Mike, Puffy and Lady Biddy—raving about what they would do to whoever it was if they ever got their hands on him. We checked and rechecked our list of customers, trying to guess who it could be. Christy and Red Cahill, another boarder, came in from work, and they too were called into the consultation.

"It wouldn't be Joe Scanlon?" suggested Christy.

"Or Bart Jordan?" said Red.

"No," my mother disagreed. "Joe Scanlon is no informer, and neither is Bart Jordan. We've known Joe for years, and as for Jordan, he comes from the same part of Ireland as I do myself, and there are so many Galway people living in South Boston that his life wouldn't be worth a nickel if he turned squealer on one of his own townspeople—and he knows it. No, it's someone else. Someone we'd never suspect." But though dozens of other names were put forward, there was none we could put a finger on and say definitely: "This is the one."

"It seems to me", remarked Christy, "that it's not you they are after at all, mam. It's Kathleen Mavourneen that they are trying to get. They knew all about her going down for the stuff, and if it had not been for Lassie she would have been caught red-handed by the cops waiting for her in the old cellar."

"By God, Christy, you have it!" my mother exclaimed. "She's been stopped on the street and questioned too!"

"But they've stopped some of the others as well as me," I pointed out.

"Not so often as they have you, though," said my mother.

"Whoever is doing the talking", put in Red, "is going to be well paid by the cops if he can get Barbara. He might try to make a sale."

"If they ever get her in court they'll do a job on her," said Mike.

Unfortunately, it was at this moment that Mary Ward returned from her shopping tour. She saw at once how worked up we were. "Is-anything-the-matter?" she asked.

"Matter?" cried my mother. "The cops nearly got ——"

With a shriek Mary dropped her bundles, ran for the bedroom, grabbed the pot of disinfectant, and before anyone could stop her was sprinkling it madly about. She didn't stop to see if there was a pot of whiskey into which she should dump the disinfectant, but ran wildly round the room, throwing generous portions of it on windows, curtains, walls, and then, to complete the damage, drenched the costume that Grahamy had pressed so carefully and laid across the bed that afternoon.

She was so distressed when she realized what she had done that no one, not even Grahamy, had the heart to scold her. "I-wouldn't-for-anything-have-spoiled-that-lovely-costume," she sobbed, "I'd-do-anything-to-make-up-for-it-Mrs.-Mullen. I'm-so-sorry——"

"Don't be silly, Mary," my mother said. "We know you didn't do it on purpose. Barbara has time enough to get some kind of a dress for to-night, and the costume can be washed and ready for to-morrow, so there's no need to make such a fuss about it."

I still had an hour to spare, and Grahamy came with me to the nearest dress store, hoping that we should find a dress green enough to serve me as a costume for that night's performance.

A precious quarter of an hour was wasted in explaining to the sales girl that it didn't matter what colour was most fashionable this season, we wanted green. No, blue certainly would not do, nor would pink. We wanted Kelly green. She didn't think she had a Kelly green in the store. No, wait a minute, she had one. She had not been able to sell it—it was put away in a back room.

"What size is it?" I asked.

"Small fourteen."

The girl brought out the dress. It was the right shade of green and I tried it on. I thought at first that it fitted perfectly.

"The skirt looks rather tight," said Grahamy.

I started to walk the length of the floor and discovered that if I didn't take very short steps, either the dress would rip open or I should fall. "It is very tight," I admitted. "But there isn't time to do anything about it now. I should be at the Garden——"

"Well, be careful when you're dancing," advised Grahamy, "or you'll trip and break your neck." Her dismal prophecy nearly came true.

In the dressing-room at the Garden that night there was more than the usual amount of conversation about the show.

"I've never seen such a flop," said one girl disgustedly.

"Lousiest show I ever played," said another.

"I heard that Mr. —— (the manager) isn't going to pony up[1] on Saturday and that we'll be left holding the bag," a late arrival cried excitedly as she began tearing off her clothes.

There was an incredulous chorus of "What? Who said so?"

"I heard it just now, coming in."

The place was bedlam; everybody was shouting at once.

"He can't do that to us!"

"We won't go on!"

"You're crazy!"

Another late arrival rushed in. "Did you hear the news?" she cried.

"Did we!"

"Isn't it a shame? He was such a nice kid too."

"Who do you mean?" we all asked together.

"The Fahey kid. You know, the youngest one in the Fahey orchestra. I thought you knew——"

"What's happened to him?"

"His car crashed last night when he was going home. He was killed."

[1] Pay up.

There was a familiar knock on the dressing-room door. "Two minutes," called a voice, "two minutes."

The girls in the opening number began to rush, keeping up a running fire of comments, calling questions back and forth.

"Is the Fahey act going on?"

"Guess so—saw them outside."

"How's the crowd?"

"Best yet. Announcer told me about ten thousand so far."

"Hurray! Mr. —— won't skip out then if the show picks up."

"Who knows? Maybe he will and maybe he won't."

The time came at last for me to go on.

In the centre of the Garden was a large ring, much like a boxing ring, with a flight of four or five stairs lead-up to it from the floor of the Garden. It was in this ring that the acts were performed.

I got up the flight of stairs, and danced, without mishap. There was a huge crowd, and judging by the amount of applause we received, they liked the act very well indeed. The act over, I completely forgot my tight skirt and Grahamy's warning. I took the usual bow and then started to leave the ring. I took one long step and tumbled from the top of the little flight of stairs to the bottom. The crowd roared and began to applaud again. Fortunately I was not injured, and because it seemed to be the only thing to do, I stood up and bowed. The crowd continued to applaud—apparently they thought it the best part of the act. "Well," I thought to myself, "if they think I'm going to do that all over again, they're daffy," and I bowed again and walked off.

General opinion in the dressing-room, after the show, was that Mr. —— "wasn't the kind of a guy that would skip out". We all felt badly about the young man who had been killed, though some of us hardly knew him at all. One girl mentioned that she was surprised that his act had gone on without him. The other girls pooh-poohed her, saying: "Of course the act went on. The crowd paid money to see the show, they want to get their money's worth. What do they care who dies or doesn't die?"

I let myself into the flat with the key. Christy, looking very alert, was standing in the hall behind the door. "Anyone follow you?" he asked in a whisper.

"No," I said. "What's the matter? Where's Mike?"

"We got raided again, a couple of hours after you left."

"Did they get anything?"

"Two gallons, right in the middle of the kitchen floor."

"Did they make a pinch?" I asked.

"Mike," said Christy. "He took the rap, goes up tomorrow."

"Did Christy tell you?" my mother asked.

"Yes," I said. "How did it happen?"

"Mike took Lassie and went down for a couple of gallons of stuff. He let the dog into the cellar first and everything seemed to be O.K. So he brought up two gallon jugs full, and left them in the middle of the kitchen floor, but before we had time to get it into the pot, the cops broke in and caught us clean."

"Where was Lassie?" I asked.

"Mike left her outside the back door," my mother said.

"What made him do that?"

"He didn't know himself why he did it."

"Christy told me he's taking the rap."

"He is."

"What will he get?" I asked.

"Probably a hundred dollars fine. I'll pay it, of course."

"The cops certainly picked the right moment to break in," I said. "I wonder if they knew he'd gone down for the stuff."

"They did," she said. "The sergeant told me."

"Told you?"

"Well not right out of course. But he did say that there were lots of telephones handy. That was enough wasn't it?"

"It was plenty," I said.

The next morning in court Mike was let off with the hundred dollars fine and the warning: "If you come up before me again on this charge. . . ."

Nothing much happened then until the following Saturday, the last day of the show at the Garden. I came home between shows as usual and told my mother of the rumour that Mr. —— had gone off to New York and that we were not going to be paid.

"That's just talk," she said. "Why shouldn't the man go to New York if he wants to without you people making such a fuss about it? He'll be back in time to pay everyone off, don't worry."

"I'm going out," she went on. "I'll be back in an hour or so. There's two half pints, bottled, and a drink in that glass on the table for whoever buys them. That's all there is in the house, and don't go down for any more till I come back. I'm going to see about a house that's to let, down the street."

"Are we going to move again?" I asked.

"We are. Be careful. Everyone is out but yourself," she said, and went out.

Shortly after she left, I heard someone at the door. It was a customer, Bart Jordan.

"Hello," he said.

"Hello," I answered.

"All alone?"

"No," I said. "I've got my dog."

"Oh no offence," he said quickly. "No offence."

"What do you want?" I asked.

"A pint."

"I've got it, in two half-pint bottles," I said. "All right?"

"Sure, that's fine," he said.

I gave him the pint and the drink, and he paid me the dollar and went out. Two minutes later he was back. I let him in, and behind him crowded in the sergeant and the raiding squad. The sergeant put his hands in his pockets and drew out the two half-pint bottles. "Where did you get these?" he asked Jordan.

"I bought them off that girl," declared Jordan, pointing to me.

"Did you pay her for them?"

"I paid her a dollar."

The sergeant turned to me. "Hand over the dollar," he said.

"Jordan's a liar," I said. "He didn't pay me any dollar and I didn't sell him any booze."

"Take her inside," he directed one of his men. I was taken by the arm and walked into the kitchen, where the cop pushed forward a chair saying: "Sit down." The sergeant and the rest of his squad searched the flat, but of course found nothing. They came into the kitchen.

"She gave you a drink?" asked the sergeant.

"Sure she did. That's the glass," Jordan pointed it out.

The sergeant took up the glass and smelled it. "She must have washed it," he said, putting it down. "We've got enough evidence without it, though." He told the cops to bring Jordan outside, and to wait for him. Then I was piloted into the bedroom and pushed into a big chair. The sergeant and the cop into whose charge I had first been put each pulled up a chair and sat one on either side of me. They began pointing their fingers and firing questions and accusations at me.

"You dumped the rest of the whiskey after you sold the pint to Jordan didn't you?"

"No," I said.

"You know you're going to be arrested don't you?"

"You've got nothing on me."

"You'll be sent away till you're twenty-one."

"So what?"

"Admit the charge and I'll see that you get off easy."

"What charge?"

"You sold this whiskey."

"I didn't."

On and on it went. My head began to ache. I wished something, anything, would happen to make them stop.

"In what part of the old cellar is the whiskey hidden?"

"I don't know what you're talking about."

"What time does the bootlegger come?"

"I don't know any bootlegger."

I wanted to scream at them, but I felt that they were hoping I would, so I kept my voice low.

Finally they tried a new line.

"We'll have to take your mother up for this if you don't admit it."

"There's nothing to admit."

"It will be simple enough to convict your mother and you know it."

"There's no charge." By this time I was nearly worn out. They sounded very sure of being able to convict my mother.

"If we pinch your mother do you know what it will mean?"

I couldn't speak.

"She'll get a jail sentence and we'll see that it's a long one. You kids will be put in a home. You'll never see your sister again, or your mother. Women work very hard in jail, scrubbing floors, washing, ironing in hot sweaty rooms, rotten food. Your mother isn't well and she won't live long if she goes to jail. Do you want that to happen?"

"No."

"Then admit the charge."

"No."

"We'll pinch your mother."

"No, don't," I said.

"It's up to you."

Whether they could arrest my mother or not I didn't know. They sounded as if they could. I didn't dare take the chance. "All right," I said. "I sold the pint."

"Where's the dollar he paid you for it?"

"He didn't pay me," I said. "He got it on tick."

"Why the dirty——" began the sergeant, and then he stopped. "Get your hat and coat," he said.

"Look here," I protested, "I've got to dance in a show to-night. I won't run away."

He thought for a minute. "Okay," he said. "But if you don't show up in court Monday morning, we'll make it hot for you."

"I'll be there," I said.

My mother rushed in white-faced and panting, shortly after they had left. "I saw them leaving," she gasped. "They didn't get you, did they?"

"They did," I said. "Bart Jordan made a sale."

"Bart Jordan——? How did it happen?"

I explained how after buying the pint Jordan had come back with the cops. "The skunk! They must have been waiting outside for him," she said. "The dollar was a marked one of course. They've got you nicely."

"They didn't get the dollar," I told her. "I caught hold of Lassie when they came in. I slipped it under her collar and told them that Jordan hadn't paid me."

"Then it's all right!" she cried. "They can't do a thing to you. It will be your word against Jordan's."

"But I admitted the charge," I said.

"You—what?" she asked incredulously.

"Well, I didn't at first, but they said they'd pinch you and send you up for a long time and put us kids in a home if I didn't, so I did."

"You damned fool!" she cried, "that was all bluff."

"How was I to know?" I said. "They sounded pretty sure of themselves and I didn't want to take a chance."

Mike and Christy came in. "What's up?" they asked when they saw my mother's face. It was red with anger towards Bart Jordan, and chagrin that I had been bluffed so easily. "Bart Jordan made a sale," she said.

"On Barbara?" Mike asked.

"Yes."

"Bart Jordan eh?" said Christy. He turned round and headed for the door. "I'll be back in half an hour," he said.

Mike followed him, saying: "So will I."

Puffy came in a minute later. "I met Mike and Christy on the stairs," he said. "Jordan make a sale on you?"

I nodded, and Puffy too headed for the door saying: "Back soon."

I looked at my mother questioningly. "There won't be much left of that squealer after this night is over," she said grimly.

Grahamy and Mary Ward were furious when they heard what had happened. They were both of the opinion that I should leave the city that night and not show up in court on Monday morning.

"If she stays, she'll go up before Judge ——, and he won't let her off easy," said Grahamy.

"He-is-known-to-be-very-strict," put in Mary.

When Christy and Mike returned they were asked what they thought was best for me to do.

"Well, if she stands trial she'll surely be put away till she's twenty-one," said Christy.

"And if she leaves town they'll probably go after her and bring her back," said Mike.

"They'll get her anyway," from Grahamy.

"There-doesn't-seem-to-be-any-hope," said Mary Ward.

After listening to comments like these all the afternoon I felt far from cheerful when I reached Boston Garden that evening. There I was greeted with more trouble.

"Mr. —— is gone and we're not going to get paid," I was told the minute I entered the dressing-room.

"Are you sure?" I asked.

"Of course we're sure. The cashier told us, and he knows."

"There's some talk of getting the police after him," one girl said.

"That'll pay our room rent and feed us won't it," said another contemptuously. "We'll be lucky if what we get covers car-fare for the week."

"I thought we weren't going to get anything," I said.

"To-day's gate receipts are going to be divided up and all hands to be paid out of whatever it amounts to," I was told.

"Workmen and all?"

"Workmen and all. But you shouldn't be worried. You're one of the lucky ones."

"Why do you say that?" I asked.

"Well, at least you've got a home to go to. Some of us are liable to get thrown out when we don't pay our rent this week, and besides, we'll have to diet till we get n another show."

"I guess you're right," I said. To myself, however, I thought: "I wish I were about to be thrown out instead of in, and that I had to go on a diet instead of being sure of getting my three squares served to me on a tin plate every day for the next six or seven years."

That night, after the show, we were paid off. What the others got I don't know, but I received two dollars and a few cents for the week.

It had not occurred to me that my mother would do otherwise than accept the two dollars, little as it was, and perhaps curse Mr. —— for running out on the show and leaving everyone stranded. Therefore I was taken by surprise when after I had handed her the money, saying: "This is all I got. Mr. —— skipped town," she flew into a rage. "You're a liar!" she cried. "Who in hell do you think you're trying to fool, handing me a lousy two dollars? Where's the rest of the money?"

"But that's all I got," I protested. "Just the two dollars and the few cents——"

"You're a liar," she cried again. "Hand over the rest of it."

"But I didn't get any more——"

"You did! I know you did!"

"Why don't you give her the money and stop all this fuss?" said Mike.

"How can I give her what I haven't got?" I snapped at him. It was none of his business, I felt.

"It will be in the papers Monday morning or maybe to-morrow," put in Christy. "But whether it is or not, Kathleen Mavourneen is telling the truth. If she says she got two dollars, then that's what she got and no more."

"She couldn't tell the truth," said my mother. "Didn't she write to her father behind my back?" She turned to me. "God help you if there's nothing in the papers about this on Monday. I'll kill you if I have to swing for it ——"

"She won't be here on Monday mam," interrupted Lady Biddy. "She'll be in court, on trial for selling Bart Jordan a pint of whiskey. Even if ye have got a fine lawyer to speak for her, 'tisn't a small matter for a child, and sure what else is she but a child?"

Lady Biddy's words seemed somehow to clear the air. "I've hired one of the best lawyers in the city to defend you," said my mother.

"That's nice," I said.

"You don't seem very much interested," she went on. "Don't you care whether you go away or not?"

"Sure I do."

"Well you don't look it."

"What happened to Jordan?" I asked.

"Nothing, so far," she answered. "We're waiting for Puffy to come in, he may have some news."

It was nearing two o'clock when Puffy returned. "Jordan's got a police guard," he announced. "We can't get next to him." He sounded very businesslike, did Puffy. "It's all over South Boston about Jordan," he went on. "Nearly everyone is on the watch for him. We'll get him before Monday."

"What are you going to do to him?" I asked. "Kill him?"

"No, we won't kill him," said Puffy. "But we're sure going to make him wish that he'd died in his cradle."

However, not one of the many who were looking

for Jordan could get near him. The following day, Sunday, was spent in what proved to be a fruitless search. Jordan, it seemed, had disappeared. Christy was of the opinion that the cops had hidden him somewhere till Monday. "Supposing he changes his mind and doesn't testify against Barbara and she gets off, what then?" Mike asked.

"It would make no difference. Not to me," said Puffy slowly.

"Or me either," chimed in Christy and Red together.

I thought that night as I was going to bed: "Well, whether I get sent away or not, Jordan's fate seems to be settled."

"What do you think about this?" I asked the lawyer as we walked up the steps to the court house the next morning.

The lawyer was not in a good mood. "I never take cases like this," he said impatiently.

"Why not?" I asked.

"Bah."

"Why did you take this one then?"

"Bah."

I began to laugh at him. "I took your case as a favour to Mr. Henry," he said. "I'm a criminal lawyer!"

"Do you mean Mr. Henry who owns the meat store?" I asked.

"Yes."

We were outside the court house. He looked at his watch. "We have a quarter of an hour yet," he said.

I saw Puffy getting out of a car. He looked around

and then ran up the steps towards us. "Feeling okay?" he asked.

"I'm all right," I said. "Whose car is that?"

"It belongs to a friend of mine," he said. "See the one in back of it?"

"I do."

"Christy and Mike and a few other fellows are in that one. They're both for Jordan." He went down the steps again.

The lawyer was looking at me intently. "Your face is familiar," he said.

"You've probably seen it about," I told him. "I dance."

"Were you at Boston Garden last week?"

"I was."

"Have you seen this morning's papers?"

"No," I said, "I haven't. What do you think will happen to me in court?"

"Nothing at all. I'm going to have the case continued for two weeks if I can."

"Will they hold me?"

"Maybe—but you'll get out on bail, so it's all right."

When at last we were before the judge, he did have the case put back for two weeks, and I was released on my own recognisance.

My mother was reading the morning papers when I reached home. I told her what had happened. "He's a good lawyer, expensive too," she said. She was silent for a few minutes, then she said: "It's a good thing for you that the papers have the story about Mr. —— running out on the show last week." I breathed a sigh of relief. I was clear of that anyway.

The following two weeks were full of excitement. We moved and were raided and caught three times; Christy, Red and Mike each taking a rap. Mike went on a drunk, and the lawyer nearly went mad. Jordan could not be found. Puffy negatived Christy's suggestion that the cops had hidden him somewhere till the day of the trial, saying: "The cops wouldn't bother to hide a rat like that. He's probably got a hole somewhere and has crawled into it."

The day before the case was to come up in court again, the lawyer rushed into the house. He looked very hot. "What's the matter?" I asked.

"Isn't there one respectable person in South Boston who knows Jordan?"

"Why?" I said.

"I want a character witness. Someone who can testify that Jordan's word is not reliable."

"The only people that know Jordan are street-corner bums like himself," I said, surprised. "Their word is no more reliable than his. Besides, the judge knows all about almost everyone in South Boston already. I could have told you that long ago."

The lawyer slowly rose from his chair. "Do you mean to say——" he broke off suddenly and sighed. "I'll call for you at eight-thirty in the morning," he said, and went out.

About what happened at the trial the next day, I remember very little. I was in a sort of daze and nothing seemed real. The court room though small was crowded. Most of the faces were familiar to me. Some people smiled at me. It made me feel good; it was as if they had said: "We're for you, Barbara." A murmur went through the court room when Jordan took the stand. I cannot recall all he said, but I remember clearly that he pointed his long, dirty finger at me and cried: "That's her."

The next clear thing in my memory is a picture of the lawyer as he said something about "tearing the cloak of innocence from the shoulders of this girl and branding her with the stigma of——" he never finished his speech. The judge cut him short in the middle of it saying: "All that is quite unnecessary Mr. Klarfield. I know all about this girl and I know that it is not through her own fault that she is here to-day. The case is placed on file."

I glanced at Jordan and saw the look of disappointment that spread over his face when he heard the decision of the judge. Suddenly I filled up inside with anger against him. Across the court room, his eyes met mine and I stood up. "You —— rat," I said slowly. The lawyer grabbed my arm. "Don't be a fool," he whispered hoarsely. He turned to the judge and said something, probably an apology for me, the judge nodded, and we left the court. "You might have been held for contempt of court," he said angrily when we were outside.

"It was worth it," I said.

He began to laugh. "Do you do American Tap as well as Irish dancing?" he asked.

"Yes. Why?"

"I think I can get you into a show. I'll let you know in a few days."

"Thanks," I said.

"Oh!" said my mother when she saw me, "you're back?"

"I am," I said. "The case was placed on file. You look very white, is anything wrong?"

"No," she said. "I was worried about you, that's all. It's all right now."

"How's Mike?" I asked.

"Still drunk," she told me. "He'll probably stay that way for a week."

Jordan got away and fled to New York: the last we heard of him he was living down in the Bowery.

A few days later I received a letter from the lawyer telling me to report to a booking office in town. I went in to the office, produced the letter and was taken into a back room where I danced a few steps for a man. "Okay," he said and told me to go into another room and wait. I did, and waited with twenty or more other girls who were already there till he came in and said: "All of you report here to-morrow for rehearsal, at two o'clock, sharp!"

At rehearsal the next day we were told that the show was to leave for Canada, a week from the following Sunday. I was very tired when I got home that night. It had been nothing but dance, dance, dance, all afternoon, rest for a few minutes and then dance some more. The day after was worse. Rehearsal was called for ten o'clock in the morning and we danced till lunch, and after lunch till six o'clock. It was the same every day after that. I asked my mother about going to Canada. She said she didn't mind, she wasn't used to having me at home much anyway.

It was now well into the summer and very hot. Some nights it was so hot that we couldn't sleep. I used to take the screens out of my bedroom windows at night, hoping for a breath of cool air.

One evening after I came home from rehearsal, my mother asked me if I had seen Mike anywhere about on my way from the subway station. "No," I said, "I didn't see him. Why?"

"Christy told me that he didn't come in last night," she said.

"He's probably sleeping it off somewhere," said I. "He'll turn up in a couple of hours with a big head."

But Mike didn't come back. We heard from one of our customers that he was sleeping down in the dump. The dump was a large piece of waste land at the foot of one of South Boston's streets. It was full of old tin cans and refuse of all kinds. Men who were so drunk that they forgot where they lived, and others who had spent their last cent on drink and had no place else to go, all found their way to the dump, and flopped there. Most of them came out of it none the worse for their night in the open—the rest were bitten, poisoned by the bite,[1] and died.

I awoke early on Sunday morning feeling very hot and irritable. I wished that I could go back to sleep again, but I knew I couldn't—the heat was too great. I turned over and gazed out of the window. At first I saw nothing but the familiar roofs of houses, and then to my amazement I saw a strange bird. Having lived in a city all my life I had never seen a bird other than the ordinary sparrow or pigeon. But by no stretch of the imagination could this bird be called either. It was very large and green. For a few minutes it flew about

[1] The bite of a deadly insect sometimes found in such refuse dumps.

outside, almost as if it were looking for a particular house, then suddenly it flew directly towards my window, flew in, and settled on the window-sill. There it perched, cocking its oddly shaped head sideways, and making funny noises at me.

As quietly as I could, I slipped out of bed and ran to my mother's room. "Mom," I whispered loudly. She sprang out of bed. "Is it a raid?" she cried.

"No," I said. "Come and see the big bird that flew into my room."

"Are you trying to be funny?"

"Honest," I said. "There's a big green bird on my window-sill."

"You're dreaming. Go back to bed."

"No fooling. I'm not dreaming."

"Then you're crazy."

"Aw come on mom," I coaxed. "Just look at it."

"A big green bird on your window-sill?" she said.

"Yes, and it makes funny noises," I said excitedly.

"Now Barbara, you mustn't get upset," she said anxiously. "I'll come with you and see the bird." She looked at me doubtfully. I could see that she was thinking: "It must be the heat that has affected her mind." However, she followed me into the room and there, still perched on the window-sill, was the green bird.

"It's a parrot," she breathed.

"Let's catch it," I said.

"Run down and get a cracker," she whispered.

I did, and when I came back, my mother had the top sheet taken off my bed and was holding it in one hand. With the other she motioned me to give her the cracker, and then she began to coax the parrot.

"Pretty Polly," she said, holding out the cracker to it. "Pretty Polly——"

The bird made a noise that sounded suspiciously like: "We're all cracked," and hopped on to the bed, trying to get the cracker. My mother quickly threw the sheet over it and so we captured it. We brought it downstairs and into the dining-room, and put it into a largish cage that had once held a pair of canaries.

"You know," I said, "I think we ought to let that bird go."

"Why?" my mother asked.

"Well, Katherine Leary used to say that if a bird flew in through an open window it meant sure death for someone in that house."

"That's nothing but a ridiculous superstition," she said impatiently. So the bird stayed in the cage, telling those who came within hearing distance of it: "We're all cracked."

That afternoon my mother received a telegram saying that Mike had been taken to the Boston City Hospital. She went in to see what it was all about, and when she came home told us: "Mike was picked up in the dump, unconscious. He's dying."

"Was it the bite?" Red asked.

"It was," she said. "He's in the contagious ward."

"I didn't know that the bite was contagious, mam," said Christy.

"It is—very. No one is allowed near him."

"What are we going to do about it?" Puffy asked.

"Notify his people. That's about the only thing we can do. Have a drink you two," she said to Christy and Red. Both men were crying unashamedly.

"Thanks mam," said Christy. "We liked him."

"I know it," said my mother.

In one of Mike's old notebooks we found the addresses and telephone numbers of a sister, an uncle, and a cousin, his only relatives who were in America. I was sent out to telephone to them, and from all three I got the same reply. "Really? In the hospital you say? Contagious? What am I expected to do? See him? Oh no! I couldn't possibly take such a risk. Why, it's silly of you to even suggest it. Funeral expenses? I'm afraid I can do nothing. I have little enough of my own. He'll be buried in pauper's field I suppose? Well let him. It has nothing to do with me."

My mother and Lady Biddy joined Christy and Red in blasting Mike's relations to hell, for a solid hour after I told them the news.

My mother went every afternoon to the hospital to see Mike; Christy and Red went every evening. On the afternoon of the third day, Mike died. More telephone calls to his relations got no better results than the first.

"They'd like to see him buried in a pauper's grave would they?" said my mother angrily. "Well by God they'll get left. I'll foot the bills myself."

"I have a few dollars mam," said Christy. "I'd like to do my share."

"Me too," offered Red.

"Buy a wreath to lay on the grave," my mother told them.

She took me with her and we went coffin shopping. The more coffins she looked at, the angrier she became at Mike's relations. "I'll show them," she'd mutter. "They'll never have it to say that Mrs. Mullen didn't do things right when she went at them at all. No,"—to the undertaker—"that looks cheap. I'll show them." She finally decided on the costliest coffin in the undertaking parlour, and arranged for Mike to be buried in one of the graves in the family lot. Then, after all that, the hospital authorities told her that they would not allow Mike's body to leave the hospital grounds until the day of the funeral, owing to the contagious nature of his disease.

It is the custom—at least it was amongst the Irish people in South Boston—when a member of the family dies in hospital and the body is not allowed to be brought home, that the wake is held just the same. So we held the wake for Mike. The undertaker pinned the crepe on the front door, and the door was left open. Lighted candles and a cross were placed in the front room, and the window shades pulled down. Christy and Red ordered a wreath of flowers, Grahamy and Mary Ward ordered another, my mother another, and Puffy and I still another. Mike was known and liked by all our customers, and most of them sent either wreaths or Mass cards. The front room was banked high with flowers. Pipes and tobacco were placed on the kitchen table, and everyone who came to the wake got a smoke and a couple of free drinks. Those who wanted more drink than what was served to them had to buy it. They all bought and they all got drunk. Lady Biddy's daughter, Mary Ellen, hearing that there was a wake at Mullen's, came down for the free drinks. Ordinarily, because ot what she had done to her mother, she would not have been allowed into the house. But in a case like this, the doors are closed to no one. So in came the tall, handsome

Mary Ellen and had her two drinks. That would have been all right, but all the men who bought an extra pint or two shared them with her, and in an hour Mary Ellen was roaring drunk. She began to keen, crying what would she do now that Mike was gone? Incidentally, she had never seen Mike in her life. Red, who was feeling merry himself, told her to pull in her neck or he'd paste her one on the jaw. Some of the men began to side with Mary Ellen, the rest sided with Red. Curses and threats began to fly thick and fast from one side to the other. It looked as though the kitchen was going to be the scene of a grand free-for-all when my mother, hands on hips, marched in, stood squarely in the middle of the kitchen floor and looked angrily around her. "I'll have you people understand", she cried, "that this is a respectable house. You ought to be ashamed of yourselves. Have you no more respect for the dead than to start a riot practically over Mike's body? If there's any more trouble in here I'll have you all thrown to hell out."

After that they were all pretty quiet, and nothing out of the way happened until the last night of the wake. On that night Christy got so drunk that he had to be carried upstairs and put to bed. About three o'clock in the morning someone said that he smelled smoke. Investigation led us to Christy's room, where we saw Christy throwing water on his bed. There was no blaze of any kind, but a lighted cigarette end had burned its way through the mattress and filled the room with smoke. Except for the hole in the mattress and an awful smell, there was no damage done. We never found out who it was that got panicky and turned in a fire alarm. In a few minutes the fire engines were outside the front door, and the firemen rushed in carrying hoses and axes; but as there was nothing for them to do they went out again. Just as the fire engines were leaving, the night police patrol pulled up in front of the house to see what the trouble was. There were four or five policemen, led by our old friend the sergeant, who was doing night duty. He came in and took off his hat. "Is everything all right Mrs. Mullen?" he asked.

"Yes, thank you," my mother said.

"I'm very sorry for your trouble Mrs. Mullen," went on the sergeant respectfully. "Is it a member of the family?"

"No," said she. "It was one of the men who stayed here, Mike."

"I'm sorry," he said. "I liked Mike. May we see the body?"

"The body", said my mother, "is not here."

For a moment I thought the sergeant was going to choke. He swallowed hard a few times, and then looked at my mother admiringly. "So", he said slowly, "someone is dead. You've got a wake with all the trimmings. In fact you've got everything—but the corpse." He turned swiftly to his men: "Raid the joint," he shouted.

Exactly how many gallons of whiskey they got that night, I don't know, but they got plenty. Christy took the rap the next morning and was fined two hundred dollars. That afternoon, Saturday, Mike's funeral took place. The funeral procession left from our house. Through an error of judgment on somebody's part, Mary Ellen and Red were put in the same car. However, everything went very well till we got to the hospital where we were to get Mike's body. There we had a shock.

In life, Mike was a tall, well-built, clean-shaven, always neat-appearing man. In death, he was long and thin, his clothes rumpled and dirty, his hair uncombed, a week's growth of beard on his face. He had been placed in the coffin, but the shininess and newness of it, with Mike, looking as he did, inside it, made the whole thing a horrible, ghastly joke. Christy was standing beside me, he clenched his hands and choked: "God Almighty—Mike," then he turned away. And so did the rest of us. We turned away and walked silently out to the cars.

All the men who had come to the funeral had brought bottles with them. When we reached the cemetery, most of them were drunk and crying. Red had a pint in each of his hip pockets, and when he and Mary Ellen got out of the car and started up the path that led to the grave, they were both staggering.

The priest who had come with us began to read the prayers for the dead. He got as far as "the body of Thy faithful servant, Michael——" when he was interrupted by a wild shriek of "Mike!" We who were standing around the grave looked up, startled. It was Mary Ellen. She began to keen at the top of her voice.

"Did she know the man?" the priest asked Puffy.

"Naw," said Puffy, "she's just a booze hound."

I looked at the priest. His face was a picture of amazed disgust. Then Red began to cry. Nothing could be done with either him or Mary Ellen, because some of the other men began to cry too, and loudly. So the priest, who looked more and more disgusted as he spoke, went on reading the prayers for the dead, and no one heard them, except my mother, Grahamy, Mary Ward, Puffy, and I, who were standing in a group at the grave side.

Half-way through the service I lifted my head and glanced at Red. He was still crying, but suddenly he stopped and looked furtively around him; then with his elbow he poked Mary Ellen in the ribs. She left off her keening and looked at him. He jerked his head sideways and walked away. She followed him, and they both went behind a neighbouring tombstone, where Red drew out one of the pint bottles, raised it to his lips and drank heartily. He handed it to Mary Ellen when he had finished, and she did the same. Red then returned the bottle to his pocket and they both walked back and resumed their keening and crying. They repeated their performance three times before the first clod of earth was thrown into the grave and we left the cemetery.

When we arrived back at the house I immediately started to pack my bags, with Grahamy helping me, as I was to leave for Canada the following morning at five o'clock with the show.

"What did your mother think of the piece that was in the paper this morning?" Grahamy asked.

"We haven't had time to look at a paper to-day," I said. "Why? What was it about?"

"About your mother," she said.

"My mother? What newspaper is it in?"

"It's in two—the *Globe* and the *Post.*"

"We've got them both downstairs," I said. "Come on, I want to see what they say."

The papers were on the kitchen table. I picked up the *Post.* "What page is it on?" I asked Grahamy.

"Page three, I think. You can't miss it," said she. She didn't look very pleased.

The story took up nearly two columns of space. I don't remember what the heading was, but the first paragraph began as follows:

"Mabel Walker Willebrandt thought she knew all there was to know about Prohibition, but over in South Boston there lives a lady, Mrs. Mullen by name, who can certainly give our friend in Washington a point or two. . . ." It went on to say how Mrs. Mullen thought Prohibition most annoying, and finding herself hard-pressed by the policemen in Station 6, "the old meanies", and having been warned by the judge before whom she had last been brought up, that if she offended again she would be sent to jail, had decided to hold a wake in order to drum up business, and perhaps make back all that she had paid out in fines. So a crêpe was pinned on the front door, the window shades pulled down, and the door left open for all who would to enter. For three days people, hundreds of people, visited the Mullen domicile, and if they staggered a bit when they came out, the police who were watching the house put it down to their grief at having been so sadly parted from a dear friend. But when the wake continued for the fourth day, the police began to wonder if perhaps they had not been too hard on Mrs. Mullen, who must indeed be a tender-hearted woman, when she could not bear to part with the corpse of the deceased. And then alas, in the wee hours of the morning, fire broke out in the Mullen home. After the blaze had been extinguished, the police, eager to do all they could to help Mrs. Mullen in a time of trouble like this, paid her a visit.

The sergeant and his men bared their heads respectfully. "I'm sorry for your trouble, mam," said the sergeant. "May we see the body?"

And wonder of wonders, no body could be found. "But surely there must be a corpse somewhere?" cried the sergeant as he began to search. In vain did he look in closets, behind pictures, and even under the carpets. No corpse could he find. Instead he found whiskey, and whiskey, and more whiskey. With reluctant admiration, the worthy sergeant had to admit that Mrs. Mullen had indeed succeeded in pulling the well-known wool over his eyes. . . .

The story in the *Globe* was much the same, although it was not so long. I was angry, but I had to laugh when I read them. "Let us all in on the joke," said my mother. I couldn't resist the temptation, so I showed her the papers. Well, talk about cursing! The air was blue with all she cursed on the two newspapers. "I'll go in to their offices to-morrow and if they don't eat these words, I'll sue them for all they are worth, if I have to beg the money to do it," she cried.

"Cut out the noise," Puffy interrupted. "Here comes Chips with the stuff."

"Get the gallon jugs Grahamy," ordered my mother. "Quick! Barbara, you go and phone for a taxi and have it waiting at the door so we can get the stuff out right away."

I was half-way across the street when I saw the police car. I turned round to shout at Christy who was on watch outside the house.

Chapter Seven

Hunt the Dollar

*

"The cops," I said. "I saw the car."

"Sure kid, sure," said Puffy. "How do you feel?"

"I'm okay, but the cops——"

"They didn't come in," he said." You just stay quiet and stop making so much noise."

And then I realized that I was lying flat on my back and that there were a number of people standing round me, all dressed in white.

"What's the big idea?" I demanded.

"You're in the hospital," one of them told me.

"What for? I haven't done anything."

"You dumb cluck. You're in a hospital," said Puffy.

"Oh," I said. "What happened?"

"You were hit by an automobile," a nurse said.

"Any bones broken?" I asked.

"Not so far as we know. Do you feel any pain?"

"No," I said. "I feel all right. May I go home now?"

"Of course not. You must stay here——"

"I can't do that," I protested. "I've got to leave for Canada in the morning. What time is it?"

"Half-past eleven. You were unconscious for two hours."

When I heard that, I was sure I must have been hurt. I sat up and moved about, but nothing happened. "There's nothing wrong with me," I said. "I want to go home."

The doctor drew Puffy aside and spoke to him. I heard Puffy say "Yeah" a couple of times, and "Okay". Then he signed a paper and we left the hospital.

Puffy went into the house before me. I heard my mother ask anxiously: "Is she badly hurt?" and Puffy's reply: "Naw, just shaken. They wanted her to stay in the hospital for the night, but she wouldn't. I had to sign a paper saying that she left against their advice. The doctor said that she should rest for a few days. She's dizzy that dame is. She should've stayed there. Maybe her insides are turned upside down, how do we know? What a woman." He sounded quite disgusted with me.

I was hugged by everyone in turn, including Grahamy, who had waited for Puffy to come in, to hear how I was.

"You'll have to stay in bed for a few days," said my mother. "The Canada trip is off. Are you sure you're all right?"

"Just a bruise on my right leg," I said. "I'm okay otherwise."

I didn't mind missing the trip to Canada. The long rehearsals had tired me, and travelling with the show didn't sound at all restful. That the show would go on the next day without me, I knew; they'd probably get someone to take my place, their first day on the road.

My mother visited the offices of both the *Post* and the *Globe* newspapers the next afternoon, and told them how Mike's relatives had refused to bury him, and that she had taken it upon herself to see that he got a decent Christian burial. How could she have a corpse in the house when the hospital wouldn't permit it? Furthermore, she had footed the bills herself and she was by no means a rich woman. What did they mean by printing such lies about her? She raised such a rumpus that both papers decided to put an apology in their Monday morning editions.

On Monday morning we looked for the apologies. There they were, four or five paragraphs in each paper, written in flowery style, and packed full of words that were twenty letters long. My mother, still suspicious and angry, made us look up the big words in the dictionary to see what they meant. They all turned out to be words of praise and she was satisfied.

Later that day Mr. Lynch came in. "I saw the apologies in to-day's papers Mrs. Mullen," he said. "Beautifully written they were, beautifully written."

My mother positively glowed. "I wrote those myself, Mr. Lynch," she said. At times my mother was an absolute joy.

The police hounded us for the next few weeks. Raid followed raid, but we always had the stuff destroyed and the police got nothing. Several times Lassie came within an ace of being shot, and one evening my mother called us all into the kitchen. "I don't want any arguments about this," she began. "I don't want to hear a word from any of you. I called up the Animal Rescue League this afternoon and they're going to take Lassie away to-morrow. It's better to send her away than to keep her here and see her get shot." Nobody moved. When my mother spoke like that she meant it and nothing could change her mind. Besides, we knew that she was right.

It was I who muzzled Lassie the next day and led her out to the small closed truck that had been sent for her. Once I looked back. Through a tiny grill in the back door of the truck I could see Lassie; she began to whine. I ran into the house. "You shouldn't have——" I said, and then I stopped. My mother was crying.

Lady Biddy, who when she had first come to us had been firm and steady as a rock, had lately begun to shake and tremble. After each raid she seemed to grow worse, and now her nerves were almost gone. She would jump at the least sound, and no one could touch her without first warning her that they were near or she would scream. My mother asked her one night if she didn't think that she would be better off in some sort of home for the aged where she would get all the care and attention that she needed. "Sure 'twill break my heart to leave ye mam, but I know well that 'tis for my own good ye are speaking, and that 'tis best that I go," was Lady Biddy's choked reply.

"Perhaps you would rather live with your daughters than go to a home? They can be made to take care of you, you know," my mother said.

"Let me have a share of peace with the few years that are left to me, mam," said Lady Biddy simply.

My mother, after a week of looking about and making inquiries, found a place that she thought would suit. It was a home for the aged and infirm. She visited the home and saw that it was well kept, and the people to all appearances happy. So she made applications, and signed papers, and at length we received a letter from those in charge of the home, saying that Lady Biddy was to be ready to leave at three o'clock on a certain afternoon, as they would be sending a car for her.

The day came when Lady Biddy was to leave. She had no belongings—just a comb that she wrapped in a handkerchief and clutched tightly in her left hand.

"The car is here Lady Biddy," said my mother.

"Ye'll come with me as far as the door mam?"

"Yes, Lady Biddy. We'll all go out to the door with you."

She gave her right hand to Puffy and he led her out to the front door. The rest of us, my mother, Grahamy, Mary Ward, Winnie, Christy and I, followed them. Nobody spoke till we were nearly at the front door, then Lady Biddy stopped. We formed a circle round her and she began to speak. "I'll not say good-bye to any of ye," she said. "I'll say only, the blessing of God and my own blessing be with ye all, always." She lifted her plaid shawl from her shoulders and placed it about her head. We stepped back and made way for her, and without another word she again gave her hand to Puffy, and he led her out to the waiting car. We didn't say good-bye to her—we all felt that she would rather she left us as she did.

The week that Lady Biddy left, we moved again, and this time good luck seemed to move with us. We were not raided until a few days after New Year's Day, four months later.

Red let the parrot out of its cage one night when he

was in his cups, shooed it out of a window, and we never saw it again.

Shortly before Christmas, my cousin John came to spend a week with us. My mother told him of the probability of our having to make a quick move to New York if we were raided and caught again. John wanted to know if she would take him in as a boarder if we did move, as his sister Peggy, with whom he lived, was going to give up her apartment and go to Chicago. My mother promised that she would.

Over the Christmas holidays we did a rushing business. My job at this time was to keep a constant watch out of a front window; Christy was on the door, and Puffy had his hands full helping my mother to serve customers. The raids got on Mary Ward's nerves so that she had to leave us, but Grahamy the ever faithful still remained.

On the night of the last big raid we had—or rather we nearly had—pigs' feet and cabbage for dinner. There were over a dozen pigs' feet boiling with the cabbage in a large pot on the stove. On a chair next to the stove was a large pot full of whiskey. Winnie had been sent to the store for disinfectant, Puffy had gone out for cigarettes, and Christy, unaware that Puffy was not in, was upstairs shaving. My mother took the pigs' feet out of the pot, put them in a large earthenware bowl and left the bowl on a table near by. I was looking out of the front window, when I heard a slight noise behind me. I whirled round and saw, running down the stairs that led from the roof, a cop. "Dump," I yelled. I heard more footsteps on the stairs and ran for the kitchen. My mother was holding the pot of whiskey and the cop was twisting her hands, trying to get it away from her. Hardly knowing what I did, I grabbed the earthenware bowl and with all my strength threw it, pigs' feet and all, at the head of the cop. It hit him just above his right eye. He put his hand up to his forehead; it came away covered with blood. He looked at me. "Christ!" he said. By this time the sergeant and the squad were in the kitchen. The sergeant took the pot of whiskey from my mother. She let him take it without a struggle, for she was laughing so hard that the tears were rolling down her cheeks.

"What in hell happened to you?" asked the sergeant in amazement as he looked at the cop. Well, he did look odd. Blood streamed from his forehead, he was covered with grease from head to foot, and around him on the floor was what remained of the earthenware bowl and the pigs' feet. "That devil did it," he cried, pointing at me. "I'm going to place her under arrest." He raved on about the charges he was going to make against me, "assaulting an officer of the law", "interfering with an officer when in the line of duty".

"Wouldn't you look nice charging that child with assault?" said my mother, still laughing as if her sides would break. "You'll be the laughing stock of the city."

"What made you do it?" asked the sergeant.

"He was twisting my mother's arms," I told him.

"You're a fool if you charge this kid with anything," he said to the cop. "Not only will she get off, but if it gets into the papers you'll be known as the 'cruel cop who frightens little girls', she has that kind of a face." The cop muttered something under his breath. I couldn't hear it, but it was far from complimentary,

I'm sure. I wasn't arrested, though at first, judging by the expression on his face, I was sure that I was going to be.

"We've got you this time, Mrs. Mullen," said the sergeant.

"I know it," replied my mother. "But, if I have to do a year for it, it was well worth it. I didn't think she had the spunk of a mouse. Are you going to take me now?"

"No—but you must be in court next Thursday."

"Not to-morrow?" my mother asked in surprise.

"No. You've still got three days of liberty," he said.

Nothing was more certain than that if my mother appeared in court to answer this charge, she would be heavily fined and sentenced. There was only one thing to do: to move to New York, and move fast. First we arranged with the furniture removers, a strange firm outside the city. For an extra ten dollars they agreed to come for the furniture at one o'clock in the morning. I telephoned to Uncle Tom, who had been on the look-out for apartments for us and asked him if he knew of one that we could move into within two days' time. "I do," he said. "There's one right next door to where I live—seven rooms and bath. I'll see both the agent and the janitor. Don't worry, things will be ready for you at this end."

Fearing the rumours of our intended move might have reached the police, and that they would come to arrest her, my mother left the house and went the next day to the home of my other half-sister, Mary. She remained indoors all that day and night until two o'clock in the morning. Then, with Mary and Nancy, she came by way of back streets to the house to pack. She left again just before daylight and returned to Mary's house. My two sisters, with Grahamy, Puffy and myself, continued to pack and tie up till all our furniture and belongings were ready for the removal men.

It was decided that only my mother and I should go to New York at first. Winnie would stay with Grahamy until such time as we had our new home in shape and had found work. Puffy would remain in Boston for the present, and go to work in a wool house.

Late in the afternoon I said good-bye to Winnie; then Grahamy took her up to Mary's to say good-bye to my mother. In the evening Christy, Red, Puffy and I went up there. Tearfully, Christy begged my mother not to leave saying that it was as if he were losing his own family to lose us. "If I stay and get sent to jail, what will become of the children?" she asked. He couldn't answer her.

"I wouldn't mind taking the rap and the jail sentence if you'd stay mam," said Red. "Yours was the only home I had since I left my own in Ireland."

"Wouldn't I do the same?" put in Christy.

"I know you would, both of you," said my mother, "but it's no use. They caught me with the stuff in my hands. It's my rap this time. Thanks all the same."

"Maybe you'd let us board with you if we went to New York?" asked Red eagerly.

"Where would you find work there, Red? You've never been to New York in your life."

"You're right mam," said Christy. "But you'll write to us?"

"I will," she promised. Then they said good-bye and left.

Puffy kept looking out of a window, his back towards us. "Well Puffy," said my mother, "I suppose you'd better be on your way too."

He turned round; he had a pair of dice in his hand and appeared to be examining them intently. "Yeah," he said, "no good in hanging around I guess." He continued to look at the dice. "I'm going to stay at Nancy's," he said, as if we didn't know it already.

"I know," said my mother.

"Well, so long," he offered his hand.

"A shake hands is it?" my mother asked.

"Aw——" and he put his arms about her and kissed her.

"Aren't you going to kiss your sister too?" she asked.

"Aw rats!" he exclaimed. "Didn't I kiss you? I don't wanta kiss any more dames."

"Stop using slang and do as you're told," she said sharply.

The only time in our lives that Puffy and I had been friendly towards each other was when we were both going to school. Once for a week we had hooked from school every day, and spent our lunch money going to the movies. All the rest of the time we were practically always at each other's throats. Though we each had a sort of sneaking regard for the other, neither of us had ever lost an opportunity for calling the other a louse, in no uncertain terms. Never before had there been any demonstration of affection between us, and the suggestion of it now embarrassed us both. He looked at me sheepishly, and I looked back at him just as sheepishly.

"Well, I suppose I better get it over with," he said; and then as an afterthought: "Don't you go pulling any fast ones and start throwin' punches at me or you'll be sorry."

"I didn't ask you to kiss me good-bye, you heel," I said hotly.

"Who's a heel?"

"You are."

"Yeah?"

"Yeah!"

"Good God, can't you two be together for five minutes without wanting to slaughter each other?" cried my mother angrily. "You started it, you idiot," she said to me.

"I didn't," I said.

"Don't you answer me back."

"There you go again," put in Puffy disgustedly. "Women, women, can't stay quiet a minute without making a fuss."

"That's enough out of you too," he was told. "A nice way to be carrying on when you mightn't see each other again for months. Kiss your sister good-bye and get going."

So Puffy kissed me and went out. He had to go back to the house to see that the furniture was sent off all right and to give the New York address to the driver of the van, before going to Nancy's.

At midnight I left for New York alone. My mother boarded the train at another station. We arrived at Grand Central Station about five-thirty in the morning, and went in a taxi to Uncle Tom's. Both Uncle Tom and his wife were much excited; they thought our manner of leaving Boston very thrilling. "Aren't you afraid that the cops will come after you?" Aunt Sarah asked.

"No," said my mother. "I've never known them to follow up people who ran away from a bootlegging charge. I suppose that they're satisfied if we leave the city."

She did not care much for the apartment that Uncle Tom had rented for us, saying that the rooms were stuffy and railroadish; which, compared to the house in which we had last lived in Boston, they were. "But"—and she shrugged her shoulders—"any port in a storm."

In the afternoon the gas and electricity were turned on. The furniture had not yet arrived, and having nothing else to do I telephoned to John. "What's your address?" he asked when I had finished telling him all the details of the raid and what followed. "872 Third Avenue," I told him. "Next door to Uncle Tom's." John turned up the next day with his luggage. The furniture had come in that morning, and my mother and I were sitting in the middle of a staggering array of trunks, barrels, bedsteads, etc., not knowing where to begin, when John arrived. "I'm here," he announced.

"So I see," said my mother as she stood up. "You couldn't have come at a better time. Take off your coat and get busy."

John, looking quite ridiculous in a frilled apron, assumed a shrill falsetto voice and a mincing walk, and turned what we had thought was going to be a long tedious job into a roaring farce. Amazingly enough everything found its proper place, and at nine o'clock we had finished and sat down to a well-earned meal.

"I have no job," said John as he lit his cigarette.

"You're in a good place," my mother said. "We have no jobs either and very little money. Still, it's better to starve with company than to starve alone. Stay here."

"That's why I brought my luggage," said John. "Babs and I will go looking for work to-morrow, over on Sixth Avenue."

"What's over there?" my mother asked.

"Employment agencies—hundreds of them. We'll each have a job inside two weeks."

"Tom is going to get me a job," said my mother. "Cooking. He'll let me know in a couple of days."

Uncle Tom did succeed in getting her in as a cook for a woman who lived in the apartment building where he worked. The salary to be paid was twenty-five dollars a week.

John and I made the rounds of employment agencies every day, without success. We usually started out at seven in the morning, returned about two in the afternoon, and robbed the larder.

"I don't get paid till to-morrow," said my mother one evening when she got home from work. "There's enough food in for a light breakfast, but you won't have anything for lunch. Do you think you can hold out for something to eat till I get paid?"

"Sure," said John. "Besides, we may strike a job to-morrow, and get a lunch thrown in."

Well, we got our lunch all right the next day, but it was by no means "thrown in".

We started off as usual at seven o'clock, after having breakfasted on rolls and coffee. Hour after hour we walked and walked, and walked some more, from office to office, street to street, in search of a job, but with no success. Before we were half-way through the rounds, it began to rain—a steady rain, that chilled us to the bone—and still we went on walking, and asking, and filling in applications for work. By noon time we were tired and weak with hunger. To look in through the restaurant windows as we passed, and to see the luncheon hour crowds devouring the meals that were set before them, was well-nigh heartbreaking. "You know Babs," said John, "it just isn't right——" and he shook his head. Seeing a billboard poster on which was pictured plate after plate heaped with somebody or other's prize muffins, I heartily agreed with him. About two o'clock we turned our steps towards home and were walking eastwards on some street in the fifties, when suddenly John stopped. "Babs," he said.

"What's the matter with you now?" I asked crossly.

"Don't you think that two people who have walked in the rain all day, as we have, deserve a meal?"

"I do," I said. "We'll think of how deserving we are and keep full that way till my mother gets home."

"Now, being a man of courage as I am," said John modestly, "I would go to any lengths to get a meal. Would you?"

"The way I feel now—yes."

"Are you cold?"

"Of course I am."

"Would you go for some hot soup, roast chicken, mashed potatoes, and green peas that would melt in your mouth?"

"Would I? And how!"

"It's ours for the asking," said he, pointing: "look."

We were standing outside a restaurant, one of the

$1.50 Plate Luncheon ones. A placard in the restaurant window told of just such a dinner as John had described. We looked at the placard and then at each other. "You see", said he, "that there is no reason why we should be hungry."

"How about money to pay for it?" I asked.

"Money," said John, quoting Winnie, "is merely a minor detail. Are you with me?"

"I am," I said. "Let's go."

"We'll have to put on the Ritz in order to look natural in a place like this," John said as he pushed open the restaurant door.

"Don't be silly," said I. "If we do they'll see right through us. Be yourself."

"How do you know that?"

"I read it in a book."

Never in my life have I enjoyed a meal as much as I did that lunch. We ate the chicken and the trimmings that came with it as slowly as we possibly could, in order to savour to the full each delicious bite.

Not until we had finished and John had leaned back to enjoy a cigarette—the only one he had, by the way—did we allow ourselves to think of the possible consequences of our rash act. "I wonder", said John calmly between puffs, "if we will spend the night in jail?"

"And I wonder what my mother will say if we do."

"Raise hell I'll bet. I can just see her."

The waiter had left the bill on the table and was standing near John. The longer he stood there the funnier he looked, and John and I began to laugh at him. He coughed politely and pushed the bill a little closer to John: "The bill sir," he said, and then after a brief interval repeated: "The bill, sir." John sobered. "Will you bring the manager or whoever is in charge here, please?" he asked.

"There is no complaint," he added as the waiter opened his mouth to speak. "I just want to speak to whoever is in charge here and I want to speak to him at once."

"Yes sir," said the waiter, and hurried away.

"What are you going to do, John?" I asked.

"Look Babs," he said, "you don't need to be in on this. You can say I invited you in here and——"

"We're both in the soup together," I said. "Stop being funny."

"Your mother's daughter," he exclaimed.

"You wished to speak with me? I am the manager."

"Eh?" said John. "Oh, the manager. Yes I did. It's about the lunch——"

"Everything was satisfactory I hope?" The manager was a little man who beamed all over his face.

"Indeed it was the best meal we've ever eaten," said John; "there's only one thing——"

"And that is?"

"We have no money to pay for it."

Suddenly all the friendliness fled from the face of the little man. He beckoned sharply to the waiter who had served us. "Bring these two to my office," he said. When we went into the office, he was standing by a desk. "Well, what's the big idea?" he barked. "And don't tell me that you forgot your wallet."

"I didn't," said John, and he began to laugh. "We were hungry and cold, so we came in."

"So you think it's funny, huh?"

I was laughing too, I couldn't help it. "Are you going to have us arrested?" I asked, "because if you are——"

"Don't give him any ideas," put in John.

"Think you're going to get off easy do you? I had the last one arrested and he got off. Well, you two are going to work it out. Take them into the kitchen," he said to the waiter who had come into the office with us, "put them to work and make sure that they don't leave till there's no more work for them to do."

"Yes sir." That waiter was grinning from ear to ear.

John took one look at the kitchen and said: "I'd rather go to jail." We were surrounded by dishes, dirty dishes, that were stacked feet high. I looked around me and agreed with him.

"When you have all those washed and dried there'll be something else for you to do," said the waiter cheerfully.

John turned on him: "When all those are washed and dried we're going, and all hell won't keep us in here," he said. The waiter pointed to the sink and left us.

We rolled up our sleeves and went to work. At first John washed and I dried, then we switched round. More and more dirty dishes kept coming in, and with each new batch the kitchen help seemed to grow more cheerful. For two hours we kept steadily at it, and then I heard a low "psst" from John. I looked at him and he winked. I knew that he was up to something, and though I couldn't guess what it was, I was prepared to follow whatever cue he sent me. "Gosh Babs, I feel as if I couldn't dry another dish," he said. "My arms are getting numb."

"I have no feeling left in my hands either," I said, as I passed him a wet plate.

"Sometimes", said John, "I find myself drying empty air."

I heard a crash and looked around me. The plate was in smithereens on the floor. "I told you," said John solemnly, "my hands are numb."

"Be more careful," said I, handing him another plate.

"What did you say?"—another crash—"my ears are ringing."

"You should be more careful."

"But my hands are numb——" Crash.

The little man rushed in. "What do you think you're doing?" he cried angrily.

"Drying dishes." Crash!

"My cousin isn't well," said I.

"We've been doing this for hours——" said John. Crash.

I was sure the little man was going to start throwing things. He began to hop up and down in his anger. "Get out," he shouted. "Get out. If you ever put your nose inside this restaurant again I'll—get out."

John and I lost no time in obeying the order.

When we got home my mother was already there and cooking dinner. "It's time you two got here," she said. "I asked to be let off early from work so that I could get you something to eat. You must be starved."

"We are," said John.

Both of us were so full that we could hardly eat. We thought it best not to tell my mother of what we had done until some evening when she would be telling us stories of the larking she had done in her youth, and when she would be in exceptionally good humour.

"For people who have eaten nothing all day, you don't seem to be very hungry," said my mother eyeing us suspiciously.

"All the walking and job-hunting we did took the edge off our appetites," John told her.

"It's queer that walking should fill you," she said. "It's usually the other way around with most people."

"We're different," said John.

She began to laugh. "There's no doubt about that," she agreed. "You didn't strike anything?"

"No, but we may have better luck to-morrow."

But weeks elapsed before we heard other than the usual "Nothing to-day" at any of the employment agencies we went to.

My mother found herself hard put to it to make her salary cover rent, gas and electric bills, as well as food for the three of us. To cut down the food expense, John and I decided that we could go without lunch every day till we found work. At first my mother wouldn't listen to us, saying that we should lose our strength and get run down. However, after talking it over we hit on a compromise. Every morning after breakfast, she agreed to lock away all the food except sugar, milk and coffee. She would give us a dime a day with which to buy buns, and though after a while John and I got so that we couldn't look them in the face without feeling smothered, during those first days, when we came in tired, hungry and despondent after walking miles in search of work, coffee and buns seemed to us like a feast.

I didn't know that my mother had told John about any of our family rows until one morning when we were washing the breakfast dishes, when he said to me: "It's a pity that you're not allowed to write to your father when you want to so much, Babs."

"I'll bite," said I; "why is it a pity?"

"Because your father is a nice man."

"How do you know what he's like?" I asked.

"I heard all about him when I was in Galway a couple of years ago. You know", he went on, "that there's nothing to keep you from writing to him if you really want to."

"Only my mother," I said.

"She needn't know."

"Tell me what you've got up your sleeve, John."

"If what I suggest isn't okay with you, you won't tell your mother about it will you?"

"I won't."

"Promise?"

"Yes John, I promise," I said impatiently. "What is it all about?"

"Well, you write to your father and tell him to send his answers to this address," and he handed me a slip of paper. "I'll collect the letters when they come, and give them to you."

"Gosh John," I said, "If my mother ever finds out about it she'll do an awful job on you as well as me."

"She won't find out unless you tell her."

"You're a pal John, thanks."

"Skip that part of it. Do you want to write before we go out?"

"Do I?"

"Then get on with it."

It did not take long to write the letter. I had been composing it in my mind for months. I told my father what had happened: how my mother had found out about our corresponding, how she had taken me back to Boston from New Haven, and how, terribly angry, she had made me write that lying letter to him. I explained that he should send his answer in care of John's friend, and finished with sending him my love and hoping that he'd forgive me and understand about the last letter I had written to him.

"Have you got a stamp, John?" I asked.

"No, I haven't," he said, "but we can get one out of the dime we've got for buns."

"And a morning paper too?"

"Yes."

"There won't be much left for buns if we do," I said.

"We have to get the paper to look up the want ads." said he, "and do you want to send that letter or don't you?"

"I'll send the letter; we'll get two buns and you can have mine. I'll just have coffee," I answered.

"Nuts!" said John. "Come on."

Noon time of that day saw John and me sitting in an employment office, trying as usual to look very intelligent, hoping we should be picked for a job. "I see one man who'll never be chosen," John remarked in a whisper, "not while he looks like that anyway."

"Who is he?" I asked.

"He's standing by the window, over there."

"I see him," I said. There was no mistaking whom

John meant. Most of the faces we saw every day were much the same, in expression anyway. They all had that look of "maybe I'll get something to-day". But the man John had noticed was different. He was about five feet tall, and very thin. The first thing you noticed about him was his hat. It was several sizes too large for his head and kept falling down over his eyes. The man would put up his hand and push the hat on to the back of his head; then you would get a good look at his face. It was a round face, full of surprise and wonder and fright. He wore an overcoat that reached nearly to his heels. There he stood by the window, almost as if he were rooted to the spot, looking thoroughly uncomfortable and scared.

"The poor guy," said John, "let's go over and talk to him."

The little man spotted us, however, and as if he guessed that we were going to speak to him he began to sidle towards the door. At the door he stopped, and with one hand on the door-knob turned and looked at us.

"Hello buddy," said John as we came up to him.

"So?" said the man, and nodded his head.

"You seem kind of lost," said John, "can I do anything for you?"

"I'm Willie," said the man. "I'm very hungry." He spoke slowly, as if he were not sure of what word to put after the other.

"When did you eat last?" John asked him.

"So?"

"When did you eat last?" John repeated.

The man took off his hat and scratched his head. He

appeared to be thinking deeply. "Not to-day," he said after a moment.

"Yesterday?"

The man thought for a minute and then he nodded. "Yesterday. At this time."

"Haven't you any money?"

"Money?" said Willie blankly, then his eyes lit up and he began to search in his pockets. "I have one cent." He withdrew his hand and showed us a nickel.

"Say, aren't you an American?" John asked him.

"Of course he isn't you dizzo," said I. "You can tell by his accent."

"Well he could be a citizen couldn't he?"

"What country are you from, Willie?" I asked.

"Germany," said Willie. "I want to go home."

"Let's get out on the street," John suggested. "Willie, you come with us."

So Willie came with us, and after questioning him for half an hour we learned that he had been in the country two days, and that he had arrived very rich and prosperous in his new hat and overcoat—he turned round in the street to show them to us—with fifty dollars in his pockets. When we asked him what had happened to his money he told us that he had gone drinking "schnaps" with a strange man, had fallen asleep over the table, and had woken up to find his money gone. He had no friends or relations in the country and he had come to make a fortune so that he could go back to Germany and get married. The night before he had slept in a doorway. He was very lonesome, very hungry, he didn't like America, and he wanted to go home.

"Well," said John drawing me aside, "what do you think of him? He sounds on the level to me."

"I think he's cute John," I cried. "Let's take him home."

"My God woman, you'd think you were buying a pet poodle or something to hear you. We'd have a lot of fun with him teaching him how to speak English and how to dress right," said John. "I know," he cried. "We'll adopt him."

"No sooner said than done," I agreed.

Willie had no objections to coming with us, and we took him along home. John and I had three cents left out of the dime. He asked Willie if he'd chip in his nickel with our three cents to buy buns so that we could eat.

"So?" said Willie, and handed over his nickel.

John and I spent the afternoon teaching Willie how to speak English. It was great fun. When Willie didn't say everything backwards, he put what sounded like a gurgle in the middle of all his words. We couldn't get him to say "Yes". He insisted on saying either "Chas", or "So?". So instead we taught him to say "Okay". He got that all right. He wouldn't say "Hello", and we hit on "Hi", as an agreeable alternative. By the time my mother came home from work, Willie's English vocabulary had increased amazingly. He refused to take off his hat and overcoat because they looked so "Okay".

When my mother came in and saw him, she took one look at the hat and overcoat and turned to John. "What", she said slowly, "in the name of God is that?"

"That", said John, "is Willie. We've adopted him."

"You've what?"

"Adopted him. He hadn't any place to go—no home, no money, no friends, and he can't talk good English. So we're going to take care of him." She sat down in a chair near by. "Well," she said after a moment, "I thought I'd never be surprised at anything you two would do, but I'm stumped this time."

We explained then how we had first seen Willie in the employment office; we repeated to her the story that he had told us about himself, "and", said John, "we decided that what he needed was a nurse, so we took him in hand."

"Whatever about Willie needing a nurse," said my mother when we had finished our tale, "there's no doubt that what you two need is a couple of keepers." She turned to our waif: "Well, Willie," she said kindly, "you might as well take off your hat and coat as long as you're going to stay with us awhile."

"Okay," said Willie.

"Was it English you said you were teaching him?" my mother asked John. "We'll have to do something about that outfit of his," she went on, "he looks like a walking tent the way he is now."

So Willie became one of the family. My mother shortened his overcoat and John rummaged in his closet and found a hat that nearly fitted him. Willie was so solemn, took everything so seriously, and spoke in such an odd manner that we couldn't help laughing at him. He wanted to learn how to dance an Irish Set. John and I taught him the figures of it, but whenever there was any kind of a crowd in the house and Willie went out to dance, he got all confused, did all the wrong things, and got wildly excited. Then he'd begin to shout in German, and send all of us into roars of laughter. He never got angry, he liked everyone he met, and they liked him. My mother often said that he was well worth his keep, because he kept us all in such good humour. But it was in the evenings, at dinner, that we enjoyed Willie most. My mother would be cooking and Willie would stand by the kitchen door shuffling his feet. Presently my mother would ask: "What would you like, Willie?" Willie would say something in German and ask her if she could cook it. "No," my mother would tell him. "I've never heard of it, and I'll bet no one else ever has either, but yourself." Willie would give vent to a long drawn-out sigh and look dismal.

"What is to eat?" he would ask mournfully. "Hash," my mother would tell him. Willie could say "Ach", in the most tantalizing way, and when he heard "Hash", he would begin to do his stuff. "William," my mother would say: "If you don't like what I cook let's see what you can do. Cook your own dinner!" Willie's face would light up with a radiant smile. "Okay," he would say joyfully, and go to work. He would emerge from the kitchen about half an hour later, bearing a large plate full of an awful-looking, foul-smelling concoction, place it on the table and sit down in his place, his face full of expectation. The three of us, my mother, John and I, would get a whiff of Willie's dinner at the same time. "Willie," my mother would say sternly. "You're a nice lad and we like you, but even if you feel that you must suffocate all New York by creating that filthy smell, you might at least have pity on us and not put it under our very noses. If you must eat junk like this you'll have to eat it in the kitchen." Willie, however, would pay no attention to her, but just keep on eating, smacking his lips after every mouthful.

"Does it taste good?" John would ask.

"Okay," Willie would say and go on eating, without a stop till his plate was empty. Then he'd lean back in his chair and pat his belly.

"My friends," he would say, and sigh contentedly, "I am so very happy."

One evening he cooked a very special meal and would not be satisfied until he had dished out a little to each of us.

John was the first to venture it, and one look at his face after he had put some of the food into his mouth, made me decide that I wasn't hungry enough to try it. My mother evidently felt the same way about it, because she didn't taste hers either. "What is it like?" she asked John.

"Poison!" he gasped as he reached for water.

After that no amount of coaxing and persuasion on Willie's part could tempt any of us to taste of his various dishes. He kept my mother in a perpetual state of amazement at the different smells, and worry for fear he would kill himself with indigestion. But while he was with us Willie remained healthy and happy. And then one afternoon, about a month after John and I had found him, he told us sadly that he had found work. John and I jumped up and began to dance round him, calling him a "lucky stiff", and telling him that soon he would have plenty of money and in no time at all he could go back to Germany and marry his sweetheart. But for some reason, Willie did not respond.

"Wait a minute Babs," said John. "He's crying."

I looked at Willie. Two great tears were rolling down his fat cheeks.

"What is the matter?" I asked anxiously.

Willie swallowed hard before he replied. "I'm going away," he said.

"Away? Why? What do you mean?" John and I were startled.

"My work is on a ship. On Monday I go to South America. I signed papers."

John began to splutter. "You can't do that Willie. We won't let you go."

"No, we won't," I joined in.

But Willie only opened his big blue eyes very wide, and his face grew more solemn as he repeated: "I signed papers."

My mother when she heard the news was very much upset and angry. "You should have known better than to let him go out by himself," she told John and me angrily. "Why did you adopt him in the first place if you didn't intend to take care of him? South America is a rough country; God only knows what will happen to Willie when he gets there. What made him take a job on a ship anyway? Did you ask him?"

We hadn't thought of asking him why he did it, so we called him out of his room to find out. In his funny, halting way, Willie explained that it hurt him to stay with us when he couldn't pay my mother something for it, and that the job on the ship was the only one he could find so he had to take it.

My mother was furious with him. "A nice thing!" she cried, "caring for you as if you were my own son. I even let you cook those rotten smells, and then the first chance you get you want to run off and leave us. I won't stand for it." She couldn't stay angry at Willie, however, because he began to cry. "I don't want to go," he sobbed, "but I must. I signed the papers." And though we argued with him all evening, telling him that he needn't go, that we'd find some way to get him out of it, it was the only reply he would make. He didn't want to go, but he must, because he signed the papers. "You'll probably get your throat cut two minutes after you land there," my mother told him darkly. But though he looked frightened when he heard that, he didn't change his mind; and on the following Monday morning Willie became a member of the crew of a small cargo boat and sailed away, bound for South America. We never saw him again. Two months after he left we received a letter from him. There was no address to show where it came from or where we could write to him. In the letter he told us that he was sick to come back to us. The first night in port he had gone drinking with some of the crew, and the boat had sailed away without him. He had no money, the people laughed at him, and he didn't know what to do. He would write to us again, he said, when he had found work and had a place to live. What became of Willie we never found out, for we never heard from him after that one letter.

Chapter Eight

Figures Make me Dizzy

★

It had never occurred to anyone in the family, I am sure, that I should ever work for my living. Puffy, yes, and it had been said even of Winnie, when she first started to go to school: "She must have a good education so that she can get a decent job when she grows up." But I have heard my mother say so often of me that I have it off by heart: "That one? She'll never have to work; why, she danced before she could walk. Her feet will earn her living for her, and it's a good thing, because she can do nothing else. It isn't as if she hadn't any brains—she has, only they work backwards. Why, she even walked backwards when she was a baby. All her ideas work backwards too, and the worst of it is that once she gets one of her dizzy ideas all hell won't stop her till she carries it out. It's from her father she takes that."

I have often heard her relating, sometimes with laughter, sometimes in the sarcastic manner that was all her own, how once, shortly after my father left for Ireland, she had found me looking out of a front window at a traffic policeman, studying him very intently. She asked me why I was watching him, and I replied that I had seen an old man leading the traffic policeman across the street. She drew me aside and explained that it must have been the other way round, telling me, also, that if ever I wanted to cross a street and there were many automobiles going past, I mustn't cross, but wait until the policeman came and brought me safely to the other side. For days I had pondered over this, and then decided to find out for myself if it were true. Without telling a soul of what I had in mind, I went out of the house and walked till I came to a really busy intersection. I sat on the curbstone for hours and hours, and still the policeman didn't notice me. Finally I became so cold and hungry that I began to cry. A crowd soon collected, and the policeman came over to see what the matter was. "Well well," he said, "have you lost your mother, little one?"

I stopped crying and looked up at him. "No," I said calmly. "Why didn't you come and take me across the street?"

"Well, you're so small that I didn't see you," he laughed. "I'll take you across now, come on."

"But I don't want to go across," said I.

"You don't? Then what are the tears for?"

"I'm cold. Why didn't you come and take me across the street?" I repeated.

"Do you want to cross now?"

"No," I said.

"Did you want to cross before?"

"No—but why didn't you come and——"

The crowd began to laugh, and the policeman becoming angry asked me roughly where I lived. I told him. He looked surprised. "You've come a long way," he said. "Does your mother know you're out?"

"No. Why didn't you come and take me across——?"

"She's off again!" he cried. "I'm going to take you—home!" Another policeman took his place directing the traffic, and he picked me up in his arms and carried me. All the way home I kept asking him the same question: why hadn't he come and taken me across the street? though I couldn't explain why I wanted to know, since I hadn't wanted to go across in the first place.

My mother answered his ring at the bell. Her face was white. "Oh where did you find her?" she cried. "We've been searching for her for hours."

"Is this yours?" the policeman asked.

She nodded.

"Then for heaven's sake take it!" he cried, thrusting me at her. "She's got me going around in circles."

When my mother was in a merry mood she would always say at the finish: "It's from me she took that," but when her back was troubling her and her temper and nerves on edge, she'd say instead, bitingly: "Just like what her father would do."

My mother did not believe that I should ever find a job, though I had often made more than $15 in one evening by dancing. For dancing was something I had always been able to do. It wasn't the result of any effort on my part, it was just something that I took for granted, because I could not remember a time when I had not been able to dance, and the whole family felt the same way about it.

Besides this, John and I were so accustomed to hearing "Nothing to-day" at the employment agencies, that

I nearly fell over from shock when I was told one morning: "Here's an address. They need somebody for office work and you might do. If you get the job you pay us half of your first week's salary. You can do office work of course, filing etc.?"

"Oh yes," I said.

"Go ahead up there and see the man. If they take you they'll phone us." The address on the card he gave me was on First Avenue near 72nd Street.

I nearly pulled John out of the agency to tell him the good news. "You haven't got the job yet," said he. "You can't do office work, can you?"

"No," I said. "I don't know the first thing about it."

"You'll have to bluff your way then," he said as we hurried to a subway station. "If you can hold it for a week you'll have a few dollars out of it. We'll spend this dime for subway fare. The job might be gone if we don't hurry——"

The address turned out to be that of a small hardware and electrical appliances and repairs store.

"Shall I go in with you?" John asked as we stood outside the store.

"No thanks," I told him. I knew John too well—he'd be just as apt to tell the man in charge to go to hell as he would to say "yes sir". It depended on his mood, and at the moment he had a queer look in his eye; so I told him to wait outside for me.

There was a girl in charge, and when I told her that I had been sent from the employment agency she took me into an office at the back of the store. There, two men began to ask me questions about previous experience. I got over that by saying that I had worked in offices in Boston, which seemed to satisfy them. "You won't have to do much office work at first," said one man who seemed to be the boss. "It's a new store and all you'll have to do for a while is keep it in order, keep the accounts straight, manage it generally and help with the repairs. Mr. Stokes here, will show you what to do. The hours are from nine to six, full day on Saturday, an hour for lunch, fifteen dollars a week to start. Is that agreeable?"

"Yes sir," I said.

"The store is on Long Island. You take a Willet's Point train——" he told me how to get there, "and be there on Monday morning. That's all."

"Yes sir, thank you," I said and left.

"How did you make out?" John asked.

"I got it. I go to work on Monday morning out on Long Island."

"Did you say 'yes sir', like I told you?"

"I did. It's an electrical repair store John. I'm going to manage it, keep the accounts and help with the repairs."

"My God!" said John. "You keep accounts! Do you know anything about book-keeping?"

"No."

"You won't last two days," he prophesied. "I know. You tell me when the boss goes out and I'll come and help you. During his lunch hour——"

"Do you know anything about book-keeping?" I asked doubtfully.

"No," said he. "But think of all the fun we're going to have learning."

"You were right," I said. "I won't last two days."

"I'll help you with the repairs too," he offered generously.

I sighed but said nothing. I had dim visions of John fooling around with electric currents, resultant explosions, mutilated bodies and a wrecked Long Island.

During my first few days at work John nearly drove me mad. He kept bouncing in and out of the store asking me the price of this or that, wanting to know how much I'd charge to repair his radio, and then saying foolishly: "Well I haven't got a radio, but when I get one I'll bring it in and you can fix it for me."

I asked him one night if he would keep away from the store for the rest of the week because the boss, Mr. Stokes, was going to be there every day teaching me how to splice wires and repair lamps. "Will he be there next week too?" John asked.

"I don't know," I said. "It's next week that I must make up the accounts."

"Are you good at addition?"

"I can add."

"I'll come in and help you," said John. "I'm very good at addition, and maybe between the two of us we can manage to get them straight. All right?"

"All right," I agreed.

Under Mr. Stokes's instruction I learned during the next few days how to splice wires, mend lamps, test bulbs, and do a few things to the insides of radio sets. While Mr. Stokes was present I was all right, because if I was in doubt about anything I could always ask him what to do, but the moment he left the store and I was on my own, I became panic stricken. I was sure that I had connected wrong wires and put screws and nuts in all the places where they shouldn't be. However, on Saturday evening, when he handed me my first week's salary, Mr. Stokes expressed himself as being satisfied with my work.

During Monday and Tuesday I was in a sweat wondering at what moment Mr. Stokes would say: "Here are the books——" and on Tuesday evening, just as I was leaving, the blow fell. He called me back and said: "You have a list of sales and money taken in for repairs haven't you, Miss Mullen?"

"Yes sir," said I.

"Good. I have expenses marked in this little book. Please enter them to-morrow and see that the accounts balance. I shall not be in to-morrow at all. Here are the keys and you can do the opening up in the morning. That's all Miss Mullen. Good night."

"Good night Mr. Stokes," I said, and stumbled out into the street. I needed air.

"Weren't you taught any book-keeping in school?" John asked me that night when I told him.

"The last year that I was in school it was taught," I said, "but I didn't like it so I paid no attention to it."

"Don't you remember anything about it?"

"No, nothing at all."

"Neither do I," said he. "But we may as well try. We'll add everything up and see what happens," he suggested. "I'll go in with you in the morning. Between the two of us——"

"Between the two of you you'll wreck the store, mess up the books and probably drive the man into fits when he sees the result of your day's labour," my mother put in at this point. But she was as proud of the $15 that I had earned for a week's work as I was myself.

"You'd better reckon what your boss owes you up till to-night," said my mother at breakfast the next morning.

"Why?" I asked. "Do you think I'll get fired?"

"Think it?" she said. "I'm as sure of it as I am that I'm sitting in this chair. God only knows what those books are going to look like when you two mad creatures finish with them. You'll no doubt add from side to side instead of up and down—you, I mean," she said, looking at me, "and as bad as you are, that article"—pointing to John—"is ten times worse."

So, just in case, John and I made up what three days' work at $15 a week would amount to. We reckoned it to be $7.50.

We arrived at the store at five minutes before nine o'clock. The books were all neatly laid out on the desk, and there was also a note telling me of two lamps and an iron that were to be repaired.

John and I examined the books. "What's debit?" he asked. "Is that what you owe somebody or what they owe you?"

"I haven't the faintest idea," I replied.

"Look, Babs, it says credit here. What does that mean?"

"I don't know that either," said I.

"Some of these things are done in red ink," said he, "and way up here"—he turned the leaves rapidly—"there's something in green ink. Not much green ink though. It's a pity. I like green. It's a prettier colour than red, don't you think so Babs?"

"I do," I said. "Hey, wait a minute John, maybe it means something!"

"No, I don't think so," said he. "What could it mean?"

"I don't know. What do you suppose he meant by 'making the accounts balance' John?"

John thought for a moment. "Maybe," he said, "he meant that all the columns of figures should be in line, or even, or something like that. Can't you remember anything at all about book-keeping?"

"No," I said. "I told you before. Besides, we didn't get this far—at least I didn't. I quit it after one day to take up French."

"Can you speak French?"

"No. Look John, there's three bottles of ink here, red, green and black. We ought to do something with them. They're here for some reason."

"Let's think," said he. "Maybe if we think hard enough we'll know what we should do with them."

Both of us fell silent, thinking deeply, wondering which was the right way to solve our puzzle. It was John who spoke first. "I've got it!" he cried. "I know what to do!"

"What?" I asked.

"We'll take all the figures that are in the book already, together with what you have, sales, etc., and what your boss has marked down for expenses, and add them all up. We'll put the sales down in one column and the expenses down in another, then we'll add that debit thing in another place and the credit in still another."

"Where does the ink come in though? Have you figured that out too?"

"I have. We'll do each column of figures in a different colour—take turns at it. I'd say that is what they're for. How does it sound to you?"

"Crazy, but I can't think of any other way, and we've got to do something, so let's go."

We were finished with the books in about three hours, and indeed they did look beautiful. Row after row of neat figures (we added up all that we could find in the book) covering page after page, each row contrasting pleasurably with the other: first green, then red, and last, black. We didn't stop figuring and adding till we couldn't find anything else to add, and then while John slowly turned the pages, I stood back and surveyed our handiwork. "It looks very neat and very pretty," I declared, "and if Mr. Stokes isn't pleased with that he'll never be pleased with anything. Now I'll hold it and you tell me what you think, John."

"Do you know what, Babs? We deserve a medal, two medals, one for each of us. It's a great piece of work," was John's opinion. "Now what else have you got to do?" he asked.

"Mend a couple of lamps and do things with an iron," I told him.

"I'll help you with those too," he offered.

We had a grand time repairing the lamps. John insisted that I was connecting the wrong wires. "No," said I. "I'm sure that Mr. Stokes said this way and these wires."

"Mr. Stokes", said John, "is out of date. Mine is a newer method. You connect this one with that one. I ought to know because I studied electricity for a year when I was in the army."

So I bowed to John's superior knowledge, and together we fixed the lamps as he said they should be fixed.

The boss, whom I hadn't expected to see that day, came in before we got to the iron. I saw him coming and called a warning to John. There wasn't time enough for John to leave, so he ducked behind the counter.

Mr. Stokes came in and headed straight for the books. "Have you finished with these, Miss Mullen?" he asked, taking one up in his hand.

"Yes sir," said I, feeling very pleased.

Mr. Stokes looked, and looked, and looked some more. His eyes got bigger and bigger till I thought they were going to pop out of his head. He began to sweat as he turned the pages; his face grew red and then it grew purple. Out of the corner of my eye I could see John's head just above the top of the counter. He was watching Mr. Stokes. He walked out from behind the counter and stood at my side, but Mr. Stokes didn't seem to hear him or to know that he was there. For fully ten minutes Mr. Stokes didn't—perhaps he couldn't—speak. Slowly he put the book back on the desk, took out his handkerchief and wiped his forehead. "Miss Mullen," he said heavily.

"Yes sir," said I.

"Allow me to congratulate you. I have never in my life seen books so completely, so artistically ruined."

He was very calm about it. He didn't raise his voice, or shout, or anything like that; he spoke in a steady, even tone that made me feel as if someone had dumped a bucket of cold water over my head. He took a pencil and began to write rapidly on paper, and here, of course,

John had to put in his oar. "It's $7.50 sir," said he. "We figured it out this morning."

"Who are you?" Mr. Stokes asked.

"I'm Barbara's cousin"—John was wearing his most angelic smile. "I helped her with the books, and with the lamps too."

"Do you expect to be paid for your assistance?"

"I hadn't thought of it," said John, "but it's not a bad idea."

"Miss Mullen."

"Yes, Mr. Stokes."

"Get your hat and coat," he handed me the $7.50, "get out, and take that"—he pointed to John—"with you."

As usual, John did the unexpected thing. I thought he would get angry: instead he began to laugh. He laughed louder and heartier than I had ever heard him laugh before, and Mr. Stokes looked on, amazed. "Was it you who did the lamps?" he asked.

John nodded.

Mr. Stokes walked over to where the lamps were standing in a corner. He examined them carefully and then he looked at us. I had my hat and coat on by this time. "I don't like to lose my temper," he said. "Will you please go as quickly as you possibly can, both of you?" Perhaps I'd better explain here that Mr. Stokes was English. An American boss would never have acted like that; he'd more probably have raised seventeen different kinds of hell.

We still had a few hours to spare before my mother would have returned from work, and John suggested that we should go up to the Bronx to his friend's house to see if there was a letter there for me from my father.

There was. He understood, he said, about the last letter, and it was quite all right. He knew that I hadn't written it of my own accord, and we were both to forget about it and neither of us was ever to mention it again. Would I write soon and send that picture? Love from both himself and P.J.

Now if there is a sentence in the English language that I heartily dislike, it is: "It's quite all right." Maybe it is because I have used it so often myself, and because I know what you can do to people with it. It all depends on the tone of voice you use when you say "quite", and the expression you put on your face. It can be quite as annoying as it is to have someone say: "My dear, do exactly as you please," or: "Whatever you like," after you have spent hours in trying to get them back into good humour by asking their advice.

"How do you think he means that?" I asked, showing the letter to John and pointing out the sentence.

"I don't see anything wrong with it," said he, after studying it for a moment. "All it would mean to me is that everything is O.K. again, and that he's not angry."

"That", said I, "depends on how he was feeling when he wrote it. It could be meant in any one of several ways."

"How?" John asked.

"Well," I explained, "it could mean 'of course I'm terribly hurt but I don't mind—it's quite all right', or he could be feeling like an unsung hero—oh several ways."

"You", said John, "have a dizzy mind. You look at

things the way no one else on the face of the earth would look at them. Forget about it."

"All the same," said I, "I hope he's not feeling too badly about it."

"Nuts! Come on home!"

"That poor man," said my mother that evening when I handed her the $7.50 and told her that I had been fired; "with thousands of good book-keepers jobless in the city, he had to get stuck with you. He deserved a better break. I wonder", she went on, "what will happen in the next job you get."

"Gosh, do you think I'll ever get another one?" I asked.

"You!" she said. "You'll no doubt be swamped with them."

"But why?" I asked, seeing that she was serious and not being sarcastic.

"I can't explain," she laughed. "Maybe it's because you're so dumb. You know what they say about luck going hand in hand with fools and blind people."

Whether she was right or wrong, I got another job two days later, as a relief girl for switchboard and elevator operating in an hotel on 47th Street, just off Sixth Avenue.

Now I knew at that time as much about elevators and switchboards as a duck knows about Latin. But doing as John said as usual, I told the bell captain who questioned me that I had an uncle who worked in an hotel and that he had taught me how to operate both an elevator and a switchboard. This was to cover me in case I was asked for references—which of course I couldn't give. If asked my uncle's name I was to give Uncle Tom's—this by pre-arrangement with Uncle Tom.

The bell captain, who was from the South, and who kept saying: "Sho' nuff," every time I answered a question, decided to give me a trial. He brought me over to the elevator and told the girl operator to let me take it for a trip or two to see how I could handle it; then he left us. This was what I had been hoping for. As soon as the girl had closed the elevator doors and we were alone in the car I said to her: "Look here, I don't know the first thing about this, but I'm awfully hard up for a job. Be a sport and let me in on the know how, will you?"

The girl—her name was Alice Ryan—looked for a minute as if I had hit her with a brick. "Boy, oh boy!" she then said, "talk about nerve!"

"Aw come on," I said. "If I get the job I may be able to help you out some day in return."

"It's okay by me," she said after a moment's thought, "only you've gotta learn fast."

Fortunately for me, the car went at very slow speed. I caught on to the workings of it quickly, and was able to judge my stops fairly accurately. When the bell captain returned in about a quarter of an hour to ask Alice how I was doing, she replied: "She'll be okay. Just wants about a day to get used to the car, that's all."

"How large a board can you handle?" he asked me then.

"I'm not as good at a board as I am on the elevator," I said truthfully, not having the faintest idea of what a "board" looked like.

"Well, the boys will help you out on it for the first

day," he said. "After that you'll be able to manage it yourself. You'll only have to work the board on Sundays anyway, and Sunday is a slow day. You'll fit the uniform we have," he continued. "It's down in the girls' locker room. It may have to be shortened, so you'd better take it home with you and see to it. You'll have broken hours, you work Sundays, and Tuesday is your day off. $17.50 a week."

"What are broken hours?" I asked.

"You come in at 7 a.m., leave at twelve, return at six and work till eleven at night, on one day. The next day your hours are from twelve to six. There are two girls on each elevator—there's another passenger car in the back of the building—not at the same time of course, one works while the other's off. The same applies to the switchboard, and they all work the same hours, alternating every day." He went on to explain that Mondays I'd be on the front car, Wednesdays on the back car, Thursdays the front car again. On Fridays I was to help the auditor, or the boss's secretary, or let the switchboard girls go for a smoke, or help the cashier in the restaurant, or any amount of other things. On Saturday I was to run the back elevator, and Sunday the switchboard. On Fridays and Sundays I was to wear my own clothes, but while running an elevator I'd have to wear a uniform.

It took me a little while before I could digest all this. The bell captain kept repeating it over and over as if he were very doubtful whether I'd ever have it straight. The hotel supplied the uniform, and from what the captain had said, I gathered that the main reason I was hired was that I was the only one small enough to fit the uniform. I was to start the next day, Friday.

John teased me unmercifully about the "monkey suit", as he called the uniform that I was to wear. However, I didn't mind because I got my own back. The Friday that I started to work John got hired as a bellboy in an hotel uptown at 100th Street and Broadway, and had to don a monkey suit too.

My first day on the new job passed well enough. I was sent up to the auditor's office, where I was given a large sheaf of papers and told to file them away.

The auditor, who had the longest nose I have ever seen, was Russian, very absent-minded, and slightly deaf. I told him that I knew nothing about filing. "I beg your pardon?" he said.

"I don't know anything about filing," I repeated loudly, whereupon he looked at me with such a woebegone expression, that genuinely distressed I added hastily, "I'm very, very sorry."

He said nothing for a moment or two, and then he rubbed his long nose and smiled: "But how could you know, little one?" he asked. "You cannot be long out of school, you look so young. Besides," he added absently, "I thought you were the girl who brings my lunch."

"It's going to be fun, working with this man," I thought to myself—and it was. He showed me how to do filing. He was endlessly patient with me and never got cross when I did the wrong thing, and would go over and over anything I wasn't sure of, a dozen or more times if necessary. I got on well with the auditor. He was always asking me if I had finished something which he hadn't given me to do. When I explained:

"You didn't say anything about it," he would look blank for a moment and then say: "Oh, so I didn't. So I didn't." I liked him.

The following day, Saturday, went well also. I arrived at the hotel at a quarter to seven in the morning, donned the monkey suit, ran the back elevator till noon, returned in the evening at six and finished at eleven, without mishap. But Sunday, the day on which I was to run the switchboard, was a day of days. I reported to the switchboard operator at a few minutes before twelve.

"Hello," she said. "Ready to take over?"

"Oh yes," said I, smiling very brightly.

"Here comes Eddie," she said. "He's going to give you a hand for to-day. See you at six o'clock. So long——" and she went off.

"So long," I said and sat down at the board.

Eddie, one of the bellboys, looked me over with a critical eye, whistled, and said: "Not bad, not bad at all! Know anything about a switchboard?"

I shook my head.

"What's your name?"

"Barbara," I said in a small voice, "Barbara Mullen."

"Boy!" he said. "They sure robbed the cradle when they picked you for this job! You ought to wear more lipstick," he went on. "It would make you look older and as if you knew the ropes."

"What ropes?" I asked.

"Forget it," he said. "I'll show you how to run this thing," indicating the board. "See if you can look as if you knew something about it when the captain comes on duty at two o'clock."

For the next two hours the hotel was in an uproar. I woke people out of their afternoon naps to give them room service that they didn't want. I gave calls to all the wrong people, sent the bellboys up with ice water to people who had called down that they were not to be disturbed, and connected the manager with the engineer when he asked to speak with an Italian Count who was a guest in the hotel at the time. Eddie was great. He took all the scoldings for the blunders I made, with a meek "I'm sorry sir", and went on teaching me as if it were all in the day's work.

By two o'clock I was able to look at more than one light on the board at a time without getting confused and forgetting which wanted what. When Eva, the regular operator, returned at six, Eddie said with a great sigh of relief: "You'll be able to work it alone next Sunday Barbara, thank God!" I never put in such a Sunday in my life, and neither, I am sure, did Eddie, or anyone else in the hotel who was unfortunate enough to lift a telephone receiver off its hook that day.

Chapter Nine

Tap-Dancing and Bell-Hops

*

Jimmy Hines had formed the habit of coming in with Uncle Tom every night to visit us. Jimmy was very helpful, and my mother liked having him about. She asked him if he would go up to Boston for Winnie, as John and I were both working and hadn't time to make the trip. Jimmy said that he would be delighted. He went up to Boston, arranged about Winnie's discharge papers from the school there, and brought her back with him, taking extremely good care of her on the way. My mother said to John and me that Jimmy Hines was a fine young man.

My sixteenth birthday came along, and with it came Puffy, down from Boston to attend the birthday party; a bracelet from Jimmy; and my mother's permission to go to the pictures with him one evening in the week.

The party given by my mother was a large one. A lot of people came that we knew, and they brought a lot of people that we didn't know. Amongst those that we didn't know was a reporter for one of the leading Irish weeklies published in New York. It was Puffy who quite by accident saw the piece in the paper. He attracted our attention by a loud "What th' hell!" My mother, who was reading something else at the other end of the table, looked up and said: "What do you mean by using such language in front of the children? What are you so excited for?"

"There's a piece in this paper about Barbara's birthday party, and it says that she's a *former* New England champion."

"Former champion!" cried my mother. "What in hell do they mean, *former*! She never lost a contest to anybody, by God!"

Well, that's where the sport was: my mother and Puffy both shouting at the same time, John standing up, roaring at the two of them that they shouldn't be using such language before the children, and the children—Winnie and I—helpless with laughter. When they finally quietened down, my mother demanded to know what I was going to do about it.

"Nothing," said I.

"Nothing?" said Puffy incredulously. "But how's that going to look when you try to get another job dancing?"

"Yes," my mother agreed. "You should go down and see the editor."

"But why?" I asked. "I'm not going to do any more dancing, so what does it matter what they say?"

They were dumbfounded. The two of them began to talk and shout all over again. John got them calmed down, saying: "Ssh! Let's hear what she has to say herself. Let me talk to her."

"Go ahead," said my mother. "Maybe you can get her to talk sense."

"Do you mean that about not dancing again, Babs?" John asked.

"Yes," I said. "I do."

"But what's the reason? I thought you liked to dance."

"Not any more," I told him. "I'd much rather do the looking on now. Besides, I think I'd be afraid to dance for a lot of people, and anyway, I don't want to. I like working."

"It's that damned hotel job that's done it!" cried Puffy. "It probably makes her feel grown up, or like a lady or something to be working. I say she ought to quit and go back to her dancing. Anybody can do that hotel job she's got. I won't stand for her being there."

"Won't stand for it, Puffy?" John asked. "What can you do about it? If the kid won't dance, she won't and that's all there is to it."

"But if she doesn't dance she'll be just another straphanger for the rest of her life," Puffy insisted. "What do you say mom?"

"You're right, Puffy," said she, "and so is John. Dancing is the one thing we cannot make her do if she doesn't want to do it. In any case this is something that she must decide for herself."

"That one decide for herself? She can't do it. If she does, we shouldn't pay any attention to her, because it will be the wrong way. She can't do anything right except dance, and you know it as well as I do."

"And you know what her dancing would be like if she hadn't her heart in it. No, we'll leave it up to herself," said my mother. "Barbara," she went on, speaking very slowly: "You know what we want you to do. Think it over carefully before you make up your mind."

"My mind is made up already," I said. "I'd much rather be working, and larking with John on my days off, than do anything else. I don't want to dance."

"Then that settles it, once and for all," said my mother firmly.

"Well—of all—the screwy dames!" said Puffy disgustedly.

"We'll say no more about it," my mother said sharply.

"But mom——" from Puffy.

"I said we'll say no more about it."

"Aw——" Puffy picked up his hat, rammed it on to his head and walked out.

The weeks flew by. Puffy found work almost immediately. When he did we prevailed on my mother to quit her job and stay at home, since Puffy's, John's and my salaries were enough to pay household expenses, with money over.

I liked my new job more with every day that passed. I met lots of people and they were all different. John and I used to swap stories every night about the guests. A good many of the people in the hotel where John worked were "always soused", as John put it, and "swell sports". The odd drinks that they sent down to John kept him continually on the borderline of being soused too, so that he was always feeling merry and always raising hell.

There were three spinsters there who kept him supplied, one with chocolates, another with cigarettes, and the third with cough medicine. "I appeal to the mother in them," said John, telling me about it as we divided the chocolates between us.

He was very well liked by the hotel manager, the

clerks, and his brother bellhops, as well as the guests, and the chief switchboard operator, Kitty. John's description of Kitty was: "Big, blonde and hefty. Drinks like a fish, curses like a trooper, and she'd rather lose her own job than do you dirt. She has a heart as big as a mountain, has Kitty, and she sure is a hard hitter." John didn't say how he found out about the hitting. He promised that I should meet all his new friends. He said, too, "You should work with me, Babs. Your people sound too respectable and dead, you can't have much fun there."

"Think of all the free meals I get," I said.

"You didn't tell me about the free meals. How come?"

I told him how the waiter brought me coffee and hot buttered rolls every morning that I was on early, tea and sandwiches when I worked in the afternoon, and coffee and pie or cake when I was on late shift.

"The laughs you'd get if you were working with me would make up for all that," said John. "You're getting too much coddling down in your place anyway, with your three squares a day duty free."

Then I told him of the little old woman who insisted on giving me a glass of sour cream every day. She used to order it especially for me, stand over me till I had finished it, eye the empty glass approvingly and say: "That is so good for you Barbara, my dear child, so good for you. It will give you lovely pink cheeks." I hated the sour cream, and the rest of the staff knew it. They used to watch for the little old woman every day, and when she came round with the glass in her hand they would all stand by for a good look at my face as I swallowed the cream. When she had gone they would pat me on the back and tell me what a nice healthy girl I should be when I grew up. "Big and fat," they would say, "with lovely pink cheeks." I would swear then that no matter how she coaxed me, I would never drink the filthy stuff again. But every day it was the same—simply because the little woman was so sweet that I couldn't bear to hurt her feelings by refusing her. The hotel staff knew that too, and Eddie the bellboy used to mimic my voice and cry: "I absolutely will not drink that filthy stuff again," after me every time I walked through the lobby.

John hootled with glee and asked: "Does she come round at the same time every day? I want to see it. I wouldn't miss it for anything."

I wouldn't tell him what time she paid her daily visit. "You know what happened the last time you came to see me on a job," I reminded him.

"You'd have got fired anyway," he returned. "It's high time I went down to see this hotel. I want to be sure that you're working with the right people."

"I am," said I. "I've got Eddie and Thad to watch out for me, so you needn't bother."

"Who is Thad?" John asked.

"I don't know," I said. "He's just Thad and he stays in the hotel."

"You mean that he's a guest there?"

"Yes. His father and mother are there too. They're Chinese and awfully nice people. Thad shares his candy with me and lends me books."

The first time I had seen Thad, he had been with another Chinese boy, named Joe. I had refused to talk to either of them because I had read so much about the

Chinese being a strange, mysterious people, and I thought that their conversation would be over my head. I lost my fear of Thad, however, when one day, not having seen Joe with him for nearly a week, I asked after him. Thad casually informed me that Joe was now shooting crap with his ancestors—meaning that Joe had died. John decided that he would like Thad.

Thad was two years older than I, fairly tall and well built, with dark eyes that crinkled whenever he smiled. We used to have long talks about football and baseball. Thad said that all I knew about either game was the name of the side I was rooting for, and that I usually got that twisted. He enjoyed explaining the games to me and I enjoyed listening. It was not unusual for us to get so interested in our subject that we would forget all about bells and passengers, until somebody telephoned down to the desk to find out if the back passenger car was out of order, and if not, whether the operator had taken the day off.

Thad spent hours in trying to train me to think before I spoke. For instance: Eddie was one day walking towards the back car carrying a pitcher of ice-water. "When he gets here," said Thad, "you ask him who's going to win to-morrow's football game. I'll step into the car so he won't see me and know that I put you up to it. Ask him before he gets in, and remember to *think*."

"Okay," I agreed. "Eddie," I said as he neared, "who's going to win to-morrow's football game?"

"Football game?" said Eddie, "this is the baseball season, Dora. Six please," he said as he entered the car, and then seeing Thad: "Oh, I get it!" and he and Thad laughed heartily.

My decision about dancing was not mentioned again until one night, about a month after Puffy had seen the piece in the paper, when I met Peter O'Dolan at a party. Peter and I had played in a few shows together in Boston, and his greeting was: "You're just the person I've been looking for. Can you take on a job with me for night after next? I need a dancer."

"I've given up dancing," I said.

"Given it up?" he exclaimed. "Stop your kidding."

"I'm not joking," I said. "I'm serious."

"But why?"

"I can't really explain why," I told him. "I only know that I don't want to dance any more. I can't put any feeling into it, and there's no sense in your asking me what changed me, because I don't know."

"Well, I guess it's my tough luck in that case," he said after a moment. "What do you think of this young lady's decision about dancing?" he asked my mother as she joined us.

"Offstage fright," said my mother briefly.

"I'm being paged," said Peter as someone called to him from the other end of the room. "Don't decide about that job right away. There's ten dollars in it for you, and you'll only have to dance a few numbers. Think it over. I'll see you again before I leave," and he walked away.

"What job was he talking about?" my mother asked when he was out of earshot.

"A church affair of some kind up in Scarsdale, night after next," I said.

"If it's only one night why not take it?" she asked. "Ten dollars is good money for a few minutes' work."

"It will be my late night at the hotel—anyway I'd rather not go."

"Well, it's up to yourself of course," she said. "But I think you're being very selfish."

"Why selfish?" I asked in surprise.

"Try and see it from my point of view," she said. "The money you'd get would buy clothes for Winnie. She needs them."

"Can't you get them for her out of my regular pay?"

"That has to go for something else. There are plenty of bills to be paid out of your salary——" She kept on about how much the ten dollars was needed and how selfish I was, "thinking only of yourself" she said. When I told her again that it would be a late night at the hotel she said that I could get off if I really wanted to. Then it was that I would rather see Winnie without shoes than earn the money to buy them for her, dancing. In the end of course I said that I would ask for the night off from the hotel, and told Peter that I'd take the job.

The following day, by agreement with one of the girls, I worked straight through from noon till eleven o'clock at night. Jimmy met me at the hotel door and walked me home. We were standing in the hall talking of music and dancing, when Mrs. Carey, who lived in the apartment over ours came in. "I managed to get tomorrow night off," I said when she had disappeared up the stairs, "I'll get paid ten dollars for it. My mother doesn't know——" Jimmy suddenly placed his hand over my mouth. "You might as well come down and join us, Mrs. Carey," he called loudly. "It's more comfortable than trying to listen to our conversation from up there."

There was an audible creak on the landing above, and the sound of a door being closed softly. Mrs. Carey didn't reply to Jimmy's invitation. "——My mother doesn't know yet that I'll be off to-morrow night," I continued when he had taken his hand away. I made no remark about Mrs. Carey's eavesdropping; it had happened so often before. "I didn't know myself till I asked Alice this afternoon," I went on. "Mother will be pleased."

"It's eleven-thirty," Jimmy interrupted. "Dead line time for you. Good luck with the show to-morrow night." We said good night and he left.

My hours at the hotel the following day were from 7 a.m. to 3 p.m. I arrived home at three-thirty. "Good," said my mother when she saw me. "You're just in time."

"In time for what?" I asked.

"Mrs. Carey. She sent down word that she was going to call at four o'clock on important business."

It was Puffy's day off and he was at home. "I wonder what her important business is," he remarked.

"When women like Mrs. Carey send down word that they're coming to see you on a matter of importance," said my mother, "it can mean only one thing."

"You or me, Puffy?" I asked.

"You of course," said he, "because of what you said to her the other day."

"I didn't hear about that," my mother put in. "What happened?"

"I met Mrs. Carey at the front door a few days ago," I related; "she stopped me and began to ask all sorts of personal questions. I silenced her by saying that I had a married sister who had two dozen children and that she had a governess for each child, teaching them how to mind their own business. She didn't like it."

"I shouldn't think so," my mother laughed. "Ssh! Here she is!"—someone was knocking at the door. "Barbara, bring out the big carving knife and leave it near me here on the table. Puffy, you open the door for her. When she finishes her story, follow my lead and we'll scare the heart out of her. You Barbara"—as I handed her the carving knife—"stay in the kitchen till I call you." I ran off. "Now Puffy, open the door."

I heard Puffy say: "Come in, Mrs. Carey," very cordially. And then my mother's voice, drooling with welcome: "My dear Mrs. Carey, I'm delighted, delighted!" She "my deared" Mrs. Carey over to an armchair, begged her several times to sit down, and then said: "Now my dear, what is the important business? Oh it's quite all right, my son is very sensible and can be trusted I assure you——"

Mrs. Carey began in the usual way: "Mrs. Mullen, I don't like to be the one to tell you this, but as I said to a friend of mine this morning over the phone, I wouldn't be a good neighbour if I didn't tell you. I always say, that's what neighbours are for." She went on: "Mrs. Mullen, remember that it hurts me to tell you this——"

"Just as much as it's going to hurt me, I know," my mother interrupted softly.

"Yes," said Mrs. Carey. "But I feel better when I

realize that you would do the same if you were in my place."

I could almost hear the "like hell I would!" that my mother said to herself at that point.

Our neighbour continued: "Mrs. Mullen"—and here she lowered her voice as her kind always do—"your daughter—is carrying on."

Puffy coughed. My mother coughed. "Which one?" she asked conversationally.

"Which one?" Mrs. Carey repeated blankly.

"Yes," said my mother. "Which one?"

"Barbara, of course." Mrs. Carey was so anxious to impart her bad news that she went on without pause: "I happen to know that she isn't going to work this evening."

"No?" said my mother.

"No," Mrs. Carey didn't like interruptions. "She managed to get off. She's going somewhere with a man, and she's going to be paid ten dollars for it. You can trust me not to tell anyone else about it Mrs. Mullen, but I'm sure this isn't the first time she's pulled the wool over your eyes. As a matter of fact I don't believe she works evenings at all in that hotel." Mrs. Carey leaned back triumphantly.

My mother waited till she was really comfortable, then she asked: "What do you think of it, Puffy?"

"Not so hot," Puffy replied. "It's not half as good as the one Mrs. Flanagan from the top floor told us yesterday."

"Barbara," my mother called, and I came out. "Lock the door Puffy, and put your back against it," she directed. "On no account let this woman get past you." She picked up the carving knife. "Now Mrs. Carey," she said, and her voice was as cold as ice, "I'm going to teach you a lesson, but first I'm going to tell you a thing or two. Don't move out of that chair!"—as Mrs. Carey started to rise—"or I'll put this knife through your heart. It wouldn't cost me a thought."

Mrs. Carey sank back as white as a sheet. "I meant no harm," she breathed fearfully. "I'm a respectable woman who minds her own business——"

My mother didn't let her get any further. "You respectable!" she said, her voice full of venom. "A woman who carries or makes up a story like you do and who has a mind as rotten as you have—why you're so low you could walk under a snake's belly with a high hat on." Mentally I gave my mother three rousing cheers; and in a way I pitied Mrs. Carey, for I knew she was in for a tongue-lashing that she'd remember till her dying day. My mother went on—"Since that child first put foot on a stage I've had filthy-minded creatures like you coming to me with stories about her. I've even received letters from Ireland about her, written by people who have never even seen her and who hadn't the guts to sign their names. The world is full of lice like them, and you come under the same heading. It's high time some of them were exterminated, and I might as well begin on you." She stood up and brandished the carving knife over her head. Her voice had risen to a shout.

"Hey ma," put in Puffy. "Not so loud. The neighbours will hear you."

"To hell with the neighbours!" my mother cried. "It's too much I've had of neighbours, but there'll be one less in the world when I've finished this day's work—mark my words."

Mrs. Carey was a small woman. My mother, who was as strong as two ordinary men, put down the carving knife, reached over, picked her up out of the chair as if she were a baby, and then shook her till I thought the little woman's head would fly off her shoulders. She began to shriek and yell. "Help! Murder! Help!"

"Sufferin' cats ma!" said Puffy, clapping his hands over his ears, "Let her go before she draws the cops in on us."

"To hell with the cops as well as the neighbours!" was my mother's answer, and she went on shaking the unfortunate Mrs. Carey until she couldn't shake her any more. "Now," she said, and I've never before heard so much satisfaction expressed in one word, "open the door Puffy, and let what's left of this bundle of rags go home to her knitting."

We didn't bother to talk about Mrs. Carey after she had gone. You may perhaps think that she would have been treated more leniently if her story had been about anyone but me. That isn't so. No matter whom she had spoken about my mother would have dealt with her in the same manner. More than once when we have had friends in for an evening I have heard my mother interrupt a conversation with: "This is not a gossipers' convention. If you want to tear your friends apart you'll have to find someone else's house to do it in, and find it right now." The gossip always stopped.

Since our earliest childhood we children were forbidden to talk about our neighbours, or to visit them unless for a gathering or party of some kind, when we would all go. I was once unfortunate enough to stop in at a schoolmate's house on my way home from school. I told my mother where I had been, and mentioned the colour of the woman's kitchen curtains. I was licked unmercifully and called a "cabin hunter". I didn't visit again.

One of my mother's favourite lectures was: "You'll find enough to do in minding your own business, taking care of your own home and keeping your self clean, honest and above board, without looking through your neighbours' windows to see how they drink their soup. Let them talk about you if they like; as long as you know yourself that you're decent and as long as you stay that way, they can't hurt you." She would invariably finish with the words: "Keep your own nose clean." And we had to live up to this teaching in its strictest sense.

The show that night went off without a hitch. Peter O'Dolan called for me at six-thirty in a car. The car belonged to a Baron something-or-other, who was Irish, fat, red-faced and full of diamonds. It was because of the diamonds that he was called "Baron". He sat in the front of the car with the chauffeur and Peter and I sat in the back. The other three acts had all piled into another car and gone on ahead of us. We caught up with them somewhere on Broadway in the late hundreds and the two cars kept nearly side by side for the rest of the journey.

Perhaps it was the fact that the Baron had two cases of champagne in the car, and had invited us all to join him in a spree after we had finished, that put us all in such good humour. We ragged the Baron, who took it like a grand sport. We teased him mostly about his diamonds. He had three or four diamond rings on each hand, diamond cuff links, diamond shirt studs; the one in his tie pin was as big as a nickel, and he carried a diamond studded cane. He was nice. He would look in the car mirror, put his hand up to his tie pin and wriggle it, and move his hands about so that the stones flashed; then he would lean back in his seat and say contentedly: "Deplorable taste! deplorable taste!" You couldn't help but like him when he said that.

When we got into Scarsdale we were in top form. Everything went with a grand swing, although no one had rehearsed. It was as if the audience had joined with the cast for the accomplishment of one aim—to have fun. And we succeeded.

The Baron, who was as jolly as he was fat, and that was plenty, got everyone of our party gloriously drunk except the chauffeur, the driver of the other car, and myself. The chauffeur didn't drink while he was on duty, the other driver said that it was his turn to carry the others home, and I—well, I had seen too much whiskey in my young life ever to want to try it. We three ganged together and had a grand time laughing at the rest. We thought the Baron, being well under the weather himself, had forgotten about us. But not he. About midnight, when the party that followed the entertainment was well under way, two waiters arrived (we never knew where from), bearing an enormous cardboard box between them, and asked for the Baron. The Baron staggered out to them, took in the box, asked them how they liked his diamonds, paid them, and sent them on their way. He called the chauffeur and told him that we three sober people were to have what was in the box; he hoped it would please us, and if we wanted anything else we were to be sure and ask for it. We hied the box off into a corner and took off the lid. Inside was every imaginable delicacy. Ice cream, boxes of chocolates, hot coffee, sandwiches, cakes, fruit, nuts, etc.; enough for a dozen people. We called the rest of the gang and then dived into it.

It was long after three o'clock when we had collected all our party and bundled them into the cars. We sang till we were half-way home, then we fell asleep.

As for the people in Scarsdale, they had as good a time as we did. They liked us so much that they made us promise to come back and do our stuff again at a card party they were going to have some night in the latter part of the next month. They said they would pay us the same money.

But before the card party came to pass, a great many things happened.

The bell captain in the hotel quit his job and Eddie was made bell captain in his place. The moment he got his new job, Eddie changed. He was no longer the easy-going, fun-loving boy that he was before. Nothing suited him, not even myself, whom up to then he had made his special charge. Before, my size had made him laugh. Now he said: "It doesn't look well for the hotel to see somebody so small working in it. People will think you're not capable." He would collar the bellboys. If one of them was delivering ice-water Eddie would stop him, look into the pitcher, and send the boy back for more ice; or when they were standing in the lobby, he would go over and busy himself brushing imaginary specks of dirt from their already speckless uniforms. I often wondered if Eddie realized how near he was to getting a swift sock on the button from one of them. He had not been two weeks on his new job when every member of the staff, myself included, hated him so much that we should have found the greatest pleasure in cutting his throat, except that he would have had us fired for it.

Every day he got worse. He got a new fad: he came up to me on Sunday afternoon and said: "You, Mullen, from now on you're to call me sir." On Sundays I worked the switchboard and so was bossed by the manager alone. I looked up at Eddie and said calmly: "Who let you out of your tree, Toots?" The desk clerk and a few of the boys happened to be standing near, and they all laughed. Eddie was wild. "I'll have you fired!" he cried. "You're talking to your superior."

"You can't fire me on Sundays and you know it," I retorted. "You're only my boss on week-days. Go hop your bells."

Of course he had a dead edge on me for that, and he made it his business to get back at me during the week. Sundays made up for it though, so far as I was concerned. The rest of the staff looked forward to it too. I used to hit the bell and call "Boy!" whenever Eddie was around, and send him on the poorest tipping calls, taking great joy in telling him to "shake a leg and snap into it".

In the meantime John was given the bell captain's job where he worked. From the stories he told me, I gathered that he had the place in a riot from morning till night.

He told me that one of the switchboard operators was going to leave, and asked if I would take the job if he spoke to the manager for me and got it. Now apart from Eddie, the job I had was pie. I knew all the guests, the work was easy and I had a lot of fun; so I refused John's offer.

Then one morning John and I decided to go down to Broadway and see a movie at one of the houses that opened at ten o'clock. We went to Broadway, but not to a movie. We decided that there wouldn't be enough time, as I had to be at work at twelve, so we bought a bag of doughnuts and went to an auction instead. When we left the auction, where John had nearly turned the auctioneer's head grey with his offer of "have a doughnut mister?" after each spiel, it was eleven-thirty. "Gosh, John," I said, "I'll have to rush or I'll be late, and Eddie——"

"Never mind Eddie," John interrupted. "I'll go in and wait in the lobby till you come up on the floor. If he says anything to you I'll tell him to go shine his buttons."

"No, don't," I protested. "You'll only make it worse."

"I'll be in the lobby," said John firmly, and I knew it would be useless to argue.

Well, to make a long story short, I was five minutes late coming up on the floor. Eddie was waiting, teetering back and forth on his heels and toes and rubbing his hands together. A few feet away from him was John, standing with his hands in his pockets, his hat pushed on to the back of his head, his face full of suppressed laughter.

"I suppose", Eddie greeted me, "that you think you'll be let work to-day."

I wouldn't have minded what he said if there hadn't been so much pleasure in his voice when he said it. He kept rubbing the palms of his hands together, and that made me flaming mad, so mad that I couldn't answer him. He went on speaking in that tone of voice, saying one thing nastier than the other, till I could feel my face burning. There were a good many people about, and they could all see that I was being taken over the coals: Eddie saw to that. And as if it weren't obvious and I wasn't feeling miserable enough, he began pointing his finger and shaking it at me, which is the one form of scolding that I can't take. It makes me feel like a little poodle when its fat mistress says: "Mamma will spank her pupsie-wupsie if it does that on the floor again."

"Don't point your finger at me please," I said. "I don't like it."

"Why, you little two by four, you'll take it and like it," said Eddie.

John stepped up to my side; he was blazing. "Where's your guts, Babs?" he asked. "You're not going to stand for that, are you?"

"No!" I cried, and slapped Eddie's face. Eddie was staggered; so was I, for I hadn't intended to slap him at all.

"You——!" Eddie gasped. "You——! You're fired!"

"Fired hell!" said John laughing. "She quit this job ten minutes ago. Come on Babs. Go and change your clothes and get your money, then come with me and learn what it's like to work in a good hotel."

I went to work with John the next afternoon. My hours were the same as his: from 8 a.m. to 4 p.m. and from 4 p.m. to midnight, on alternate days. The salary was $20 a week, and we got every second Sunday off.

I met Kitty, who told me some of the facts of life on the very first day, and said when she'd finished: "John asked me to tell you. He thought you should know."

Afterwards I heard her talking to John. "Lord!" she said, "imagine finding a kid of sixteen in this man's age, not knowing what it's all about. You'd never think she'd been on the stage all her life. More as if she were kept in a convent since her baby days."

"Her mother", said John, "made that her business."

Chapter Ten

John has a Wedding

★

Kitty worked late for me on the night I went to Scarsdale again.

This time the Baron couldn't make it, and even before we started there was no kick or spirit in any of the members of the show.

Half-way to Scarsdale I turned to Peter and said: "I shouldn't have come. I haven't danced since we were here last and I'm scared."

"Scared? What of?"

"I don't know," I admitted. "I'm just scared silly. I don't want to go out before all those people to-night. I can't."

"Don't be funny," said Peter. "Of course you can. You'll be all right once you get out on the stage."

"I doubt it," I answered. And I was right.

I had to sing. My voice shook and broke and squeaked all the way through the song—the same one that I had sung there before and put over with a bang.

Just before I was to dance somebody handed me a flask and said: "Take a drink quick, you need it!"

"No thank you," I said. "It won't do any good."

I was shaking. My feet felt as heavy as lead when I

went on again. As my mother would put it, "all the heart for dancing had gone out of me". So far as the audience was concerned, I might as well have been dancing to a brick wall.

Peter was very angry. When our part was finished he turned to me and said furiously: "You flopped!"

"I know it," I said. "I told you I couldn't do it."

When he heard that, he was all for making me go back on to the stage again. "Go out there and raise hell," he said. "I'll go out with you. If you don't put it over to-night you'll never be able to face an audience again."

Some of the others gathered round; they all agreed with Peter and coaxed and bullied. But though I knew they were right I couldn't get up nerve enough to leave the wings. I made two or three starts; Peter even went out and announced something or other, but still I couldn't make it, though they were nearly shoving me from behind. Finally I burst into tears, begged them to leave me alone and ran off to my dressing-room.

I don't know who went on the stage for me that night, but I didn't care. When I reached the dressing-room, I took off my costume and make-up, dressed, and went out and sat in the car till it was time to go.

Peter didn't speak to me during the drive home. Some of the others asked me what had made me go to pieces like that. All I could say was that I didn't know.

Life in my new job went on smoothly enough for the first two or three weeks. Then I began to get calls from nearly every room in the hotel from people who said that they were going to complain to the manager about the poor telephone service. It was awful. The better service I tried to give, the more complaining calls I got. It was always a man's voice, and I finally found out that it was John's. He gave the game away by bursting into laughter in the middle of a long rigmarole of complaint. He could disguise his voice but not his laugh.

Then it happened that every night when I was on late a call would come in at eleven-thirty. It was a man's voice, and he always asked the same question: "May I take you home? I'll meet you outside the hotel door. I'll be in a cab." For a while I thought it must be Kitty for whom he was asking, so I used to say: "Kitty isn't on duty to-night," and cut him off. But one night he started on a different note. It was: "Please don't cut me off because I'll keep calling back again till you talk to me, and I *don't* want Kitty."

"I'm sorry," I said. "Is it a guest in the hotel that you wish to speak to? If so, who will I connect you with please?"

"I don't want to speak to anyone but you," said the voice impatiently. "You're the little one aren't you?"

"I am," said I. "What do you want?"

"I want to take you home to-night, may I?" said he. "I'll be outside the——"

"Hotel door," I interrupted him, "and you'll be in a cab. Stop being funny and please don't call again." With that I cut him off. He was back in a few minutes. "Good gracious!" I exclaimed when I recognized the voice: "Will you stop pestering me?"

"No," he replied.

I was beginning to get scared. "Just a minute," I said, "I've got a call."

"I'll wait," he said.

I called to John who was standing in the lobby. "Pick up the desk phone and listen in to this," I said. "He's been calling up every night for a long time. I cut him off a few minutes ago but he's back again."

"Who is it?" John asked.

"I don't know," said I. "Listen in and tell me what to do."

"Okay," said John, and picked up the phone.

I made the connection and opened the keys. "Hello," I said.

"Hello," replied the unknown.

"Now will you explain why you keep calling me every night?" I asked. "What is it you want?"

"I want you," said the voice. "I want to meet you—to take you home."

I looked over at John. His lips were forming the words "play up". I nodded.

"But I don't know who you are or anything about you," I said to the voice. "And anyway why pick on me? It would be different if I'd ever seen you, maybe I have, but I don't know your voice. Besides, how do I know that it's home you'd take me?"

"You can trust me," came the reply. "We'll go to a midnight show first and I'll take you home afterwards. How does that sound to you?"

"Sounds okay," I said, obeying John's violent nodding. "But just the same——" I went on as if reluctant.

"Please, really I won't do you any harm."

"Well, if you promise to take me right home after the show——"

"I do," said the voice, "I promise. Is it a date?"

"It's a date," I agreed. "I'll meet you outside at five minutes past twelve."

John hurried over to me. "Now what?" I asked.

"Get the house detective," he directed, "and tell him to come down here right away."

"I'll get him," I said, "if you'll tell me where he's to be found. He could be anywhere." Usually when I called the house detective, whether I tried the roof or the cellar, or any floor in between, or all at the same time, I got the same reply, "Well, he was here a minute ago—just left—if I see him I'll send him down——"

"Try the engineer's office," said John. "Tell him it's murder, kidnapping, anything, only get the house detective. That's where he most likely is."

So I called the engineer's office. "I want Bill," I said, "right away. It's urgent. Is he there?"

"Bill?" said the engineer. "No, not now. He left here a minute ago——"

"But good gravy he's got to be found!" I cried. "The manager is up here in the lobby——"

"Manager up there?" interrupted the engineer. "At this hour? Wow! Hey Bill," I heard him call. "It's something serious. You'd better scram."

I heard the sound of a chair being pushed back, then a familiar complaining voice: "Hell! Can't a man ever get any rest around this joint? I suppose some old dame thought there was a man in her room and now she's squawking 'cos there isn't. Oh, my feet. Well, I suppose I might as well go up and see what's eating them. Don't know what they'd do if I wasn't here. . . ." his voice faded. I heard a door being closed.

"Babs!" said the engineer excitedly, "what's it all about?"

"Wouldn't you like to know?" I said sarcastically. " 'He left here a minute ago.' Baloney!"

We heard the house detective's heavy breathing and footsteps long before we saw him. When he did appear, he was walking as slowly as he possibly could.

"Hey lightning," John called to him. "Where'd you leave the rest of the funeral?"

"Smart guy huh!" said Bill. "What's the idea? What do you want? What's the matter?"

"He's awake at last," said John admiringly. "Come here till I tell you a pretty story."

"Spill it," said Bill.

John told him. Bill listened intently, saying nothing but "huh, huh," at odd intervals, till the story was finished. "And you don't know who he is?" he asked me then.

"No," I said.

"How long's he been calling up?"

"Every late night for ages," I replied.

Bill glanced at the clock. It wanted ten minutes to twelve. He picked up the desk phone. "Get me the nearest police station," he said briefly. He beckoned to John and spoke to him in a low tone while I made the connection. When Bill began to speak into the mouthpiece John called the bellboys together. They all joined Bill and waited till he had finished his conversation. They talked with him for a few minutes, then they came over to me. "You'll have to be in on this with us," said Bill. "There'll be two plain-clothes men here—here they are now," he broke off, and went to meet two men who had just entered the lobby. He brought them back with him.

"Is this the girl?" they asked.

Bill nodded.

One of the men began to speak. He spoke so rapidly that I couldn't understand a word he said. When he had finished, Bill turned to me. "This is what you've got to do Babs," he said. I listened carefully while he outlined his plan to me. It was this: I was to get the man to come out of the cab if possible. The two plain-clothes men, Bill, the bellboys and John were to be standing by, ready to nab him the moment he stepped on to the sidewalk.

"I won't go near the cab," I demurred. "My mother warned me about men like him."

"But we'll be right there," said Bill.

"That doesn't make me feel any better," I returned. "Besides, I don't see what all the fuss is about. Maybe he's just soft in the head. It'll make me feel like a rat to trap him that way."

"Now you listen to me," said Bill. "There's a man in this town who makes a practice of calling a half-dozen hotels every night and asking the operators to go out with him. Some of them did. They never came back. We have reason to believe that this is the man. It's five past twelve. Will you do as we ask or are you too yellow?"

"Why didn't you tell me all that in the first place?" I said. "I'll do my part."

"You know what to do?"

"I've got it," I said. "Don't mind me. You do your stuff." I didn't like being called yellow.

A few minutes later I was standing outside the hotel

door. Bill and the others were posted in corners all about me. I felt somehow as if it were the opening night of a big show. I hoped I'd remember my lines. I coughed, and as if it were a cue, a cab came speeding down the street. It came to a stop at the curb in front of me. "So you did turn up," said the now familiar voice. "I was afraid you might change your mind. Come on——" the cab door was thrown open.

"You're not afraid of me are you?" as I made no motion towards getting any closer to it.

"Well, no," I said and hesitated. "But I'd kind of like to see you first."

"You can see me in here as well as on the sidewalk."

I laughed. "Now who's afraid?" I said. "Come on out, I won't bite you."

There was no answer. Someone nudged me from behind. "I only want to have a look at your face," I went on. "After all, you can't expect a girl to go out with a man who won't even let her see what he looks like——" I saw the figure as he leaned forward in the seat, I could see his hand as he grasped hold of the inside door handle, He pulled himself up out of the seat, and his head and shoulders came part way out of the cab—then suddenly he shot back into it, the door was pulled shut with a loud bang, there was a shout, and the cab shot away up the street, turned the corner, and disappeared.

Bill and the others rushed out. They were all shouting and blaming each other for bungling the job. "If you'd had a car there you'd have got him all right," said one of the bellboys.

"He wouldn't have stopped at all if there had been a car anywhere near him," said Bill. "Well he's slipped us anyway. We'll never get another chance like that." He shook his head mournfully. The other two detectives went off, the boys went back to their posts, John went downstairs to change, and I waited in the lobby for him to take me home.

Kitty, hard-boiled as she was, was entirely loyal. Many a time she excused John and me to the manager when, off larking somewhere, we arrived late for work. She would keep thinking up excuses till we got there, at the risk of her own job. We could always depend on Kitty, we knew that she would rather sink with us than swim without us.

Now Kitty was a boozer: as John often expressed it, "she'd drink the seven seas dry". But we all loved her. There was something charming in the way she said "Me and Henry Ford," when the boys asked her for cigarettes or borrowed lunch money. And when she had done you a favour and you said breathlessly "Thanks Kitty. You're a peach!" she would say "Nothing to it kid. Me and the manager—just like that," indicating the two first fingers of her right hand, which she would place close together. There was something even in the way she chewed her gum that made you love her.

The day of the big battle was one of my early days. I went in at 8 a.m., and was to work till Kitty relieved me at four in the afternoon. Four o'clock passed, five o'clock passed and there was no sign of Kitty. John, who was supposed to be off at four also, said: "I'll stick around till we hear from her," and stayed on duty.

Kitty arrived at six-thirty, too drunk to work. I told her to go home. She insisted that she had never been so boozo that she couldn't hold down a job. I called John. "Put her in a cab and send her home," I said. "If the boss ever sees her she's sunk. I'll work her shift."

"Okay," said John. But Kitty wouldn't hear of it. "No!" she cried. No one was going to work till midnight for her, she was perfectly able to do it herself. John and I looked at each other in despair.

"What do you think?" he asked.

"It's no use asking that," said I. "She's not able to run the board, that's all there is to it."

"Yeah, but what will we do?"

"I've got it," I said. "You take over for a few minutes. If the boss comes along tell him that the operator has gone to supper. I'll take Kitty in to the Ladies' Room and put her lying down. Get her another drink. It'll knock her out and she'll sleep it off."

John agreed to the plan, and sent one of the boys out for a bottle of whiskey, which he sent in to me in the Ladies' Room.

I poured out a stiff drink and gave it to Kitty. It had no effect, but the second one made her sit down, and the third put her to sleep. I put a sofa pillow under her head, made her as comfortable as I possibly could, and left her.

Now every job has its rat, story-carrier or squealer. Our job was no exception. We had long suspected Leo, one of the bellboys. We never let him in on our conversations, secrets or fun, since the day he had said to Kitty that Bill was lazy, and didn't she think the manager should be told about it? Kitty had told Leo what she thought of him in no uncertain terms, and he had held a grudge against her ever since.

Unfortunately Leo was on duty when Kitty came in, and he saw her. Unfortunately, too, the manager chose to take a walk round the lobby before going out that evening. He stopped by the switchboard when he saw me and said, surprised: "What are you doing here at this hour Miss Mullen? Didn't you work the early shift to-day?"

"No sir," I replied. "Kitty and I broke up the day. I owed her a night off."

Leo was standing by and heard all this. John was standing by also: he was watching Leo. Try as I did, I could think of no reason to send Leo off anywhere. If we could only get him away from the manager, or if the latter would only go out before Leo told him anything, to delay his hearing the story till Kitty got sober, then we could all deny it. Leo wouldn't have a leg to stand on. But Leo was already plucking at the manager's sleeve, clamouring for attention. I could see John's face, it was flushed with anger. I knew how he felt: I would have strangled Leo myself if I could.

"I'd like to tell you something sir."

"What is it, Leo?" the manager asked.

"She's not telling the truth," said Leo. "They didn't break up the day. She's got to work because Kitty came in drunk and had to be taken to the Ladies' Room to sleep it off. It's happened more than once——"

"You skunk!" John's fist connected with Leo's chin.

I was very pleased. "Give him one for me John!" I cried. "And remember we'll get fired now anyway, so do him up brown."

"Watch my smoke," returned John, and laced into Leo to the best of his ability, which wasn't bad at all.

The lobby at that time was crowded with guests in evening dress, all on their way to the dining-room to dinner. They formed a circle round John and Leo, and began to take sides and make bets on the winner. Some of them were half boozo; those who weren't stood around with the others to see the fun. The fight wasn't stopped until a woman seeing the blood on Leo's face became ill. There were a few remarks, and a man stepped into the circle, lifted John's arm above his head and shouted: "The winnah!" on which the crowd dispersed, laughing.

The manager was too angry to speak at first. When he did, it was mostly splutter. "Rowdies!" he cried. "Hooligans! You've disgraced the hotel. You're both fired."

"Are you telling us?" said John. "Come on, Babs."

"Coming," I said. "How about Kitty?"

"We'll collect her on the way out," said he. We, or rather I, succeeded in rousing her enough to get her out of the Ladies' Room, and between us we walked her out of the hotel. The three of us got into a cab—and so ended another day's work.

"The two of you take a week off before you look for another job," said my mother. "You need rest."

We accepted the suggestion with pleasure.

John announced one morning that his sister Peggy was returning from Chicago and was going to live in her old apartment. She had already arranged by letter about renting it, and a friend of hers was to do the furnishing, so that it would be all ready for her to walk into and resume housekeeping where she had left off. John looked at the letter in his hand. "She's probably moved in already," he said. "She was to leave Chicago the day she posted this."

"Will you be going back to stay with her, John?" my mother asked.

"I will not," John replied. "This is my home, and here I stick till you throw me out."

"Then I've taken on a life job. But what will Peggy say?"

"Peggy", said John, "didn't know that you'd come to New York to stay. If she did she'd be living with you or on you too, you know that. We'd all park here if you'd let us."

"You'd better go up and see her," said my mother.

"That's where I'm going. Coming, Babs?"

"No," my mother answered for me. "She has work to do right here."

"And you said we'd have the week off," said John plaintively. "I thought there was a catch in it somewhere."

"You're not getting away with a thing," my mother said. "The windows are to be cleaned first thing in the morning. Will you be back for dinner?"

"I will," John laughed and went out.

"John is very late," my mother remarked anxiously as we sat in at table that evening, after holding the meal back for an hour. "I hope nothing has happened to him."

"Nothing has," said Puffy. "You needn't worry about him, he'll be——" he broke off suddenly, staring at the door. We turned our heads to see what was causing him to stare so. The door was opening, slowly, inch by inch.

We couldn't see anybody, but we could hear heavy breathing. It was a full minute before the door was all the way back, and then John stepped in.

John's usual entry was preceded by a loud merry whistle and a throwing open of the door; we always knew when he was coming. It was no wonder that we gasped when we saw him come in the way he did.

He looked at no one, but walked over and sat by the window, slowly, like a person walking in his sleep.

My mother broke the silence. "Aren't you well, John?" she asked. John made no reply, but sighed, a deep sigh. "Is anything wrong with Peggy? You haven't quarrelled with her have you?"

No reply.

My mother motioned to us to go on eating as if nothing out of the ordinary had happened. "Come and have your dinner, John," she said casually, and then went on eating as if she had forgotten about him completely.

It worked. After a few minutes during which no one paid the slightest attention to him, John came over and took his place at the table. He began to eat, slowly, as if he didn't know what he was doing.

"What on earth is the matter with you John?" my mother spoke impatiently. "Stop doing that!" as John sighed again. "You sound like a bellows. What is it?"

And John spoke. "Ah!" he said and sighed rapturously. "I've met an angel."

"Good God!" my mother dropped her fork in amazement. "You've met a what?"

"I've met an angel," he repeated. "I'm in love."

"Well for goodness' sake!" I exclaimed.

"My gosh!" said Puffy.

Winnie looked on questioningly. She wasn't quite sure whether he was being funny or not. "Does he mean it Mama?" she asked.

My mother looked at John intently. "I believe he does," she said at last. "He's serious. When did this happen John? Where did you meet her and what is she like?"

"Up at Peggy's," said he. "Oh! she's an angel. She's not like anyone else. She's different."

"They all are," said my mother briefly. "But tell us about her."

John went into raptures. "She's beautiful," he cried. "She's perfect——" He kept on in this strain till we were so thoroughly fed up on his angel that we couldn't listen to him any longer.

"Can she walk and talk?" Puffy asked heavily.

"She must be very queer," put in Winnie.

I was too disgusted to speak.

"Tell me John," said my mother, beautifully sarcastic, "does she eat and drink like an ordinary human being?"

"Yes," said John. "But not very much, hardly anything."

"I suppose", said my mother, "that when you first saw her, she was picking, just picking mind you, at a dainty little salad?"

"She was," said John.

"Do you by any chance know her name?"

"Stella. Isn't it like music?"

"No," said my mother bluntly. "It's like anything else but, and she sounds like anything but the kind of a person I'd like to have around the house. Don't bring her down here, I'm warning you. Angel indeed!"

For weeks we heard nothing from John but Stella, Stella this, Stella that, Stella here and Stella there. We got it for breakfast, lunch and dinner. He mooned and sighed all over the place. Then one night he asked my mother if he could bring his Stella to visit us.

"No," said my mother firmly. "I will not have any angels parading around this house. This family is quite content to wait till judgment day to see its angels, human or otherwise."

We were all so tired of hearing about Stella by this time that we nearly hated her. Winnie, who was then nearing her tenth birthday, was the only one who had any sense in the matter. "Let him bring her down, Mama," she said. "Maybe she acts as funny as he does."

"There is wisdom" said my mother with a wicked gleam in her eye, "in young heads. By all means, John, bring your Stella to see us."

John was delighted. "You'll be awfully nice to her won't you?" he asked. "And have the house looking especially neat because she's very particular about things like that. And have something special for dinner, nothing greasy, she doesn't like greasy foods. And don't get any beer or wine, I think she doesn't like them either. Have something dainty, she likes dainty things ——" Do you wonder that we almost hated her?

"John," my mother interrupted him. "You may bring Stella to dinner to-morrow evening, but right now you'd better run—and don't mention her name again or I'll strangle her on sight."

"I know of no dish greasier than pigs' feet and cabbage," she said the next morning, "and of nothing that goes down so well with it as beer. That is what we're going to have for dinner to-night."

Stella was the subject of our conversation for the rest of the day—we were trying to guess what she looked like, and wondering if she acted as stupidly about John as he did about her.

John stood by Stella's side when they came in. "Here she is," he said proudly. And he had reason to be proud. She was nearly as tall as John, blonde, slim and lovely. My mother eyed her approvingly. There wasn't a hair out of place.

She walked over, holding out both hands to my mother. "Thank you so much for allowing John to bring me," she said warmly, sincerely, and won my mother's heart.

"This is Babs of course, the dancer——" and I was hooked too.

"Oh, and I know you're Puffy, you're so strong-looking and broad-shouldered." I could see Puffy's chest swelling as he joined the rest of us round her little finger.

"And Winnie, why you're nearly as tall as Babs——" I didn't like that so much, but when I saw Winnie looking so pleased I was pleased too.

She had a way with her, had Stella: she made us all feel like special people.

"Isn't she grand?" John asked. "Just like I told you?"

"Not a bit of it," my mother retorted. "She's no more like an angel than I'm like the bearded lady." My mother was flustered. She was sorry now for the pigs' feet and beer, but she didn't know what to do about it, because the smell of both was all over the house.

"Beer!" said Stella suddenly, spotting the pitcher. "Hooray! I haven't had a drink of good beer since the batch I made myself last summer." She began to sniff. "And a boiled dinner! I'm sure it's a boiled dinner."

"It is," said my mother. "It's pigs' feet and cabbage."

"How sweet of you to have it. John must have told how much I like it."

"John", said my mother, on her way to the kitchen, "is a worm."

"She's grand, John," Stella laughed, "exactly as you said she'd be." John was having the time of his young life. "I told her you liked dainty this and thatses," he said. "I knew she'd have pig's feet and beer. Don't forget what I told you. We'll have some fun."

The dinner was a great success. Stella ate till she was grease to the ears, and drank till my mother said: "If you take much more you'll be frothing at the mouth." The only thing that in any way tended to spoil the evening was that she and John called each other "darling" and "sweetheart" all over the place. My mother, after listening to them for a while, eyed first one and then the other. "If you two can't behave any better than that," she said, "leave the table. I've never seen two sottier people in my life."

"John, she's priceless," Stella gasped.

"You bit, ma," said Puffy. "They just wanted to get you started."

Then followed the two months of John's hectic courtship. The more we saw of Stella, the more we liked her. The more John saw of Stella, the crazier he got. He used to get ideas about her in the early hours of the morning. He would wake up wondering if she loved him, rush madly to the nearest telephone, call her up and ask her. One night, or rather one morning, she said: "For goodness' sake go back to bed and sleep it off!" John, in the depths of despair, woke us all up to tell us that he was going to end it all. Stella didn't love him. "Who would?" said my mother, glancing at the clock, "at four o'clock in the morning? She couldn't and be human. Take an aspirin."

John paced the floor of his room till daylight. Then he woke us up again with a loud shout of "Now or never!" and rushed out, banging the door after him.

"Shall I follow him, mom?" Puffy asked. "He may be going to bump himself off."

"Not he," my mother replied. "And stop using slang. John will come back when he's hungry."

John returned in time for breakfast. He had his beloved in tow, and announced joyfully that they were going to be married.

"When?" my mother asked.

"We're going down for the licence as soon as we have something to eat——"

They were married at the end of the week. The wedding was held in Peggy's apartment. Peggy, as delightfully irresponsible as John, left all the arrangements to my mother.

Everything went very smoothly till it was time to cut the wedding cake, then it was found that John and Stella had disappeared. My mother was worried. "I do hope they're all right," she said anxiously. "Of course

John is crazy enough to do anything, but Stella has a bit of sense, she'd never leave her guests this way."

First we hunted up Peggy. We found her sitting on top of the piano, eating nuts. We asked her if she knew where Stella and John had gone. "Last I saw of them they were wrestling with a bottle," said Peggy, and went on eating nuts.

We searched every room but the pantry, and that of course was where they were. Winnie found them. They were sitting on the floor with five or six others, playing dice. "And what", said my mother, "do you think you're doing?"

"Shooting crap," said John. "We haven't the price of our train tickets."

"Train tickets? Where are you going?"

"Boston," said Stella. "We're going to live there."

"When did you get that idea?"

"A few minutes ago. We're going to get the midnight train."

"Midnight hell!" said my mother. "Come out and cut your wedding cake. A nice thing—playing dice at your own wedding!"

John and Stella did go to Boston to live. They opened a small grocery store, and proceeded to keep the neighbourhood in which they lived supplied with laughs as well as groceries, while they made money hand over fist.

I sent a hasty letter to my father telling him not to write till he heard from me again, as I could no longer get his letters at the old address. I would not go there without John, and six months passed before I found another address. It was that of a new job, and a badly needed one.

Chapter Eleven

Ship for Aran

★

Shortly after John left us, Puffy was out of work. I was still "loafing". Daily, Puffy and I tramped the streets looking for work. I even tried to get a job with a show, but that fell flat too. The money my mother had saved went quickly. There was no joking now about lunch money. There was no money.

My job-less months were from November till May. The winter was a fierce one: cold below zero, snowstorm after snowstorm; we had no fire, no light, no heavy clothes—we had nothing. Day after day we saw Winnie come home from school with her hands blue with cold, her feet nearly out through her shoes, her body nearly frozen under her threadbare spring coat. All we could do was to stand by and watch her thin little body grow thinner.

Then one day I saw a sign outside an employment agency: "Elevator operators wanted. Twenty dollars per week. No experience necessary." Twenty dollars seemed a fabulous sum to me that day. My feet ached, and it was weeks since I had eaten a real meal. I was sure I should not get the job, but I thought as I looked at the sign that at least I could sit down and rest my feet for a few minutes. However, when I entered the office I hadn't a chance of sitting down, for there were no other applicants waiting, and I was attended to at once. "Ever run an elevator before?" the man asked.

"Yes," I said.

"Thank God!" he exclaimed fervently. "It might be a help. Every other girl I sent down there got sick from the motion of the cars. You might be able to stick it, having run an elevator before. The only thing is—" and he hesitated "—you should be five foot three and good looking, pretty."

"I'd be five foot three in high heels," I said.

He studied me for a moment. "You wouldn't be bad looking," he murmured, "but you're so thin and sort of tired. Been out of a job long?" he asked abruptly.

"Yes."

"Hungry?"

"I've been hungry for months," I said.

"Mmmn—poor kid. My lunch will be here in a few minutes; wait and have a cup of coffee. It'll make you look better and feel better. In the meantime I'll telephone down and have them hold that job for you. You may be lucky."

"Thanks."

"Got car fare?" he asked a few minutes later, as he handed me a glassful of hot coffee.

"No," I replied. "I can walk to wherever it is."

"I doubt it," he said. "It's the Transportation Building, down near City Hall. You'd never make it. I'll advance you a dime and you can pay me out of your first week's salary."

"And if I don't get the job?"

"You will," he said. "It's eight dollars, by the way, to be paid in advance; but we can let that slide too till you get paid."

To find a man like that in charge of an employment agency, where they are usually as hard-hearted as a lobster and sometimes as nippy, is so rare that I have often wondered since whether he was just naturally decent, or whether I looked so done up that it got the better of him. You can't help mistrusting employment agency men; after a few clashes, you have to.

The superintendent at the Transportation Building looked me over: "You're a bit short," he said, "but they need one more to make up the crew. It's a new building."

"Is it as high as this?" I asked.

"No," he replied. "It's only thirty-five storeys, but you break in on these cars."

He put me in charge of a girl dressed in a very smart uniform, and told her to see whether I should do. I did. The elevators went at lightning speed, nearly a floor a second. They worked automatically: all the operator had to do was press the buttons for the floors, close the doors and start the car. The doors and the "start" motion of the car were controlled by a small lever or handle. It was so easy that I immediately suspected a snag.

Down on the main floor was a board, full of numbers and lights. There were two or three "starters", who kept their eyes almost continually on this board, watching the numbers and lights. I found out the reason from the operator who was breaking me in.

"Every car has a number," she explained, "and every number is shown on that board, as well as the number of every floor in the building. The starter can tell by watching the board exactly how long you stop on a floor, what floor you're on, whether you skip a stop, whether you're going up or down, what switch you're using—he's got a much tougher job than ours."

"What's tough about this job?" I asked. "It looks simple to me; and why does he have to watch what we're doing?"

"His job", said she, "is to see that no one has to wait more than twenty seconds for elevator service, no matter what floor in the building they're on."

"Oh," I said vaguely. "And what's the snag about the operator's job?"

"The operator? She has to get from the bottom to the top floor and back again, making her required number of stops, in a given number of seconds. To do that, she has to hurry the people in and out of the elevator as if she were a subway guard, and yet keep them all in good humour. She is not allowed to talk to them, yet she can't be rude. She's got to have a quick eye, a quicker brain, and self control in case of accidents. She's got to look at all times as if she had just stepped out of a band-box, spick and span——"

I interrupted her at that point. "Spare me the rest," I said. "I'll take it by degrees."

I was hired and told to report to Mr. Hogan, who was head starter in the thirty-five storey building at the foot of John Street. There were fifteen elevator operators including myself. They were all five foot three or over in flat-heeled shoes. After one day's work on the elevator I wore flat heels too, which made me look so much shorter than the others that I was christened "Pee Wee".

The motion and speed of the cars made me violently ill the first day. It was even worse than sea sickness, but after a few days I became accustomed to the motion and it did not affect me any more.

I had never worked with a group of girls like these before. I had known and worked with chorus girls of course, but these were of a different type. Amongst them I felt like the man who woke up to find himself in a strange country where the people spoke a different language from his own. I could not understand the girls, and to be honest, I did not try to. After a bad beginning, I got into my shell and stayed there. One of the girls, during the first week, remarked: "Why the false accent, Mullen?" Now my accent wasn't false. It was just Boston, and a Boston accent is almost as different from a New York one as Chinese is from Cockney. But it was no use my saying that, in fact there was no use in my saying anything, so I let it slide. Once they invited me to a party. I could not give a definite answer to the invitation because I did not know whether or not my mother would allow me to accept it. "You don't mean to say that you have to ask your mother's permission?" one of the girls asked in amazement.

"Of course I do," I replied.

"Well, of all the sissies! Don't you know that nobody does that any more? Asking your mother about anything went out in the gay nineties." Nevertheless I did ask my mother, and was told that I was not to attend the party. More amazement and jeers were occasioned by the fact that I accepted my mother's decision. Catcalls of "Mother's little darling", "Sweet young thing" and "Goody goody", followed me all over the place.

Everything I said and did was commented on and laughed at. There is no worse feeling than that of knowing that the people you work with think you a freak. Their remarks, which at first I could not understand, became through constant repetition fairly clear to me. I would come up from lunch with my face burning, ashamed to look anyone in the eyes. Finally I asked my mother to let me quit. "They'll leave me nothing to believe in," I sobbed. "I don't want to be like them."

"Do you think I want you to be there?" she replied. "But Puffy isn't working, and if you leave it—well, you know what hunger is like."

So I stayed in the job. I admit that if I had made any attempt to understand the girls, my first two years at John Street might have been happier ones. As it was, they were so near to hell that there was no fun in them.

My father's letters, which I now received at John Street, became less frequent and shorter. He was very busy, he said, and had a great undertaking on hand which he would tell me about as soon as he could. He knew that I should understand and be patient. In the meantime, P.J. was going to write.

It was fun to become acquainted with the little brother whom I had never really known. P.J.'s letters bubbled over with fun and good-natured raillery. He told me tales of Aran, of the sea, of long talks and yarnings by a turf fire on winter nights; of his friends, and the things they did and talked about. He was impatient to see me. Would I never come to Aran? he asked. He would take very good care of me, he said, and it wasn't right for sister and brother to be separated. We should be together, know each other. I thoroughly agreed with him. Aran grew on me. My love for my father and for P.J. grew with every letter. Then suddenly the letters ceased. At intervals a short note arrived from P.J., telling me how busy he and "Paw" were. Once he mentioned that they were working on a film, but no more than that.

I grew to rely more and more on Jimmy Hines's company. We became engaged when I was eighteen, and planned to be married the following year. There was no one with whom I could talk about the wedding. Whenever I mentioned it to my mother she would change the subject. Winnie of course was too young. The girls at work were out of the question. At last I did what I ought to have done in the first place, and wrote to John. John answered the letter in person. He was before me when I got home from work the night after I had written to him. "Your letter came in this morning's mail," he said; "I got here as quickly as I could. What's on your mind? Start with the biggest things."

"Well," I began, "Jimmy and I are going to be married."

"Oh, oh, oh!" said John.

"What's the oh, oh, oh, for?" I asked.

"What kind of a job have you got, Babs?"

"What's my job got to do with getting married?"

"Well, getting married is a good reason for quitting—or hadn't you thought of that?"

"Of course I hadn't, you egg."

"You won't get married, not to Jimmy anyway," he said seriously.

"Why not?"

"It's not in the cards. Your mother wouldn't let you."

"She hasn't said anything about that to me."

"Well, she has to me. One of her reasons is that you're too young. Do you mind very much, Babs?"

"I mind terribly," I said. "Suppose we get married whether she likes it or not? I'm over eighteen, she can't stop me. She won't. We won't let her."

"What will you do?" John asked.

"I don't know. Run away, elope or something like that."

"No, you won't."

"I will!"

"What do you keep on saying you will for? You know perfectly well that you'll do as your mother tells you."

"I won't John. I mean it."

"Listen to me Babs, and don't get excited."

"I'm listening."

"Are you certain that you want to marry Jimmy?"

"I am."

"Your mother will never forgive you if you do. Do you care that much for him? Think before you answer."

I couldn't answer.

"Do you?" he asked again.

"I—I think—John, I don't know!" I said desperately.

"You ought to know. You ought to be sure, very sure."

"I was sure till you came."

"And now?"

"Now I'm miserable. I don't know."

"Let's change the subject," said John abruptly. "We'll come back to this later. How's the job going?"

"Awful. I hate it."

"What do you hate most?"

"Everything."

"Hmm . . . sounds like a good job. Tell your cousin John about it."

I gave him a detailed account of the girls, the cars and the passengers at John Street, which took nearly two hours. "You", said John when I had finished, "are the wrong one."

"Wrong one for what?" I asked.

"You're wrong for that job, but you're wrong too in the way you've judged the girls there, and the way you take the things they say."

"How do you know whether I am or not? You don't even know what they look like."

"I know the type. And remember this, you're probably as hard for them to bear, as they are for you."

"But John——"

"Listen to me. You've never met anything like those girls before; they've probably never met anything like you before either. They don't understand your way of thinking and living any more than you understand theirs."

"But I don't need to, John. I don't bother with them at all. I hardly speak to them."

"Why don't you?"

"Well——" I stumbled, "they laugh at me and poke fun at me, and as for the things they say—why they're terrible."

"Why don't you give them as good as they send?"

"Well—I couldn't."

"Why?"

"I—I don't bother."

"You think they're not good enough for you to bother with, is that it? Babs, you've developed into a damned snob."

"I have not!"

"You have. If you weren't a snob you'd like those girls, be able to get along better with them, and they'd like you. No wonder they keep their conversations dirty. It's their way of bringing you down to earth."

"You're wrong John, dead wrong."

"Oh am I? Well look here——" and so we argued back and forth for hours. The end of the argument saw me giving ground and John teaching me a lesson in how to be a human being. Then we returned to our first discussion.

"I've got to get this straightened out John," I said at last. "I'm going to ask mother about it, right now. I want to find out just what her objections to Jimmy are. Maybe we can get around them some way."

"You won't get around them," said John.

"I'm going to try, anyway."

My mother was in the kitchen preparing supper. "If you please mom," I said, "I'd like to speak to you."

"There's nothing to stop you," she said. "Go ahead."

"It's about Jimmy."

"Well?"

I found it difficult to go on. "I was talking to John just now," I managed.

"Well?"

"He was saying that——" I couldn't find the right words.

She stopped what she was doing and looked at me. "He told you that I object to Jimmy, is that what you're trying to say?"

"Yes," I said.

"He told you the truth," she said. "You'll not marry Jimmy."

"But why?"

"Because I say so. You're too young in the first place, and you're not a well-matched couple. You'd never be happy together."

"But we get on well enough now," I said.

"You're not married to him now. Keeping company and marriage are two very different things; get that through your silly head. You'll get over it after a while."

"Do you think so?"

"I know so," she said. "If you really cared for him you wouldn't stand there and take this so quietly. You couldn't. No girl could. If I thought you did care," she went on, "I wouldn't interfere. If you married him you'd not only wreck your own life, you'd make a mess of his too. You're not to see him again."

"Ever?"

"Don't be ridiculous. I'm not a warden. After another year or so you may see him as often as you like. But not now. You're not in love with him, he's just a habit. I'm right. You'll see that for yourself when you're a year older."

"But I'm sure——" I began.

"How can you be sure," she interrupted, "when you've never been out with another man but Jimmy?"

"I don't want to go with anyone else," I said.

"That's what I object to," she said. "Eighteen is too young for any girl to tie herself in a knot. You should be eager to go places and make friends, lots of friends. Oh no you don't"—as I turned to leave—"You don't leave this kitchen till you promise me that you won't see Jimmy again." Then the fun began. I would not promise and my mother barred the kitchen door. This lasted for a solid hour, but she won of course: she always did where I was concerned. "I promise," I said. "How shall I let him know? By letter?"

"No; by telephone, right now. Take John with you."

Outside the telephone booth I weakened. "I can't do it John," I said.

"Here's the nickel," said John. "I'll wait outside for you. Make it short."

The memory of that telephone conversation is a sort of a blur. Jimmy refused to listen, and insisted that I was playing some kind of a joke. When he finally realized that I was serious, all he could say was: "Why? Why?" over and over again. But I got him to promise not to write and not to try to meet me. "Why?" he asked. I wouldn't tell him. "Is that the way you want it?" he asked finally. "Yes," I said. We did not argue any more. I said good-bye and hung up the receiver.

When Jimmy inquired for me at John Street he was told that I no longer worked there. This I arranged with the boss, Mr. Hogan. When he inquired for me at home, he was told that I had gone out.

Attention to John's instructions worked miracles in my job. I began to make friends. On the day after the break with Jimmy, I went in to work without my engagement ring. One of the girls, Jeanne, noticed it immediately. "Hey girls!" she cried, "Pee Wee's hocked[1] her sparkler!"

Now, I didn't like Jeanne: I thought she hadn't a right feeling in her whole carcase; but I remembered John's lecture. "You're in the wrong pew, Jeanne," I said.

"What? You no hockey?" she asked.

"Me no hockey," I returned. "Me busty."

"No kidding, Pee Wee?" she said unbelievingly, "is it all off?"

"It's all off," I nodded.

I saw Jeanne again at lunch time. She was with another operator, Rose. The two of them came over to me. "Hw'ya Peanuts?" said Rose. "I suppose you're too high-toned to have lunch with us?"

"She couldn't see the plates," Jeanne said. "Holds her nose too high in the air."

"I'd love to have lunch with you," I said. "That is, if you're sure you don't mind?"

"We don't mind," said Rose. "We're not particular."

"Neither am I," I returned.

"Did that crack come out of you?" said Jeanne in surprise.

"It did," I laughed.

[1] Pawned.

"Why, the gal's human!" Rose gasped and caught hold of Jeanne in pretended shock.

"How's the old ticker feeling, Pee Wee?" Jeanne asked during lunch.

"Not so hot," I replied.

"What you ought to do is get another boy friend," she said seriously.

"Aw give the kid a chance to pick up the pieces," Rose put in.

"Do you know about it too?" I asked in surprise.

"Of course I do. What do you think I am, a Rip Van Winkle? All the girls know it by now."

"I think she ought to get another boy friend," Jeanne repeated.

"Are you still tuning that fiddle?" Rose exclaimed impatiently.

"I don't want another boy friend," I said.

"Then you ought to get a job or something to keep you busy at night, otherwise you'll think too much, and the next thing you know—pht! cracked goes the old cranium!"

"Jeanne is right, Pee Wee," said Rose. "What can you do besides run an elevator? Something you could do at night."

"Wait till I think," I said.

"Better swallow your mocha first," said Jeanne. "The strain might throw you."

"Heh, heh, heh, bright baby," Rose answered for me.

"I know what I could do," I said after a moment's reflection. "I could have a night dancing class. You know, from eight to eleven at night."

"What would you use for feet?"

"My own feet. I taught dancing before."

"Honest? What kind of dancing?"

"Irish dancing."

"Boy oh boy!" cried Rose so loud that all in the restaurant looked round at us. "Pee Wee's an Irish Jigger! Whee!"

"Hey, what did you three have for lunch?" somebody called over to us.

"Mexican Jumping Beans, wise guy," Jeanne retorted.

After two or three nights I realized that the girls were right in what they said. I tried to read, but could not concentrate. I went to the pictures and found myself looking at the screen without seeing what was on it. So I spoke to my mother about a night dancing class. "No one can work day and night too," she said.

"I'd rather for a while."

"Oh, I see. All right then," she agreed. "I'll attend to the advertising part of it."

The dancing class was a boon. I had an average of four or five pupils every night except Sunday: it kept my mind busy, and tired me so that I used to roll into bed exhausted every night.

I was now more confident with the girls at work, fairly sure of myself while there were no men about. But the memory of those first two years stuck in my brain. I have often wondered since whether the girls knew what their everyday conversation did to me. They joked and talked about men in a way that first disgusted and then terrified me. Marriage became something horrible to me, and men in general seemed loathsome creatures who had been put into the world for one reason. I was not quite nineteen, but I was as miserable and bitter as a sour old maid of fifty. This went on until one day Jeanne, who had gradually made herself my godmother, big sister and adviser, said casually: "I was talking to some of the boys to-day. They like you."

"I don't like them," I returned. "I don't like any man."

"Why?"

"They're all the same," I told her; "judging by what I've heard on this job, anyway."

"Yeah?"

"Yeah."

"We could talk about women that way too, Pee Wee, but it gives us more satisfaction to pan the men. There's good and bad of both."

"That makes no difference."

"It does make a difference. You've let your thinking apparatus grow crooked listening to things. That's what's wrong with you. Snap out of it before you turn into a lemon. Now take Fred for instance——"

"You take him," I interrupted, "I don't want him."

"Will you listen to me and stop cracking wise? Fred won't bite you. He's a good sort. Even if you don't want to go out with him, you might be polite and civil. Aside from anything else, it's what your job calls for."

"He didn't ask me to go out with him," I said in surprise.

"He's afraid of you. All the boys are. You bite their heads off if they come within a yard of you. Come off your perch Pee Wee, and don't judge either men or women by what you hear in this dressing-room. Take people as you find them yourself. Most of what we say down here we don't mean. We try to be wise, and hell, we've got to talk about something."

"Does it have to be men all the time?" I asked. "Can't you talk about anything else?"

Jeanne paused for a moment. "Who cares about music, art and politics?" she asked then. "That's only in books, like the bees, the birds, the flowers and the sunshine. And poetry, that's a lot of bunk too. Nobody ever reads it and you never hear of anybody talking about it —only authors and people like that. Men", she finished, "are what make the world go round."

"But——" I started.

"Put a lid on the 'buts', Pee Wee," she went on seriously. "Never talk about books or things like that on this job. It's no dice, and the girls will think you're either half-baked or else putting on a show. Try and act like we do and you'll get along better."

From that day on, the job became a completely different one for me. Gradually I was taken into the circle and treated by the girls as a human being—"reads too much, a bit odd, but on the square". The people in the building began to notice me too, and from the thirty-fifth to the bottom floor I was known as the "Pee Wee", and the "Irish Jigger". My size, which at first had been a drawback, I now discovered to be an asset. All the other girls had to be polite and dignified while on duty; never for a moment could they relax. I, not quite five feet tall and with a round baby face, could get away with nearly anything. I was not more than a year younger than most the girls, but I looked only sixteen beside them. I was teased from morning till night by everyone, and loved it. Even the very staid and business-like lost some of their sternness, and unbent enough to say: "Aren't you afraid that you'll get lost in this great big elevator, Pee Wee? You're such a tiny little thing."

Amongst the most dignified and distant men in the building was one who was known to us as the "English Captain". He had never been known to unbend to any of the operators, or to speak to them except to wish them a curt good morning. So I was nearly bowled over when, one day as he entered the car he said: "Aha, the pee wee operator is it not? You're looking very chipper this morning, if I may say so."

"Oh?" I gaped at him in surprise, and then recollecting myself said: "Thank you."

"Yes indeed." He was wearing a rose in the lapel of his coat, and suddenly he put his hand up and unfastened it. "Allow me," he said, offering me the flower; "an American Beauty for an American beauty."

I could hardly wait to tell the girls about it. The English Captain had been the subject of much discussion in the dressing-room, and there was a sort of wager as to who would be the first to "melt the iceberg". It was my triumph, and I gloated and preened till Jeanne said: "We ought to duck your head in a bucket of water three times and pull it up twice, Pee Wee, You're a wicked rubber inner."

A couple of hours later the joke was against me. Rose, choking with laughter, rushed pell mell into the dressing-room and shouted the news. "Hey Pee Wee! They just sent the wagon for your American Beauty boy friend. They're going to put him in the looney bin. He threw a couple of fits up in his office, went completely screwy, bats, burpy. Oh my American Beauty!"

I didn't hear the end of the American Beauty till the day I left the building.

The first edge of unhappiness began to wear off about three or four months after the separation from Jimmy, and slowly I discovered that life was full of fun and good after all. I gave up the dancing class and went to a night school. This kept me busy four nights a week. The other nights were filled with dinner dates, show dates, dances, etc. In the midst of all this, the bombshell arrived—a cablegram, saying "Be on lookout for registered letter posted here August 21" from P.J. The registered letter contained a money order for twenty pounds and a note, short and to the point: "Get the first boat from America. Wire me when you sail and I'll meet you. Love, from P.J." And this with no warning. I was at first amazed, then overjoyed, and lastly, as I thought of my mother, scared. I knew that she would be extremely angry and hurt, but because she knew—though she rarely mentioned it—that the thing I most wanted was to see my father, it never occurred to me that she would refuse to let me go, any more than it occurred to me to try and sail without her knowledge.

It took me two days before I could gather enough courage to speak to her about it. I approached her one night after dinner. "Will you come into my bedroom Mama, please?" I asked. "I have something to tell you. It's very important."

"I'm busy," she said. "Can't it wait?"

"It's very important," I repeated.

"Righto. Go in, I'll be in after you."

"Well, what is it?" she asked as she sat down.

"You're going to be very angry," I began.

"Don't hedge, out with it. What's on your mind?"

I took a deep breath and made the plunge. "I've been writing to my father and to P.J.", I said, "for quite a long time now."

She said nothing. Her lips came together in a tight hard line.

"The other day I received a letter from P.J. containing twenty pounds——" I hesitated.

"Go on," she said coldly, "What else?"

"He asked me to take the first boat leaving New York for Ireland—that's all——" I finished haltingly.

"What are you going to do?" she asked.

"I want to go," I said. "May I?"

She didn't answer for so long that I looked up, wondering. Her face was as white as chalk, her body rigid. She turned her head slowly and looked me full in the eyes. "I'd rather see you dead," she said.

I shrank away from her, hurt and frightened at the bitterness in her tone. Finally she went on, slowly, deliberately: "When I, who have never seen Aran, have had my heart broken by its people—strangers—what will they do to you?" She paused for a long moment. "You're small and gentle, you've been protected all your life. What will the people of Aran with their lying tongues and gossip do to you? You'd have no one to stand between you and them. No, I'd rather kill you with my own two hands than let you go."

"There's my father and brother," I said softly.

"Your father and brother," she repeated. "Yes, they

are there, and they've gone through a hell on earth there. Stay here with me, Barbara. I don't want you to go."

"But it's what I've wanted all my life——"

"You'll not go."

"Please," I pleaded. "I'll go some day anyway——"

"Give me the twenty pounds," she demanded suddenly. "If you haven't your fare you can't get there."

"I couldn't do that," I said aghast. "It isn't my money. It's P.J.'s."

"Give me the money at once!" The battle was on.

She coaxed and bullied and pleaded for hours, but I would not give in. At length she went to an old trunk and took from it a small packet of letters. "Read these," she said, handing them to me. "They were sent to me from Kilronan, Aran, and remember while you read them that I don't know and have never seen the writers, nor have they seen me. They will show you what the people of Aran are like."

There were six letters in the packet, dated fourteen years before, and every one of them contained unbelievably malicious gossip about my father. Some of the letters were signed, some were not.

"Do you see now the kind of a place you want to go to?" she asked when I had finished. "Do you see the kind of people that are there?"

"I want to go all the same," I answered.

She raged and stormed. I felt myself be ng beaten down slowly but surely. Dawn was showing in the sky when, tired and broken, I gave in.

But—and this was the strangest part of all—the moment I handed over the money, I changed. Not outwardly, but inwardly I seemed to shrivel up. My mind was terribly, frighteningly clear, with only one thought in it. All my hopes, all my dreams, since I could remember, had been centred in my father and P.J., and theirs in me, and now I had deliberately turned my back on them and let them down.

The change was gradual but definite. At first I felt numb: I ate, but didn't know whether I was eating or not. Then food began to sicken me; I could not eat at all. My mother wore herself out in cooking the dishes I liked best to try and tempt my appetite. I would push them away and have nothing but coffee. The next thing that went haywire was my sleep. I would wake up in the middle of the night, drenched in a cold sweat, shivering with terror. This got so bad that I could not be left to sleep alone. My mother had first to sleep in the same room with me, and then, as it got worse, to sleep in the same bed and hold me all night long. I nearly went out of my mind with fear—or with what? I did not know. Then it began to affect me in the daytime. If anybody—my mother, Puffy, Winnie, no matter who it was—spoke to me suddenly, I would scream and get hysterical. In six weeks my weight dropped from 132 to 102 pounds. My mother got more worried every day. Then one night when I was sitting at the dining-room table reading, and Puffy came up behind me and touched me on the shoulder, I fell across the table in a dead faint. The next day my mother sent for the doctor.

"Heart and lungs are sound, but her nerves are completely gone. At the rate she's going she won't last six months. She needs a complete change, quietness, and building up. Get her to eat, otherwise——" was the doctor's verdict.

My mother did not take long to make up her mind. The doctor had not been gone two minutes when she came to me: "You heard what the doctor said?" she asked.

"Yes," I said.

"Well?"

"I don't care," I answered dully. "One way or the other, it doesn't matter."

"It matters to me," she said. "I have a proposition to make to you."

"What is it?" I asked.

"This—if you let me build you up, eat the food I prepare for you, drink the medicines I get for you, and make an honest effort to overcome this nerve business, I'll let you go to Ireland next summer and give you my blessing into the bargain."

I couldn't realize what she was saying at first; I couldn't believe it. "Don't say that unless you mean it, Mama," I said after a long time.

"I'm not in the habit of making promises that I don't keep," she said roughly. "What's the answer?"

"I'll do my best," I said.

It was tough going. The struggle to overcome my fears and fainting spells, the effort to make myself eat and drink, was agonizing. My mother was kindness itself, but there was no getting away from the raw eggs, wine, tonics, broths, etc.: she was as firm as a stone wall.

My mother wanted to give me the money that P.J. had sent to me. I wouldn't take it because I had given it to her in the first place. In order to be able to look myself in the face again I knew that I should have to earn the money myself to pay for my ticket, because it seemed to me as if I had stolen money, spent it, and now had to pay it back. I told my mother how I felt about it. "Ridiculous," she scoffed; "I have the money here. It hasn't been touched since you gave it to me. What's wrong with it?"

"I did give it to you," I said, "that's what's wrong with it. I should have sent it back to P.J."

"How do you propose to earn the money?" she asked.

"I'll get another job, at night," I said. "I can work Sundays too. If I can't do it that way I'd rather not go to Ireland at all."

"I wouldn't give much for your chances of living to a ripe old age if you hang on to that idea for long. You'll kill yourself."

"That doesn't matter, so long as I get to Ireland before I kick off."

"Well," she said after a moment's thought, "since that's the way you feel, keep a grip on yourself and go to it."

I used the typing, shorthand, etc., that I had learned at the night school, and found no difficulty in getting a job from seven-thirty till ten at night, and another from eight till four on Sundays.

Three months before I was to sail I told the girls at work about my prospective trip.

"Little woman, what did you ever do to deserve such a lucky break?" Rose asked. "What's your Poppa like?"

"I don't know," I answered. "I haven't seen him for fourteen or fifteen years."

"So that's what's been eating you for the last umpteen weeks," said Jeanne. "Hey Rose!" she cried suddenly, "what do you bet that Pee Wee bumps her head on the well-known altar rail out in Ireland? She'll fall in love with a farmer."

"You're on," Rose agreed, "I say she'll marry a cop —bobbies they call them out there. She'll go for the tall, shiny hat."

"No she won't. It'll be a farmer. Little Pee Wee, what would you do if you had to milk a cow?" Jeanne asked.

"Flop," I replied laughing; "I wouldn't know one end of a cow from the other. I've never seen one in my life."

"Who has?" said Rose. "But I'm glad about the trip," she went on, "for your sake. It's good to see you sitting up and taking notice for a change. You've been looking dead enough to have been buried months ago."

I arranged to sail on the 9th of August, nearly a year after I had received the money order from P.J. I wrote to him—my first communication with him in the year, for I had never answered the money order. In my letter I told him the sailing date and the name of the boat, and described myself as best I could, so that he might recognize me. P.J.'s answer was short and characteristic of him:

"Dear Barby,

Don't worry, I'll be there to meet you.

Love,

"P.J."

Things went on in much the same way till the week when I left the job. But in any case I was too tired to notice anything that went on around me: I was aware of only one thing, and that was that I must work to save money to get to Ireland. And work I did: I stopped only to sleep and eat.

The girls at John Street gave me a send-off from the Hollywood Club in New York. They sent fruit, candy, and farewell messages. One of them got off early and rushed to the boat. But all that, even the actual sailing and trip across, is like something that happened in a dream. Many uncles, aunts, and cousins came to see me off. Nancy, Winnie, Puffy and my mother were there. I remember very little of it clearly. My mother's face. It was white and streaked with tears. "You'll come back Barbara? Promise me that you'll come back?" She kept saying that over and over again. I remember Winnie too: Winnie, the other part of me, saying: "You belong to me, Babs. Why did he send you the money? Don't leave me Babs, don't, don't." The next thing was the call of "All ashore!" My mother caught me by the shoulders: "Promise to come back," she said again.

"I'll come back some day," I promised faintly.

"If you want anything you'll go to Scoby?" she said.

"I will," I answered. I dimly remembered Scoby. He was a sailor on board, and my mother had pointed him out to me as a man who had seen my father and P.J. a year or so before.

I was too tired to look back at the shore as the boat left the harbour. I went down to my cabin and turned in. The trip was long, dreary and monotonous: there were days when I prayed desperately for the sight of land, any land. I wasn't seasick. I was exhausted. Every day on board was a repetition of the preceding one. The passengers were polite and friendly, but they were all fairly well fed up after five or six days on the sea. Then, on the morning of the last day out, an air of suppressed excitement hovered over the ship. We all felt it. Some of the passengers were crying, others laughing hysterically: it was the longest day of the trip.

The sun had just gone down when we got our first good look at Ireland. I could see the Aran Islands plainly from where I was standing on deck. "The Aran Islands" I thought as I looked at them: "How small they are, and how bare and lonely, in the middle of the ocean. What kind of a world is this I've come to? Who are my father and brother? What will they be like to live with? Will they like me? I shouldn't have come. This isn't my home. The Aran people aren't my people. How could they be? They are strangers. Oh why did I ever leave America, the people I knew, Winnie——?" I wasn't happy after all.

My thoughts were interrupted by the sound of the dinner gong. I went to the dining-room in a sort of daze. This would be my last meal on board: in an hour the passengers would be leaving the liner for the tender that would take them to the shore. My father and P.J. would be on the tender to meet me. How should I know them or find them in all that crowd? Then I remembered the sailor my mother had pointed out to me, Scoby. He knew them. If I could find him I would ask him about it. I had last seen him on the for'ard deck doing something with a lot of ropes. The food was choking me. I gave up trying to eat my dinner and left the table before I was half-way through the meal. I was so anxious to find Scoby that I almost ran to the door of the dining-room, unmindful of the astonished glances of those around me. On reaching the corridor I became confused. For the moment I could not remember whether I should turn to the right or the left to reach the for'ard deck. Fortunately there was a sailor standing by. "Have you seen Scoby?" I asked.

"Scoby?" he repeated. "He's on the for'ard deck Miss. Just turn to the right and go up the stairs at the end of the corridor. You'll find him."

I could feel the sailor looking after me as I ran off.

I was out of breath and panting when I reached the deck. Scoby was still there. I ran to him: "Scoby!" I gasped.

"What's happened?" he asked, alarmed.

"Nothing," I said, "only——"

"Well, what are you so excited for?" he interrupted.

"I'm not excited," I denied, "but——"

"Don't tell me that when I can see for myself."

"For goodness sake will you listen?" I almost shouted, "I want you to do something for me, please."

"I will if I can," he said. "What is it?"

"It's like this, Scoby," I explained. "In a few minutes the tender will be alongside and I'll be getting off. My father and P.J. will be on the tender to meet me. They don't know what I look like, I don't know them either, and I thought you might sort of—well—be around——"

"You're all mixed up," Scoby interrupted, "but I get what you mean. You want me to get you together, kind of introduce you. That right?"

"Yes," I said, relieved. "Will you?"

"Sure, sure I will. Don't worry, I'll see you right."

Anxious and eager, I searched the faces of the people on the tender, hoping that in one of them I should see some sign of recognition, some resemblance that would mean I had found those I sought. Scoby had completely disappeared. The tender was packed, and everyone was kissing, hugging and shouting joyfully. I wandered from one end of the ship to the other, heartbreakingly alone. They hadn't cared enough to come and meet me. The strain of the past year began to tell; I could feel myself breaking. I wanted to scream, and clenched my fists to hold it back; my fingernails were digging in through my flesh, my head felt as though it would burst —"We've been looking all over for you, Miss. This is your brother, P.J." It was Scoby's voice, behind me. I turned slowly round; my body felt stiff and aching. I saw Scoby first, and then lifting my glance I saw a face very like my own, and two blue eyes, dim and misty. "Barby?" he asked softly, holding out his arms to me. "Oh P.J." I sobbed, and ran to him.

Scoby, with blessed understanding, left us.

P.J. held me very tightly, and didn't speak until I had stopped crying. "Gee, aren't you small?" I heard him say wonderingly. His voice was strong and deep, his rich brogue delightful. He towered over me in height. "Come over here Barby," he said, leading me to a seat. "Why are you so frightened?"

"Is—my father—here?" I asked timidly.

"Your father? Sure, isn't he my father too?"

"Gosh, that's right, he is."

"You haven't a bit of a Yankee accent Barby, how is that?"—he sounded very pleased. "I've waited so long," he went on, "and now I have ye, sure I'll never let ye go."

"Where is he, P.J.?" I asked again.

"He couldn't make it. I'll be telling you about it later. Are you very tired?"

"I was," I said. "But I'm not now. Why?"

"Why do you think? Haven't we the past fifteen years to catch up on?" He drew a long breath, as if he had suddenly made up his mind to do something that he had been afraid of doing up till now. "Let me see your hands, Barby," he asked.

"They're clean," I said as I showed them.

"It's not that," he said. "I wanted to have a look at your fingernails."

"What on earth for?" I asked wonderingly.

"I can tell a person's character by their fingernails," he explained. "I didn't want to look at yours but I had to. You're all right, Barby, I can tell. Gee but it's queer to have a sister. You're not lonely for America?"

"No," I answered; "I was at first, but I'm not now. Isn't it odd, P.J.? I feel as though I'd just come home and that I knew you all the time."

"Sure, this is where you belong," he interrupted; "and wait till you see Aran."

"What time will we get there?" I asked.

"Not till to-morrow. It's three hours from the mainland."

"Must I go on another boat?"

"Well, how else do you think you'll cover thirty miles of ocean?"

"And will I see him to-morrow? What do you call him, P.J.?"

"Oh, just Paddy Mullen or Pop——"

We got through the customs rush at Galway without much trouble, and went directly to an hotel where P.J. had booked rooms for the night. We didn't stop talking for a second. Explanations had to be given, questions answered. Why hadn't I answered the money order? What was America like? What made me so small? What did I like to do? Could I ride a horse? No, I couldn't ride a horse. I had never been close enough to a horse even to say "how de do". Could I swim? Yes, I could swim a stroke or two. Could I ride a bicycle? No, I had never been any closer to a bicycle than I had been to a horse. Well, he would teach me to ride both. What was mother like? What was Winnie like? etc., etc. He told me why Paddy Mullen hadn't come to meet me. He had to be in Aran when the boat went in the next day, as there was to be an excursion. Paddy Mullen drove tourists around on his side-car; he also wrote books. I should see him on the quay when the *Dun Aengus*, the Aran boat, arrived. It was five o'clock in the morning when we stopped for a breather. "Gosh Barby, I'd better let ye go to bed," said P.J. contritely. "I'll call ye at eight o'clock. The boat leaves at nine ——" he paused at the door on his way out—"I can't believe it yet," he said, and turned and went to his room.

I fell asleep immediately. It seemed only a minute until I heard P.J. knocking on the door. I called to him to come in. He looked so frightened that I became alarmed. "What's the matter?" I asked.

"I called you three times," he said with a break in his voice, "and you didn't answer." He came over and sat on the bed and took one of my hands. "I thought then that you were sorry you came, and that you'd gone away. Sure, you'll never go back to America Barby?"

"I've got to go back some day." I said.

"You won't go back because I won't let you."

The *Dun Aengus* pulled out sharply at nine o'clock for Aran. The boat was crowded, but P.J. found a seat for me. He stayed by me as if he were afraid that I should disappear if he left me out of his sight. I kept thinking: "When the boat stops I'll see my father." Sometimes the boat seemed to be flying, sometimes crawling. I was anxious to get to Aran, yet I was afraid too. "What will I do when I see him P.J.?" I asked. "Will you point him out to me?"

"Stop worrying Barby," P.J. answered; "everything will be all right. Do you see Straw Island Lighthouse?"

"Yes," I said.

"Once past it we're landed, ye might say."

We passed Straw Island. "Look P.J.!" I shouted. "I saw a fish! A big one, jumping out of the water. There's another one!"

"Those are porpoises. Did you never see any before?"

"No, never." I watched the porpoises in amazed incredulous wonder. They were leaping all round the boat, dozens of them. I watched them and noticed nothing else, till "Here we are," said P.J. We had arrived.

There was a great number of people on the quay. I walked down the gangway, P.J. behind me. Several people came up to me and shook hands. "I knew you out of your brother," they said, "you're welcome to Aran, Miss Mullen."

"Thank you," I said gratefully. Again I had the feeling that I had been away on a visit and had just come home. There was a sort of pause. Everyone seemed to be waiting for something to happen. "Here he comes!" someone shouted suddenly. All heads turned in one direction, mine followed suit. Coming down the road that led to the quay was a side-car, the big white horse running at a terrific gallop, its long mane and tail flying in the wind. The driver was a powerful figure, grey-haired, brown-skinned—you could feel the force and strength in him as he made the horse go faster and faster. He pulled in the horse as they reached the quay, and jumped down off the side-car. As I ran to him he yelled to another driver who was standing near: "Hell's fire Patcheen! A crowd is looking for a side-car up the road. Hop to it. Damn it man, hurry!" Then he put his arms round me and said softly: "Babs child. It has been so long, the waiting. Thank God to see you again." I felt all the worry and strain of the past year fall away from me as he nearly smothered me in a bear-like hug, and my spirit soared sky high as I thought to myself: "Well, for goodness sakes! I've struck oil at last."

THE END